I0418371

Sauté Them Babies

Sauté Them Babies

Sauté Them Babies
Copyright © 2025 by Vinnie Oakes
All rights reserved
Reproduction in part or in whole of any work contained within is strictly prohibited without permission from the author.

Published in print and digital e-book
by Moderator Press Publishing

ISBN: 979-8-9985981-0-4
Library of Congress Control Number: 2025907092

Cover Design
Copyright © 2025 by Dustin Howard
All rights reserved
Reproduction in part or in whole of any art contained within is strictly prohibited without permission from the artist.

Praise for "Sauté Them Babies"

Mark Erickson, Provost, Retired, Culinary Institute of America

"A witty, candid, and captivating reflection—not just on an individual, but an entire profession—passing through a phase of reckless, exhilarating innocence before maturing into a respected pillar of American culture.

Vinnie Oakes' story embodies a generation of young cooks and restaurant professionals, a tribe of swashbuckling 'pirates' wielding knives and fire as they helped shape America's culinary identity and build an industry that employs nearly one-third of all Americans at some point in their lives. Among them were figures like Anthony Bourdain, whose bold spirit defined an era.

Reading this collection of serendipitous, chaotic stories and sharp insights, I found myself nervously laughing out loud—immersed in the reality of someone living life by the seat of his pants and having the absolute time of his life along the way."

Matt Russell, CEO, Russell Public Communications, Former Food Writer and Broadcaster

"Whether you're just getting started in the hospitality industry, a seasoned veteran, or simply someone who loves a great story shared over a memorable meal, *Sauté Them Babies* dishes out heaps of wisdom through the deeply personal and professional experiences of one of the best in the business, Vinnie Oakes. On his page-turning adventure, Vinnie chronicles some of the milestone moments and lessons learned on his journey, from his first glimpse of a commercial kitchen as a busboy in a New Jersey motel restaurant to working with the nation's hospitality elite in Manhattan and beyond. The characters in Vinnie's beautifully stitched-together vignettes, with whom I found myself connecting emotionally in every chapter, are real people whose contributions to his career are immeasurable. Vinnie's stories left me chuckling, choked up, and everything in between. His abundance of passion and boundless gratitude was food for my soul, and it's gratifying to know how this book will inspire readers today and for generations to come."

Paul J Lee, Director of Culinary Operations, Retired, Harrah's & Harvey's Hotel Casinos

In his *Sauté Them Babies*, Vinnie Oakes tells story after story about restaurant life in the towns bordering Teaneck, New Jersey, Manhattan's Central Park, and Madison Square Garden, to the casinos in Lake Tahoe, Reno/Sparks, and Las Vegas. The characters in these recollections are colleagues, family, and lifelong friends, that make you feel like you're reading a sitcom, subtitled 'the life and adventures of Vinnie Oakes'. This masterful storyteller puts his characters in the limelight and builds the story around them in places and times remembered. I was compelled to turn the pages to immerse myself in the next unbelievable experience.

Vinnie ends his emails with an image, a silhouette of Peanuts, Woodstock and Snoopy in a full moon with a quote: "The best times in our lives were not about what we had, but who we were with." I think that's just what you'll find between the covers of *Sauté Them Babies.*

Amber Barnes, Leadership & Culture Developer, StartHuman

"In *Sauté Them Babies*, Vinnie doesn't just recount the hustle of a life spent in the fast-paced, gritty world of food and casinos. He paints a portrait of resilience, courage, and the quiet, often invisible work that makes all the difference: the relationships we build, and the people who shape us when no one's watching.

From his early days in Jersey to the high-stakes world of Harrah's Lake Tahoe and the uniqueness of Silver Dollar City Theme Park, Vinnie's story is one of grit, wit, and a rare kind of bold authenticity. He's seen it all — and still believes in the power of a good relationship, and in showing up for the people who matter.

What I love most about this book is how Vinnie gives credit where it's due: to the people who helped him when he stumbled, to the bad examples who taught him what not to do, and to the good ones who made all the difference. It's the kind of leadership I believe in — rooted in presence, connection, and the courage to be fully human.

If you're looking for a story that's raw, real, and full of heart, *Sauté Them Babies* is exactly that. A reminder that success isn't just about climbing the ladder; it's about who you become along the way."

Rose Levy Beranbaum, Author of "*The Cake Bible*"

"Following Vinnie's career in the hospitality industry is as exhilarating as a roller coaster ride. His evocative voice speaks with strength, humor, and authenticity. It is enlightening to know the details of his life story."

Jim Macphearson, Vice President, Tarrant Area Food Bank, Feeding America

"In *Sauté Them Babies*, Vinnie Oakes recounts his travels through commercial kitchens and dining rooms essentially from coast to coast. In a series of short stories covering decades, Vinnie's energy and enthusiasm for the next adventure compels the reader to move forward, yet not wanting to arrive at the last page."

Dedication

This book is dedicated to the chefs and entire staff - past, present, and future - of the Culinary Institute of America.

Anything good that happened in my professional life, and in most of my personal life as well, can be traced back to one night in late 1962, where I bumped into a hometown acquaintance at the Cedar Lane Grill in Teaneck, New Jersey. He was just getting out of the Navy, and he told me he was looking into a cooking school in New Haven, Connecticut.

In less than a year I became a student there. It was a modest place; a collection of converted old turn-of-the-century wooden houses and a carriage house, situated between Yale's School of Divinity and School of Forestry at 393 Prospect Street.

After years of steady growth between 1946 and 1971, the school moved to its current home in 1972, where it is located on 170 scenic acres overlooking the Hudson River in Hyde Park, New York. In addition to the main campus in Hyde Park, there are satellite campuses in St. Helena and Napa, California; San Antonio, Texas; and Singapore.

— Vinnie Oakes

Contents

Sauté Them Babies

"You're going to feel like hell if you wake up someday and you never wrote down the stuff that is tugging on the sleeves of your heart: your stories, memories, visions, and songs – your truth, your version of things – in your own voice. That's really all you have to offer us, and that's also why you were born."

-Anne Lamott

Duckboards

We walked on duckboards in the kitchens where my friends and I grew up in the business. There were no soft, comfy thick black rubber floor mats, no microwave ovens. We didn't have disposable paper chef hats, or hand sanitizer on the walls, or quartz-powered, wall-mounted cheese melters. We had to *earn* a chef's hat. Nobody wore clogs, a print-patterned cooking uniform, or had his name and fancy title embroidered on the left side of his jacket (except maybe if he was *truly an executive*, like Eugene Scanlan at the Waldorf-Astoria). I don't think I saw a professional chef on TV until the middle of the 1980s. I'm not telling you that we all rode to work in a covered wagon, but the times were definitely different. People didn't enter the biz for fame and fortune, although as time went on, some of the lucky ones with the right amount of talent and charisma did quite well.

Please don't misunderstand me: I'm happy that things got better for people in kitchens and bakeshops, and I'm glad that women were finally accepted in the culinary world, but the 'back of the house'—when and where I started—was often inhabited by some pretty rough characters.

We worked a hell of a lot of overtime, and most of us never saw a dime from it. But here's the thing: *we loved the work*. It was an amazing adventure. We were learning . . . entering a career with its own lexicon, not only in English, but a smattering of words from all sorts of western European countries; and we were taught dozens of little culinary tricks to do a job better, quicker, cleaner, neater. And we worked for those moments when somebody more senior than us would walk by our station, see our work and say, *"Soigne."* Hearing that word describing our work from somebody we respected was worth all the blood, sweat, and yes, occasionally, tears.

Before We Start

This book is a collection of some of my more memorable moments in the hospitality industry, but also a few non-work stories sprinkled in, because many were just plain fun times, and anyway, they almost always involved food people.

This is not just my story. It's also about the people who have been around me over the years: the crazies, the characters, the big personalities, the leaders, and the talents. I have fondness and great appreciation for those who have had a positive impact on my life and my career, so there are a lot of words devoted to their stories as well, because without those people I wouldn't be me.

Throughout my schooling in Teaneck, New Jersey, I was never much of a student. I tried. I really did. These days people tag kids like I was as having A.D.D., but back when I was in school, if you were disruptive or not paying attention the teachers would just put you in the corner of the classroom, maybe one or two would smack you around a bit, or worse, send you to the principal's office. A.D.D. wasn't a thing back then. So I guess subconsciously I came to the conclusion that I would grow up to live a life in some sort of service job, and that if I was to be successful, it would mostly come from hard work, not my S.A.T. scores. Maybe that's why one of the first jobs I agreed to was digging a grave.

July 1951 - A Summer Morning

Mer's pet bird, a canary named for the bright yellow box of cereal, is "Cheerio." We take it to Gram and Gramp's farm with us when we move up there for the summer. I have just completed the first grade.

Cheerio's cage is placed in the big formal dining room, where it chirps and sings, most likely to keep its mind off the full-sized alligator that is mounted on the stone chimney above the river rock fireplace at the west end of the only somewhat darkened and spooky space in the entire 19th century farmhouse. The nervous bird can't know that the gator has been dead and stuffed for decades.

My older sister Merilee and I are the early risers of the house, and her first stop is always the dining room, where she feeds the bird. But on this morning, she calls for me in a concerned voice, as she discovers that Cheerio is in a bad way, struggling on the floor of the cage.

No one is around, so Mer goes upstairs to wake Mom to ask her what to do. Thinking perhaps of the legendary Saint Bernard dogs trotting through deep snows in the Swiss Alps reviving half-dead travelers with brandy from their neck-mounted miniature casks, my mother in her semi-conscious state tells eight-year-old Mer to give the bird some brandy.

Mer leaves our mother's bedroom, locates an eyedropper in the bathroom 'drugstore,' and then proceeds downstairs to the liquor cabinet where she gets the bottle of brandy. She goes to the kitchen and fills the eyedropper from the bottle, then heads back to the ailing Cheerio.

The canary and my sister are old friends, so it's no problem for either party when Mer puts her hand through the little door and around the bird, picking it up off the cage floor in preparation of administering a few drops of brandy. Cheerio takes a gulp, actually its last gulp. Then, fully re-energized, it flies up to the top of the cage, lands on its little swing up there, and immediately plummets down to the cage floor, stone cold dead. An overdose!

Merilee then takes on the role of the funeral director: planning, organizing, recruiting the labor (me) to immediately dig the grave, and then presides over the actual burial ceremony. I am asked to dig a grave in the wild grass southeast of the barn. Mer finds an empty shoebox, gently places Cheerio in it, and surrounds the little canary with freshly picked daisies. I shovel dirt onto the 'coffin,' and Mer recites a bible psalm, learned in school, no doubt. We both have a vague recollection of placing a marker of some sort, maybe popsicle sticks.

We do not replace the canary.

September 1962 - Chocolate Pudding for Four (by Four)

By some miracle I get out of high school on time, graduating with the kids that surround me since we begin kindergarten in September of 1949. I manage to get into a junior college in upstate New York, far from civilization. During this era, people go to a junior college for two years, try to get respectable enough grades—because if you tried to get them in high school you wouldn't be at a junior college in the first place—so that you can transfer to a senior college or university. If you can't trade up, you walk away with an associate's degree and go to work.

I'm not happy with the place. I'm there to study Hotel and Restaurant Management, but their cooking classes are pathetic, and there are very few girls there. Nothing to do but drink and try to stay warm during seriously cold time. The temp hovers not too far above zero for much of the winter, and when it's *really* cold, it drops below. I do manage to make some good friends who will be in my future, and I do have some fun times also, but by Christmas break of my first year I want out.

7

I *know* their cooking classes are pathetic at this place because the summer before I start there, I am working as a busboy at a motel restaurant in Fort Lee on New Jersey's Route Four, about a half mile west of the George Washington Bridge. During my breaks, I hang around the kitchen. I like watching the action; I like the guys in the crew and they like me. Pretty soon they start teaching me how to make dressings for the pantry area.

Not only do I learn a few things in the kitchen, but I am exposed to a number of little moments that both shock and amuse me. Like the time thirtyish waitress Ramona is more than ready to pick up a couple of hot entrees, but has to cool her heels behind the middle-aged, slower, and very un-hip Eve. This isn't a large enough kitchen to have an expeditor, which means that Ramona has her own method for directing traffic at the pick-up station, and impatiently snarls at Eve, *"Get the fuck outta my way!"*

I'm thinking, "Hmmm . . . nobody talks that way in my kitchen at home. This restaurant business is kinda fun."

I learn enough to know what a real kitchen is: the noises, the action, the pace, the precision, the aromas, even the drama, and I fall in love with all of it. And I know that a bunch of kids in groups of four, standing around a little stove at the junior college, making chocolate pudding *for four*, being directed by a dietitian dressed in a white 'nurse's uniform' (including white shoes) is not going to help me learn how to run a restaurant.

8

During the Thanksgiving break, I am in Teaneck, and one night down at the diner, I run into an older guy I know. He's getting out of the Navy and thinking about going to a cooking school up in New Haven, Connecticut. I'm interested and get all the info on the place. By the time Christmas break is over, I've driven up there, visited the place, and applied for admission for the following fall. It's called The Culinary Institute of America (years later it is relocated to Hyde Park, New York), and it's located on nine acres between Yale's School of Forestry and the School of Divinity.

I return upstate, and later in January of 1963, take finals, ending the first semester and also my career at the j.c. My grades are okay, but I am ready to move on. My good high school friend, Ann Lesser, gets me juiced-in to a restaurant job. It's a steak house being built on the cliffs (Palisades) overlooking the Hudson River on the Jersey side. They tell me that I can help with the construction, and later I can work in the kitchen after the place opens.

Working winter construction is an education. I am working out in the winter wind carrying decorative bricks and mortar, high above the Hudson River in Englewood Cliffs. The restaurant, Sid Allen's, is famous before it even opens because the owner, Sid Allen, is a long-time restaurateur in Bergen County where I grow up.

Ten days before we're to open, we hammer in a new plywood floor over the sub-floor, and it's ready for the carpet. But Sid Allen hears a creak as he's walking across it one morning, and we spend the next two days tearing up the plywood and replacing it with a thicker sub-floor and floor. This is a tough guy, who comes up the hard way, working in his youth for Toots Shor (Google: Toots Shor. More about my connection to Toots later). It is a good restaurant lesson for me: *everything must be perfect . . . and if it isn't, do whatever it takes to make it right.*

I'm making $1.25 an hour during construction, but in the hiring process, I'm promised a raise as soon as the restaurant opens. We have a big grand opening party, and I'm in heaven: working for a chef who's going to teach me everything, and I'm in a real kitchen. I put in 105 hours the first week and still have the energy to go over to Ann's late at night.

The morning after night number three, I wake up and can't open my eyes. They're stuck shut from problems related to my contact lenses. Contacts are still in relative infancy at this point, and overuse from my long work hours creates major irritation. Luckily, Dad is still home when I wake up, and gets me to our ophthalmologist who fixes me up with some eye drops. I go right back to work for another 17 hours . . . but wear my specs and hit the drops at prescribed intervals.

Tuesday of week #2 is payday. I have dreams of the big check that I'm going to get. I run the numbers over and over in my head.

I'm setting up my station in late afternoon when the lady who works in the office brings my check. Same pay as construction: $60 ($1.25/hr x 48 hrs - that's what we'd been working during construction: six eight-hour days/week). I am more than disappointed. I'm angry.

I talk calmly to Danny the chef who tells me to go check with the lady in the office. She's in there with a real accountant from the firm that oversees the books. He's showing her how to do some bookkeeping stuff, when I pop in and explain my situation. The guy is flabbergasted, asking, "You worked 105 hours?"

"Yeah," I answer.

Clearly the guy is concerned. The lady is nice, but sends me back to the kitchen, saying she'll have to "check with Mr. Allen."

About 30 minutes later Sid Allen is at the urn in the kitchen getting a cup of coffee. He's about 20 feet away from where I'm working. He looks over his shoulder at me and says he understands I have a question about my money. I tell him that I worked seven days and 105 hours; I was promised a higher hourly rate after the opening. Then I ask, "And what about the overtime?"

I tell him I'm going to cooking school in the fall and need to save the money. He tells me his son Roger is at Cornell, "standing in still water, compared to what he learned from Chef Danny over the years."

I tell him, "Come on, Mr. Allen, cut the bullshit." He can't believe I'm talking to him this way. Neither can I.

Allen responds, "Maybe you want to leave right now."

I answer, "Maybe I do."

"Wait a minute," he says. And then, "Danny, come over here a minute." Danny comes over to me. Sid Allen is on the other side of the stainless worktable.

"Danny, Vinnie worked an extra day. We need to take care of him," Allen says. Danny reaches into his pocket and gives me a ten-dollar bill.

Sid Allen, who maybe at this point is waiting for me to apologize and act grateful for the ten spot, then says to me, "You need to think about this overnight. You need to think about whether you want to stay here."

I answer, "Yeah, OK."

The next day I go in and set up my station. Nobody says anything to me about making it all up to me or about a new pay rate. Not a word. Ten minutes before opening time (5 p.m.), I yell for Danny to come and see me. I ask, *"You remember when Mr. Allen told me to think about whether I wanted to still work here?"*

"Yeah," he answers.

I tell him, "Well, I don't. I'll come by and pick up my check another time."

I walk, leaving them with an unmanned station ten minutes before dinner service.

Summer 1963 - The Jewish Alps, aka The Borscht Belt, aka The Sour Cream Sierras (affectionate nicknames for New York's Catskill Mountains)

After I leave Sid Allen's I find a job at a little diner where I'm 50% of the kitchen crew: the cook's helper. It's okay work and has its fun moments, because just about every diner in New Jersey has a resident smartass working the grill behind the counter, a poor man's Don Rickles who tosses out insults to the clientele seated on the stools a few feet away. This joint is no different.

One morning a crew of regulars from a moving company sits down for breakfast. There's a new kid with them, a rookie, and when it's his turn to order he's trying to be cool, to be one of the boys, and asks for 'an egg on a hard roll.' If you're not from the northeast, this is a fried egg on a butter-grilled Kaiser roll. Jim, the cook, a regular ball-breaker, slices a Kaiser in half, slaps it on a dinner plate, and puts a raw shell egg between the two halves of the roll. He's got his back to the counter, so no one can see what he's doing. He pivots around, quickly placing the plate in front of the kid, and immediately walks down the line to take care of other tasks. There's no smile from Jim, not an insulting remark, no nothing. He's still got his back to the rookie and busies himself with both real and imaginary food prep duties. At this point the kid is left trying to figure out what just happened, and if or how he should respond. It's too late: the regulars are already having a good laugh. Diner life. Fun, but not permanent if you're dreaming of bigger things.

I begin looking for a better place to work, and through family friend, Dr. Mel Elting, I gain an introduction to a former executive chef who is now Restaurant Associates' Director of Purchasing, Harold Simpson. Mr. Simpson, in turn, provides entre to an interview with Executive Chef Eugene Scanlon at the Waldorf where I begin to explore the possibility of a formal culinary apprenticeship there. I ask Jim for the afternoon off so I can go get my interview at the Waldorf. He's greatly amused. How could his assistant, working in a wooden shack of a diner in the morning, finish his day interviewing on Park Avenue at the Waldorf? He tells all the regulars, and they have another big laugh. I just smile.

But I *do* meet with Chef Scanlon, who is a real gentleman: I'm told I need to wait patiently for an opening at the Waldorf, and to go to school at CIA for now.

A couple of weeks later I get in contact with one of my former high school teachers who helps me get a job at one of the resort hotels in the Catskills in upstate New York. During this time period almost all the hotels up there have one thing in common: they work you seven days a week, but they give you room and board along with your pay. We work from 6:30 every morning till 2 p.m.; take a break till 4 p.m., come back and work through dinner service and clean-up.

There's no job interview. I'm just told where and when to show up. I am assigned to work in the pantry at the New Morningside Hotel in Hurleyville, New York. It's an hour and a half from home. They give me a room in employee housing, really a building that feels only slightly more refined than what pioneer settlers' cabins would have been like.

On my first morning I'm introduced to Tom Velasquez, who is the head guy in the three-man pantry section of the kitchen. Tom's a great teacher and I'm learning every day. The kitchen is high volume and fast paced. Guests are on the American plan, which means that they get breakfast, lunch, and dinner along with their hotel room. There's no limit on what they can order.

Most of the cooks are from Germany, the dishwashers are all on summer break from Tuskegee University, and the waiters and waitresses are all college kids. The kitchen has its old-world culinary traditions. For example, herring comes to us in wooden barrels, and must be butchered and then marinated in either a sour cream blend or a red wine vinegar sauce. All fruit at this time is packed in wooden crates and must be brought—on one of my shoulders and on the run—up a steep flight of stairs from the basement. Even cream cheese comes to the hotel in little wooden boxes. No cardboard for the good stuff at this time. Nothing is done slowly in this place. As a matter of fact, after about a month, Tom is ready to give me a five-dollar-a-week raise, up from my starting salary of 55 bucks. In order for the raise to be approved, hotel owner Mac Weiner must come by and watch me speed-slice through a couple of prone bananas on a cutting board. Speed is everything in this kitchen. I get the raise.

The place is a bit of a nutty atmosphere, which is fine with me. Most of the kitchen crew in the summer resorts at this time work the northeastern summer spots, then head back to their seasonal jobs for the winter in Florida. My roommate is the hotel butcher, a Florida guy, an unhinged middle-aged dude who often wakes up in the morning, grabs his ukulele, and starts singing (howling) at about 6 a.m. I enjoy this freak show and am particularly amused one day when he comes upstairs from the butcher shop to the kitchen during the breakfast rush, stands in the middle of the chaos, and starts playing his uke and singing. The uptight German chef goes ballistic on the guy. I look back on this particular day, in this particular kitchen, and am reminded of 'The Burbs,' when actor Corey Feldman, playing Ricky Butler, says, 'God, I love this street.' *The street* for me is any restaurant or hotel kitchen, and I love it.

It's incredibly ironic to me that really only two decades after Hitler's defeat in WW II, so many of the Jewish hotels in the Catskills were manned by German chefs. Mostly these guys were pretty stern, pretty serious; they'd seen tough times. One day, though, during a slow lunch, with no warning, the chef grabs waitress Merle, throws her up into a prone position on a cutting board, and begins pawing over her body for a few seconds. His way of courting, I guess. Not a word was ever said. Different times, for sure.

After about six weeks, Tom and the chef come to me with a situation. The chef says, "We have three of you in the pantry, and business volume is not what the owner expected. Either you or Quincy (a Tuskegee University kid) must go by the end of the week. We're leaving the decision up to you."

I tell them, "Look, my home is only an hour and a half away from here. I'm not gonna make that kid go all the way down to Alabama. I can get a job back home in a few days. I'll be the one to leave."

Two days later the chef tells me he's got a buddy at another hotel up the road who has a bad back and needs someone to carry heavy pots of food for him, to be his helper. The job is mine if I want it, and I can have a day off before they want me to start. I take the job.

It turns out that the hotel I'm going to is bigger and more successful than the New Morningside. It's called the Brown's Hotel & Country Club, and it's pretty famous during this era. Comedian Jerry Lewis got his start there, so his image is plastered on the Brown's billboards up and down the local highways. It's about 15 minutes from the New Morningside.

I drive down to Teaneck for an 18-hour visit and get back up to the Brown's early the following evening. I find the kitchen steward (let's call him Sheldon) at the hotel. He gets some bedding for me and takes me to a four-man room. If the employee housing at the New Morningside was an upgraded version of pioneer settlers' cabins, this room with its inhabitants is like a wooden drunk tank. My three roommates are a different breed of cat—basically, hobos. I take one look at these guys and decide to leave everything I own locked up in my VW. Everything except a knife.

My suspicions are later validated by what I'd have to call a rumor, or a myth: When Sheldon is occasionally short of dishwashing help, he drives the hotel's station wagon down to the Bowery, drags passed-out drunks out of the gutter into the vehicle, and they wake up two hours from the city in the Catskills.

As the story went, when they'd wake up, he'd offer them a meal and money if they would wash dishes. What choice did they have? They had no idea where they were! And while there's no proof this sort of 'recruitment' ever occurred, if you ever saw the three gents I had to share that room with, you'd certainly figure that there could be a fair chance for truth to the story. I stay in that room for two nights, then tell Sheldon, I have to leave if he can't find a non-hobo-inhabited room for me. He does, and I remain happily employed for the rest of the summer.

The kitchen at the Brown's is clean and efficiently run. It's the same work schedule as most of the joints in the area: work breakfast and lunch, take a 2 or 2½ hour break, come back and handle the dinner. At the Brown's I actually get one dinner a week off. Pretty good! Working right alongside the chef in that kitchen is a perfect spot for me at the time. It is a food prep job, and I learn how to handle a knife in high volume circumstances and get some valuable experience in heavy production. On my breaks I hang around in the meat cutting area and am taught how to trim beef.

Every day after the lunch service, I walk through the line and put together a meal for myself, then go to sit down and eat in a children's dining room just off the kitchen. On one memorable day, I walk in with my tray of food and begin having my lunch. As always, the little kids are already gone by the time I'm ready to eat, and the room is empty. My food is nothing unusual: some braised beef in brown sauce on a pile of wide buttered egg noodles, a buttered roll, a dessert, and a glass of milk.

A thirty-something lady and her little boy come into the room. They're late arrivals, but of course they are hotel guests and take their seats a couple of tables away from me. Lunch is over, but somehow a waitress is found to take their orders. It's ok for me to be eating in there, but they are guests, so I am careful to not make eye contact with them. I'm eating, minding my business, and suddenly this woman jumps up from her table and begins screeching and yelling, pointing at me. The chef hears the commotion and quickly arrives.

I'm actually pretty calm watching/listening to this lady having a fit, not at all aware of what I'm doing to upset her. I just figure she's upset because she and her son are being subjected to sharing a kids' dining room with a hoi polloi kitchen worker. The chef comes to my rescue, smoothly ushering me and my lunch tray out of the room and back into the main kitchen, where he begins a gentle irony-filled explanation of why she is unhinged: she catches me eating meat and having a glass of milk on the same tray, a definite no-no in a kosher-styled resort. This is ironic because the chef is a Hungarian Catholic, and I am a Jewish boy from Teaneck, New Jersey—one, who I might add, obviously hasn't a clue about the rules of 'keeping kosher.'

September 1963 - CIA: Year One

During my initial weeks at the Culinary Institute of America (CIA), school feels different. I'm no longer the disruptive comedic presence that I was from kindergarten through the twelfth grade. I am being drawn to the world of food, I am finding my passion, and almost instantaneously, my father and I are getting along better. As a matter of fact, the only strong words he throws at me during this time are when he makes it clear that I am not to bring my laundry home on weekend visits unless I'm doing it myself. It's not my mother's job. I'm an adult.

Alan Hills

I meet Al Hills at CIA at the beginning of my first year there. He becomes my roommate of sorts, living across the hall from me in a tiny cul-de-sac of three small sleeping rooms located on the third floor of the school's main building, Angell Hall, a large, old, turn-of-the-century house.

The rooming situation isn't in CIA's original plan. At first, I am placed in a large room with six other guys. OK, fine. But on the first weekend after school begins, I go back down to Teaneck for a couple of days and have a stomachache most of the two days. I return Monday morning late, due to the stomachache, about 8 or 9 o'clock, after classes already start. I go upstairs to my shared room, and find my bed messed up. It is not drastically torn apart, but clearly people had been sitting on it. I remake the bed, and then tear up all six of the other beds; then head downstairs to Registrar Barbara Meyers' office and tell her that I'm not putting up with this behavior. She offers to give me another room, and that's how I end up in the little hallway adjacent to Al Hills' room.

Oh yeah, and the issue of the six messed-up beds gets resolved pretty quickly. Naturally, these guys complain to me, and I tell them I don't care. One of them or their pals have messed my bed, and I'm not putting up with that shit (we don't use the word "disrespect" in 1963, especially if we're from New Jersey).

A couple days go by and Hillsy tells me that one or two guys around the school want to fight me because of what I do to their friends' beds. Al warns them that they'd better bring a brick along. This is all based on the fact that I have a set of weights in my room, and he's seen my county champions high school wrestling jacket. They disappear (thanks, Al, that was easy).

Al is a year ahead of me at CIA. He starts there in 1961, but transfers after his first year to the Hotel and Restaurant Management program at U. Mass. He doesn't care for U. Mass and returns to CIA in 1963 to complete his schooling there, as a 'storeroom major.'

This guy is a hustler's hustler, a raconteur, a hip, street-smart dude who is always thinking, scheming about how to make a buck. He is a very good friend and frequent dinner companion. Years later, he becomes a millionaire through his association with Carriage Trade Diner's Club, a 'Two Fer' restaurant marketing model which he falls into in its very early days.

CIA was co-founded by Frances Roth and Katherine Angell. The school was started in 1946. In the context of the time I attend, the CIA is barely out of its infancy. It has made a remarkable rise to a world-class facility over the years, thanks to its continued visionary leadership, faculty, and alumni success stories.

When I am in school there, the faculty is an eclectic collection of characters who are our teachers. Unquestionably the most unforgettable, for the wrong reasons, is 'Mr. G.'

Aldo Gratziotin, aka 'Mr. G.'

OK, this guy is kinda nuts, frequently displaying kooky behavior. His notoriety among the students carries itself along from year to year as if it were a floating leaf moving forward on the waters of a flowing stream.

He is half English (with a Brit accent) and half Italian, and often just crazier than a hopped-up monkey on fermented bananas. He teaches in a theater-styled demo kitchen complete with large mirror over his worktable, and he shows us what we'll be making the following week in another chef's production kitchen.

At least once or twice during any given week we spend in demo class with him, when he has his back turned and is working at the stove, one of the guys will yell out, "The Queen!" Then 20 feet away in our bleacher seating, a second guy chimes in, "Goes! " And finally, a third, way up high in the seats, finishes up with, "DOWN!" *THE QUEEN - GOES - DOWN!*

Then Mr. G. whips around, looking quickly back and forth at the 60 souls in the bleacher seats, all dressed in whites, all looking very much the same as each other, and asks in his British accent, "Who said that, man? Who said that?" Silence. This is carried on week to week, month to month, all school year long, by all junior groups who experience demo class several times during year number one at CIA. Then it's repeated the following year by the incoming class of first-year students, who learn it from the seniors.

Every group at some point or another gets to see Mr. G. climb into an empty stainless-steel pot sink and stomp his feet when he's particularly upset about something. It's craziness. Yes, CIA is the best cooking school in the country when I go there, but it is certainly NOT the CIA of today, not even close. It is an eclectic collection of mostly talented, in some cases classically-trained chefs—many from Europe—and a few odd ones (none as odd as "G.") teaching students who run the gamut of some who are dumber than a side of asparagus to very bright and talented young men. Three alums from my time at the school will later become stars on the American culinary/hospitality scene: two guys from my class, Marcel Desaulniers and Rod Stoner, and Richard Schneider, a year ahead of us.

Marcel became a highly successful restaurateur who authored ten cookbooks and was the recipient of a number of awards from the James Beard Foundation. Rod spent 29 years at the world-class Greenbrier resort hotel in West Virginia and retired as its vice president of food and beverage. Richard Schneider worked in his family's New Jersey restaurant for a number of years, but later moved on to the corporate world, where he found enough time to try out for the American Culinary Olympic team. He eventually became captain of the team, winning four gold medals, and was named national chef of the year by the American Culinary Federation.

For twelve years, from 1986 to 1998, I am fortunate enough to be a 'Member of the Corporation' of the CIA. In the earlier years, right at the start of the holidays the school sends a Christmas tin of pecan diamonds (cookies) to my home. We have to ration them out because we all love these little treats. We keep them in a sealed container and they retain their original quality for many days. But we never really have to worry about that at my house, because the cookies are gone within 72 hours!

I smile whenever this tin shows up, because in the mid-60s, when I am a student at the school, the annual holiday gift to dignitaries and supporters of the school is a Christmas tin of fruit cake. And my memories of the craziness that goes on at CIA during this period, of course, makes me silently laugh. These fruit cakes are sent to the White House, the governors of Connecticut and surrounding states, restaurant industry luminaries, big financial supporters, etc. Most of the tins go out just fine, but every once in a while, a few little balls of aluminum foil find their way into the batter; or there are notes folded in (*'Help! I'm a prisoner in a Korean fruit cake factory'*). One time, the head of bake shop, Joe Amendola, is entertaining some important people for dinner at his home. He is bragging about what nice boys his students are when one of his guests grabs a baguette made in the bake shop that morning, and cuts into it only to find a wooden dowel through the entire length of the bread. *Whoops.*

November 22, 1963

One Friday after lunch we are listening to Mr. G. lecture. It is early afternoon. Suddenly a senior student comes rushing in from the advanced demo classroom immediately behind ours. He is carrying a radio and excitedly tells Mr. G. that we all need to hear what is going on. Mr. G. nods his approval, and the guy plugs in the radio. Immediately the news is unfolding from Dallas: President Kennedy has been shot! We listen very quietly. It is, at the time, a shocking and foreign concept to grasp.

The America that I grow up in doesn't prepare its children for the assassination of anyone, let alone such a popular president. We can't relate. That sort of thing happened way back in time, to Lincoln and some distant figures of history: Garfield and McKinley. About three years before this event, I saw a documentary on TV, in which a man attempted to shoot FDR and Gov. Long during the 1930s, down south in Louisiana. But that, too, was a long time ago, before I was born.

When you're nineteen and you're told about something that precedes your birth or your age of understanding, it's an abstraction. The event might just as well have been a hundred years ago for all the relevance it has in your nineteen years of life experience. Besides, stuff that happens in the deep South always takes place within a sort of gothic, spooky, swampy fog, sometimes literally.

So it really doesn't count as a reality that anyone would try to shoot our beloved American president at this time in my life. Soon enough, after a short time we are told that Dean Hausmann is closing school until further notice. I pack up some stuff, jump into my VW Bug, and head for Teaneck.

As I'm driving down Prospect Street in New Haven, I slow for a stoplight, right next to a black Ford station wagon full of nuns. With the exception of the driver, they all have their rosaries out and are praying. I never forget the scene. Many years later, I write about that moment:

At a Stop Light in New Haven

It happens at a corner
in New Haven, Connecticut,
on the mind-numbing day
of November twenty-second,
in nineteen sixty-three.

As I slow for the red light
in mid-afternoon traffic,
I pull up next to a black Ford station wagon
waiting in the next lane.

The driver is a nun.
She is chauffeuring four of her black-clothed sisters,
who are in sorrowful prayer over their rosary beads
on this blackest of American days.

And I know exactly why and for whom they pray.
I watch them. I stare at them.
And although I am only nineteen,
I know this scene will imprint onto my memory for life.
It will always be with me:
The stoplight, the Ford, the nuns, their rosaries;
and the blackness of it all.

On November twenty-second, nineteen sixty-three.

I get home, and for the first time in our lives, we (my mother and I) are really glued to the TV. Prior to that, we really don't watch as much as you might think, even though the 1950s are described in contemporary terms as the 'Golden Age of Television.' I think that is more a reflection of the *innovation* associated with early TV, rather than its popularity. We are in front of that TV for much of the next few days because most of what is happening is really unfolding live before our eyes. (Taping is in its very embryonic stage and is introduced primarily as a limited way of replaying sports action).

Late Sunday morning, Bill Cannon and I return from playing our weekly touch football game, organized by Bill Schneeloch, over in Tenafly. We immediately land in the Cannon's living room. The TV is on, and we are just in time to watch as Lee Harvey Oswald is taken out of the Dallas jail (back door) into a waiting car. I believe he is being taken to a court arraignment. He's about 10-12 steps out the door, under close security, surrounded by all kinds of official-looking cop types. I have seared into my memory a stern-looking older man, in light clothes and wearing a light-colored cowboy hat, gripping Oswald by the arm; perhaps he's *the* Dallas Sheriff.

From the bottom right side of the screen a figure emerges, an arm extends toward Oswald, and from a foot or two away, fires a pistol right into his belly. We not only see this LIVE, but HEAR the shots, and HEAR Oswald's grunt/scream of pain and surprise—all of it LIVE. Oswald dies, and with him the story of who, how, why, he kills JFK, the most popular president of my young life.

It's remarkable. All of it. A whole weekend of shock and drama. It's America's first reality show—only we don't call it this at the time. The shooter is Jack Ruby, a local night club owner, known to many in the Dallas police fraternity. *And that's it*: if people are gonna be killing each other LIVE on TV, then we ain't movin' ('we' meaning America). And WE spend the next days glued to the TV, witnessing the hastily-planned funeral-related rituals, and

Monday's big state funeral, an event that is remarkable in its attention to detail and flawless execution (a bad word to use here). We watch the tube until we all have to return to the progress of LIFE, which is Tuesday of the week following the JFK assassination.

Much later in my life, as food bank friend, Dustin Howard is helping me ready this book for publication, we both read a retrospective of the "Kennedy Weekend" and the effect it had on our country. Dustin adds a beautifully written summary, which he's given me permission to include:

The Day the Grown-Ups Cried: On Reflection of JFK's Assassination:

There are moments in American history that don't just change the course of politics—they change the emotional weather of the country. The assassination of President John F. Kennedy was one of those moments. It has been recounted countless times, framed in documentaries, dissected in classrooms, and woven into fiction. In his 2013 piece for CBS News, contributor Bill Flanagan offered something quieter and more intimate: a reflection on what it felt like to witness that rupture—not as a historian, but as a child watching the adults around him fall apart.

"Those of us who were children when President Kennedy died absorbed the assassination through the effect it had on the grown-ups around us," Flanagan writes. It's a simple sentence, but it holds profound truth. Children are often emotional mirrors, reflecting the world not through comprehension, but through atmosphere. And on that November day in 1963, the atmosphere was heavy with something they had never quite seen before: adult grief, unfiltered and raw.

Flanagan remembers "the shock in the faces of the teachers as they whispered to each other before dismissing school... the grief we encountered in adults we met on the way home... and most of all, the pained reactions of our parents." These are not grand historical images; they are quiet, domestic ones. They remind us that for millions of Americans, Kennedy's assassination wasn't just a geopolitical crisis—it was the moment their parents lost something intangible, yet deeply felt: their sense of youthful possibility.

Looking back across five decades, Flanagan sees that moment as a generational turning point. "It seems to me that November 22, 1963, marked the moment when the World War II generation stopped thinking of themselves as young." It's a stunning observation. Kennedy, after all, was their reflection: a decorated war veteran, a product of the Depression, articulate, witty, driven. He was, as Flanagan puts it, "how the children of the Depression liked to see themselves." When he died, so too did a version of their identity.

The commentary takes a poignant turn when Flanagan shares his father's belief that "the day JFK died was the day our country went from optimism to cynicism." Whether or not that's literally true, it captures a deep emotional truth about the shift that followed. The World War II generation, once the face of bold rebuilding and American ambition, soon found themselves labeled the "Silent Majority." Their children—the baby boomers—began to question everything, from Vietnam to segregation to the very notion of institutional trust. "Don't trust anyone over 30," became the rallying cry. Kennedy's absence seemed to hasten that divide.

Flanagan evokes the literature of John Updike and John Cheever, where once-hopeful men now look back on "lost glories." He recalls Sinatra singing about the "September of My Years." And he imagines all the disillusioned Don Drapers of the world nodding along, sipping something strong, wondering how they got so old so fast. The emotional shift wasn't just political—it permeated the stories people told, the music they played, the way they talked about love and purpose and time.

But the most haunting exchange comes near the end, when Flanagan quotes journalist Mary McGrory: "We'll never laugh again." To which Kennedy aide Daniel Patrick Moynihan replied, "Mary, we will laugh again. It's just that we will never be young again." There's something in that sentiment that feels eternal. It's not just about the assassination—it's about the sudden awareness of mortality, the collective loss of innocence. It's about watching the people who raised you suddenly look small and uncertain in the face of history's cruelty.

Flanagan closes with a simple reflection: "It was the moment when our parents went from believing in all the great things that were going to be, to regretting what might have been." That line stuck with me. Regret, not just for a man, but for a version of the future that died with him. Kennedy's death marked a hinge between eras—between belief and disillusionment, between youth and aging. And fifty years later, we're still trying to understand what was lost that day, not just in terms of policy or politics, but in terms of possibility.

Winter 1964 - Joel Kunkel

At some point during my first year at CIA (probably in the winter of 1964), Al Hills has a visitor come up to our little three-room hallway in Angell Hall. This guy begins at CIA with Hills and graduates during that time that Al is up at U. Mass. Prior to meeting the "Kunk," Al tells me some pretty amazing stories about this guy. I believe they are all true.

Al brings him over to my room because I have a repurposed (glass) gallon mayonnaise jar filled with saltwater that houses a group of miniature sea horses. I buy them via an ad on the back of a comic book. I guess this is a 'must-see' item in Al's mind, and that's how Joel Kunkel and I meet. Over my two years at CIA, Kunk visits two-three times, even after Hillsy has graduated. We stay in touch but are really just acquaintances during this period.

A Prisoner at Betsy's

In the winter of 1964, I am going to CIA during the day, and U. of Bridgeport two nights a week. To make matters more challenging, for a short while during this period, I must hitchhike the round trip from New Haven to Bridgeport in the darkness of winter nights on the Connecticut Turnpike— not exactly a bucolic, tree-lined country road. It is one of those times my license gets suspended, so I cannot use my car.

My relationship with Betsy, a CIA student, has gotten to a point where she begins trying to persuade me to stay over after my returns from Bridgeport. On two or three occasions I stay over there, but I am never comfortable. See, her place isn't really her place. She rents a bedroom inside the apartment of an old widow.

About the fourth time I sleep there, it's the same routine: the old lady is watching TV way around back in the 'parlor.' I call to let Betsy know that I'll be there in five minutes. She opens the door for me, and I quickly go down the main hall, unseen and unheard, into Betsy's room and lock the door.

The usual routine in the morning has been that I peek out of the bedroom, look across the hallway and make sure that the old lady is asleep, and then I make a hasty exit down the main hallway and out the door to my car. Betsy then re-locks the front door behind me. And I drive around the corner and up the hill to my room at CIA, where I get ready for classes. It's all very dicey, very crazy, and VERY risky.

The old lady's bedroom has two sliding doors that are pulled toward each other, sealing off the room from the center hallway of the apartment. Usually, the doors are drawn together when she sleeps. When I wake up the morning of my fourth stay-over, I peek out of the bedroom to see that the sliding doors are open, and the old lady is in her bed, propped-up with pillows behind her. For the life of me I can't tell if she's dead or just alive and staring straight ahead or maybe asleep in a semi-sitting position. It's simply too far away, with my lousy vision, to see her eyes.

I know this could be disastrous for Betsy and me, and I must think very fast before this old bag, assuming she's awake, gets out of bed. Minutes tick by as I'm trying to get a better look. Betsy, who is also not blessed with the eyesight of an eagle, tries a few peeks but it's useless. Pretty soon the old lady gets up and out of bed. (*Oh hell, we're in for it now!*)

Soon enough, she goes up to the kitchen, where it sounds like she's making an early breakfast for herself. What I'm hoping will save me is the fact that it's 1964, and most people in apartments have just one phone. The phone is located in the parlor and has the world's longest cord—a cord that stretches, just barely, about 25 feet all the way into Betsy's bedroom. I tell Bets to bring the phone to me, while the old lady is in the kitchen.

For some crazy reason, I know the phone number of the payphone one floor down from the little hallway where Alan Hills and I have rooms at CIA. When I get the phone, I call the payphone, and wait until somebody in the dorm picks it up. Now I just have to hope that whoever it is will not only agree to run upstairs to Al's room, but actually find him there. It's early enough in the morning so that Al should be there getting ready for school. The minutes tick by, but finally I'm talking to Al. *"Al,"* I say, *"you gotta do me a BIG favor. I want you to wait at least one minute (time enough for Betsy to place the phone back into the far reaches of the parlor), then call this number. Betsy will answer. It may take a while, but she's going to put an old lady on the phone. I need for you to keep the old lady on the phone for at least 30 seconds. Use her name in your conversation, so she thinks you know who she is. Her last name is (whatever - I forget now). Just do this for me. I'll explain everything later."* So now I tell Betsy to put the phone as far away into the back reaches of the parlor as is possible.

Moments later I hear the ringing of the phone. Bets picks it up and yells for the woman, telling her there's a call for her. She doesn't bring the phone out to her, so the old lady has to go from the kitchen all the way down the hallway into the parlor, hunting for it, and finally answering. As soon as I know the woman is in the parlor and that I'm out of her view, I tear out of that bedroom, making a hard left down the main hallway toward the front door. My speed is such that I actually throw a small rug up in my wake. I don't stop. I gotta move fast. I get to the front door and fumble my way through two difficult locks, getting out what feels like just in time. I walk to my car and head up to school. I find Hillsy up in our hallway on the third floor of Angell Hall, and tell him, "Al . . . thanks, man. What did you tell her to keep her on the phone?"

Hills is showing me a big smile, saying, "Oh, I went through this whole morning DJ thing, you know: Hello, Mrs. so-and-so? My name is (famous New Haven DJ), and you're on the radio. I'm going to ask you a question and if you get it right, you're going to get a big breakfast prize. Are you ready for the question, Mrs. (so-and-so)? OK, here we go, "What ship brought the Pilgrims to Plymouth Rock (a good New England question)?"

"Why, it was the Mayflower," the old lady answered.

Hillsy is responding lightning fast, "That's right, Mrs. (so-and-so), and do you know what you've won?"

"No, what?" she asks.

"A big bowl of SHIT!" says Al.

Not only does Hillsy save my life, but he gives me an unexpected laugh imagining the scene back at the apartment.

Later I run into Betsy at school. I'm effusive in my praise of Al and tell her what happens when he runs the phone scam. But it doesn't quite go so well at her end.

After the call, the old lady leaves the parlor and heads back to the kitchen. She's walking down the main hallway looking straight at the front door and sees that both locks are unsecured. She immediately asks Betsy if she unlocked the door. Bets says, "No." But this smart old bag smells a rat.

"Hmmm. There's a mystery around here, and I'm going to get to the bottom of it," she says.

And before Betsy can get out of there and head for school, the woman bugs her three more times about 'the

Mystery.' All I know is that I've escaped. And there will be more escapes in my future, although I don't push my luck in *that* apartment ever again.

A Martha's Vineyard Summer 1964

The days and nights on 'The Island' are filled with every kind of learning and adventure, culinary and otherwise. I am working for 'Cadillac Jack' Griffin, a former CIA instructor who I first meet through Al Hills. I work for Griffin at the Jug End Barn, a rural resort hotel in the Berkshires (Mass.). I help out in the kitchen on a handful of weekends during the late winter and spring of 1964. Luckily, someone drops off the chef's Martha's Vineyard roster, and I get a spot working for him at what is, in 1964, the best hotel on the island, the Harborside Inn in Edgartown. Griffin is quite a character; I'll say that for him. He's full of what Hillsy calls verbal 'Bop Slop.' In other words, he uses a lot of 'be-bop' phrasing (popular at the time with musicians and the like), trying to create an image of the hipster chef. All of this is OK with me . . . for a while. My favorite thing he does while I'm cooking on the line during the dinner service, is to stand at the waiters' pick-up area, lifting one leg waist high, whistling through his teeth, making a sautéing motion with both hands held together, and yelling to me, "Sauté them babies!"

One afternoon early in the season (late June), I happen upon him at his favorite girl-watching/tourist-fisherman hustling spot (hustling to have his cooks clean and filet the tourists' day's catch for cash tips). It's the small receiving dock a couple of feet above the adjacent sidewalk of Main Street in Edgartown—so lots of foot traffic.

He's standing there acting for all the world as some sort of Main Street/harbor area master of ceremonies—in his whites and very tall (after all, he's *the* chef) toque blanc, commenting to all who will listen. For instance, whenever he sees a pretty girl(s), he immediately rolls into, "Hi ladies. down for the summer, or just the weekend?"

This day it becomes apparent that he has previously met the object of his attention. I'm just in time to hear Griffin's changed-up schtick, "Little Egypt, she walks, she talks, she crawls on her belly. One thin dime, folks, just one thin dime, one tenth of a dollar. Just step right into the tent."

And without skipping a beat he introduces me to a very pretty Boston College girl, who is, in fact, from Egypt, but really, she is the daughter of an emigrated Spanish/Jewish family. Her brother Andre is a Cornell hotelie who is running the Colonial Inn, a few blocks away. That's how I meet my first island girlfriend, Jocie Barcelone.

Music Break: Listen to "Little Egypt" by The Coasters.

The summer of 1964 in Edgartown on Martha's Vineyard is a paradise contrasted with my trip back to the island in 2015.

During the two summers I spend there in the sixties the place seems to be known only to rich people and those who serve them. There are no crowds of touristas milling around in the ubiquitous tee-shirt shops of the new millennium, and no traffic-halting presidential motorcades. During my summers there, the island is a beautiful, relatively non-commercial place of New England whaling history, with fishing boats and lobster pots strewn about, not for atmospheric effect, but because they are actually used. The beaches are classic Cape Cod, in their look of wild grasses on the dunes with their protective, weathered picket fencing. And those of us working in the bigger well-known hotels are given room and board along with our wages. Yes, it's a paradise in the 1960s.

I work six days, from 6:30 a.m.-3 p.m. cooking breakfast and lunch. I go to South Beach after my shift, and later I shower in my dorm and head back to the kitchen, where I get a head start on the next morning, laying out sheet pan after sheet pan of bacon and sausage, so that when I walk in I can just pop them into the ovens. Afterwards it's time for my supper, and I can eat anything I want from the dinner menu. Then I leave and get ready for whatever the night may bring my way.

In the mornings, during my walk of about three blocks to the Harborside kitchen, it is all peace and quiet. The only sound accompanying my footsteps are the absolutely charming buoy bells activated by the moving waters of the harbor, and the chorus of the gulls overhead. Those two sounds bring joy to me at 6:15 a.m. Pure joy. I love cooking the breakfast at the Harborside Inn. My job is to cook everything on the morning menu except pancakes and waffles. It's really a great opportunity to learn cooking a unique regional menu for the well-to-do New England crowd. Along with what is expected on any good hotel breakfast menu, guests will ask for just about anything. If we have the ingredients, we honor the request. I'm new at this business, and sometimes must ask for a definition of the item. John Vignone, who is a year ahead of me at school and who had the breakfast job during the previous summer, teaches me the ropes: it's all about being ready, being organized, about your 'mise en place,' i.e., having everything you'll need all prepped and within an arm's reach. 'Vig' teaches me for three mornings, and I'm ready. I learn Newburgh Omelets, Sauteed Lobster, Broiled Scrod, Broiled Mackerel, Roast Beef Hash and eggs – eggs any style, many of them, frankly, that are mostly new to me. Shirred Eggs, Eggs Benedict, Ham and Eggs Country Style, Jelly Omelets, etc. Not exactly the diner fare of northern New Jersey in 1964.

I learn a very important art, which will in a few years become obsolete: how to cook on and care for blue steel egg pans. There is no such thing as Teflon or anything that is a non-stick surface. The care and frequent 'burning-out' or 'salt conditioning' of the pans is so crucial to a smooth breakfast operation, that I learn in order to protect the surfaces of the pans, I must lock them up every night. It's a great summer job experience.

Edward M. Kennedy, U.S. Senate

One evening, I decide to treat myself to supper in a restaurant a block away from the Harborside Inn where I work. It's the Seafood Shanty, and I've got friends and CIA acquaintances working there. Island life is intimate among the people who work and/or own restaurants/hotels/inns there. And so even though I'm new to Edgartown, I already know the owner of the place. It's a nice little joint, not nearly as big as its 2015 relocated and rebuilt version when I visit the island with my New York family. But like so many people and things on the island, I learn about it from Alan Hills. He and I go for an occasional beer, but I've never eaten there. It's got very tight seating, and has a classic Martha's Vineyard menu for the times—lots of lobster dishes, bluefish, swordfish, scrod, sole, crab, etc. It sits right on the Edgartown Harbor facing 'Chappy' (Chappaquiddick Island, where in 1969, Ted Kennedy would somehow escape the most scandalous event of any American politician in history)—until Bill Clinton, anyway.

The place also has a very talented Japanese/American college girl singer/guitarist who entertains while I wait for my dinner. To this day I recall her rendition of "Try to

Remember" that I hear several times that first summer on the island, and like a handful of special songs from my youth, hearing it usually brings on a strong wave of nostalgia.

It's not unusual to see or deal with celebrities in Edgartown, and I am seated a few feet away from Ted and Joan Kennedy, who are hosting a group of their friends, a party of eight or so.

I'm eating alone, and occasionally someone I know will stop at my table to say, "Hi." The Kennedys receive their check and I watch Teddy sign and hand it to the waitress; afterwards, they all leave. I keep eating, and a few minutes later the owner, Bobby Carroll (who years later becomes mayor of Edgartown and is an extra when they film "Jaws" on the island) comes over to me and throws down Teddy's guest check in front of me and, exasperated, asks, "What the hell am I supposed to do with this?"

I look down at the check and pick it up. The tab is for about $250, which in 1964 is *a lot of cash*. It's signed, 'Edward M. Kennedy - U.S. Senate.' No phone number, no contact information of any kind. Bobby goes into a small rant about the tracking job he's going to have to do to find "this guy's people" to get the money, and he and I talk about the possibilities of ever even seeing the payment.

"What am I supposed to do," asks Bobby, "chase 'em down the dock to their boat?" And so it is in Massachusetts in 1964, when the Kennedys are at the peak of their power.

Labor Day 1964

One of the most poignant memories of my entire life occurs when I am only 20. It's on Labor Day night 1964. I have just completed the first of two summer seasons cooking on Martha's Vineyard. Of course, Labor Day is the last big weekend of the summer for island visitors. And it is also the period of the biggest few days of exodus for the many working people who spend the entire summer on the island. Most of us never leave because it's work, work, work; beach, beach, beach; party, party, party. Why would you ever leave to go to the 'mainland,' as it is called?

So leaving is a time of very strong feelings. Young adults away from parents, away from, 'What time did you get in last night?' 'Where were you last night?' and 'Who were you with last night?' etc. It's the bittersweet blend of walking away from the great friendships and the unreal culture of island life, which consists of working and playing hard all summer in a resort environment, knowing you'd never be there were it not for the fact that you are in service to those who can *actually afford* being there—and an awareness that the party's over. And now it's time to get back to the real world: a return to the old friends, family, school—the life one leaves in June—and the anticipation of the future, 'on the mainland.'

Back in the middle of that summer, I get a letter from the state of New Jersey, that they want my driver's license for a few months (again), so a co-worker who is quitting the job early does a favor for me and drives my car down to NYC, dropping it off at my grandfather's business. But then I'm without wheels for the rest of the summer. So when it's time to head home at the end of the season I arrange a ride with a bunch of southern college girls from the Seafood Shanty, who are going to drop me off in Teaneck on their way back to Charlottesville and Chapel Hill. The night we are leaving, we park their car on the lower deck of the Island Queen ferry and go up onto the top deck at the Vineyard Haven dock. We're standing at the ferry's rail, looking down through the late-night darkness at the crowd of well-wishers who are illuminated by a long string of overhead lights on the dock. I'm not expecting to see anything or anyone special in this group of people who drop off friends and family at the ferry, when out of nowhere, someone on the dock begins singing "Auld Lang Syne." Others on the dock began to join in, singing up at those of us crowded around the rail. Pretty soon we begin singing back at them. It's a special moment. I don't know, maybe I'm just sad, anticipating having to get out of the car and leave five very pretty college girls with their charming southern accents when we get to Teaneck at 4 a.m.

But that night, between the song and the circumstances, I experience an emotional feeling that previously never occurs to me. I 'get' the song. I 'get' its meaning. I think about it, and I know it is a moment never to be repeated. Even when I hear that song later in life, I will never again have that emotional response. Never. And that's okay.

September 1964 – CIA: Year Two, October 1964

A field trip to a poultry farm in Rhode Island is unusual for CIA seniors. It's my second year at school, but this is the first time they load us into buses and take us *anywhere*. Mostly this is because classes who precede us at CIA misbehave while on field trips. When I attend the school, CIA has a blend of miscreants and people who are serious about getting a culinary education. Currently it's quite different; yet in the old days, it was still the best this country offered in culinary schooling, just a crude and financially limited version of what it is today.

Of course, the farm is out in the country and they give us a nice tour. Everybody behaves. They have a bunch of picnic tables where we'll be served a turkey dinner, but they're not ready, so we're told to take a break. We're just hanging around having cigarettes and talking. There are about a hundred of us. I get bored and find my way into a small wooden building adjacent to the picnic area.

It's pretty dark inside the little building, but as my eyes are adjusting, I spot a trough attached to the wall. Above the trough is a long wooden plank perpendicular to the wall, and it's holding custom-made funnels with wider lower portions than normal. I realize this is where they kill the birds. They turn them upside-down, push their heads and necks through the bottom of the funnels, and then hack their heads off which then land in the trough below.

I look into the trough and it's filled with dried bloody chicken heads and feet. A goldmine. I load an ample amount into the pockets of my sport jacket (we're well-dressed for the outing) and head for the picnic area. I'm just in time to see classmate Dennis Kilcoyne doing his scrawny best to imitate an Olympic hammer thrower—only Dennis is doing this with a live turkey, which he is temporarily holding by the neck with both hands and twirling round and round, finally flinging it to the blue October skies over Rhode Island. Nobody in authority sees any of this, so our behavior on the field trip is deemed satisfactory by the chefs and other instructors who accompany us. We eat lunch and leave for school.

In the evening, Rod Stoner and I go over to the apartment of some female art students we've been chasing back in New Haven. We don't know these girls very well, but well enough for Rod to have bought the ingredients for a Shoo-Fly Pie, which he's promised to teach them how to bake. I sit watching my friend, this talented Lancaster, Pennsylvania, native, make the most famous dessert of his entire state, but as usual I get bored and take a walk.

I go into one of the two bedrooms in the apartment and unload a bunch of the dried bloody chicken heads and feet into an underwear drawer in a dresser. I know that I'll miss the fun when the girls discover them, but I can imagine the result, and that's enough for a good private chuckle. It's just a little fun.

The pie is very good.

November 1964

Spending a lot of time with CIA chef instructor, Art Jones, I begin to hit my stride as my second year at the school gets rolling. But in planning for what to do after graduation, I am entertaining divergent ways of moving forward: I desperately want a formal culinary apprenticeship, but only if I can get into one of the two best: either the Greenbrier or the Waldorf program. And then there is college; college, because now I feel that I am truly ready for an education. I feel a void that needs to be filled, an emptiness. I'm serious now, and *'I can at least get B's at any school - just let me in.'*

At this same time I am chosen for a four-man team to work under the direction of Chef Emile Delorme to create a show piece for the Culinary Salon at the 'New York Show,' the National Hotel Show that takes place in the N.Y. Coliseum.

Although clearly, we couldn't have done it without the chef's guidance, the team does take "First Prize for Student's Work." It's a thrilling moment.

1965 - Graduation Looming...What to Do?

Over the late winter and early spring of 1965, any college Hotel and Restaurant Management program that I apply to says, 'Not so fast, Buster.'

Nobody wants me. It's a trap of sorts: they know about me. There's a Seinfeld episode where Elaine has an itchy rash, but she's a difficult patient. In the show, the docs all have a secret network, and soon enough, every dermatologist who she goes to refuses to see her.

The colleges must be the same: they get a peek at my high school transcript, and it's all over. Rejections pour in from every school that has a decent Hotel and Restaurant Management program. I redouble my efforts to get into the Greenbrier or the Waldorf, and also entertain the idea of doing an apprenticeship of sorts in the meat-packing houses of Manhattan.

The Greenbrier is not happening, but after a lot of effort on my part, including two trips to the Waldorf kitchens to meet with its famed Executive Chef Eugene Scanlon, we meet again on Easter weekend. He tells me he took eleven applicants from all over the globe, and I am his first choice.

The Waldorf says, "*Yes!*" Yes, to a two-year apprenticeship! This is an honor that has me floating in the clouds. Of the various recognitions I later receive in my career, this is still the highlight, the most genuine, and is totally devoid of politics or insider help from anyone.

Between these two occurrences—the Easter weekend meeting with Chef Scanlon and his official letter of acceptance—a CIA friend tells me on a Friday afternoon that the University of Denver (DU) is going to be interviewing the following day in Manhattan. I make an appointment.

I am interviewed by Dean Curtis of the Business School, and after he looks over my high school and CIA records, he says, "Look, I doubt very much you have a chance of getting in, but I'd like you to apply."

This makes no sense to me, and I tell him so. He is a very nice guy and explains that the turn-around I have made since starting at CIA (vs. my high school record) shows that I have grown up, and continues, "What if you found out 20 years from now that you could have gotten in? You'd kick yourself in the ass." How could I not like this guy?

So I apply to DU and then go about my business, sure in the knowledge that it will join the other schools who already refuse me. I continue planning to attend the Chef Magazine's late September tour of Europe's most renowned kitchens. After the tour, I am scheduled for early October start at the Waldorf. I'm not worrying too much about a summer job: that'll happen.

A lot is happening in my life now, a period of excitement. Along with three other senior students at CIA, I am chosen to work the school's booth at the National Restaurant Association Show in Chicago in May. The four of us drive out in a van owned by one of my classmates. He is chosen because the school can transport all the booth materials, etc., in the van—a marriage of convenience. We will meet up with school administrators in Chicago. Going to the show is a major big deal in my young life, and on one afternoon, I manage to get cousin Max Ostrow (a student at Northwestern) onto the exhibit floor, and we have a great visit walking and eating samples for a few hours. I also have an opportunity to visit with Dr. and Mrs. Wilson of the University of Denver's Hotel & Restaurant School.

There are dinners, seminars, and important lunches to attend, and we get to sit with Mrs. Roth, CIA's founder, and the school's newly appointed president, Jacob Rosenthal, who arrives in March but will take over officially in September. We always are seated in VIP locations because of Mrs. Roth's status in the restaurant world. One of the lunches is put on by the American Culinary Federation (ACF). We eat a nice but uncomplicated meal of roast sirloin and a brown sauce (I forget which variation), a vegetable, rissole potatoes, and of course, dessert. After the meal, ACF President and Master Chef of Heinz Soups, Paul Laesecke, a highly respected man in the industry, is introduced. Chef Laesecke stands at the podium and rhetorically asks, "If anyone here doesn't think that was the greatest meal he's ever had, I'd like to know about it." And right then and there, Jake Rosenthal doesn't merely raise his hand from a table front and center in a banquet room with 200 seated chefs but is actually waving his arm for attention. It's a stunning, brash move—insane for somebody who must make friends with industry bigwigs in a constant effort to raise funds for CIA in its infancy. I'm trying not to fill my diaper from embarrassment, sitting next to this virtual stranger, and I realize he's putting the culinary world on notice: he has higher standards than the ACF's president, and higher aspirations for the students of CIA and the school itself. Chef Laesecke is a classy gentleman and either doesn't see Rosenthal's waving arm or ignores it. Peace returns to our table in the crowded banquet room.

A few years later Chef Laesecke's son Paul Jr. joins the DU Hotel School's faculty while he's working on a doctorate degree. He is my teacher in a catering class. He's only a few years older than me, and we become friends while I'm at DU. The other connection that goes back to the lunch in Chicago is that Laesecke Senior's protégé at Heinz is a young Ferdinand Metz, who takes over when the chef retires, and eventually is brought onto the CIA's Board of Trustees by Rosenthal. Then when Jake himself retires, Metz is tapped to run the school, and we also become good friends during his time there.

During this window of time, in late May, girlfriend Ernie and I go to a Joan Baez concert in New Haven. Baez is the reigning queen of single act folk singers as the genre is winding down, courtesy of the 'British Invasion,' and I am still a big fan. We have to wait and wait for the show to start, and before we can hear her, we suffer through what appears to be a novelty act—some guy we had never heard of, half-singing/half-talking, playing a guitar, and occasionally blowing in and out of a harmonica. All I want is JOAN BAEZ, not some sideshow act, '*what's his name? Oh, yeah, somebody Dylan.*' Needless to say, he becomes world famous, and years later, I learn to enjoy Bob Dylan's music very much.

After the concert we stop in at a well-known downtown New Haven basement folk music club, and who should be there at a table full of cigar-smoking guys and their dates? Joel Kunkel. He tells me he's going to begin the Hotel and Restaurant Management program at Denver in the fall. I tell him I've applied and will stay in touch. I do call him once during the summer, just to catch up on any news.

June 11, 1965 - CIA's Graduation Day

Resulting from circumstances beyond their control, this is the only time in my life that my parents will see me graduate from anything, and it is a very nice experience all the way around.

The graduation takes place at Sprague Hall, a building at Yale. As we're leaving the ceremony, it's a beautiful sunny day in New Haven. The exalted Chef Emile Delorme is stationed just outside, near the doorway, ready to congratulate his students as we walk out of the ceremony. He is the former chef de partie at Hotel Plaza Athenee in Paris, one-time corporate executive chef for Air France, and *the* opening executive chef for Le Pavillion, perhaps the most prestigious Manhattan restaurant in its time. Le Pavillion was built as a successor to the French Pavillion's famed restaurant at the 1939 NYC World's Fair. As we approach the chef he looks up and sees that it is me, accompanied by people who are obviously my parents and girlfriend. I know that I am one of his favorites, so it doesn't surprise me when he shakes my mother's hand and gives her a glowing report. As we begin to move away heading for the car, and to the reception lunch for graduates and guests, my mother, not fully understanding, or maybe more accurately, not fully believing, the transition from the Teaneck schools' Vinnie to the CIA student Vinnie, remarks to anyone listening, "That guy's looking for a tip" (as in . . . 'how could anybody in the teaching profession sincerely say anything nice about Vinnie?'). It's really not her fault. If you had a kid like me and had to live through umpteen disappointing report cards and parent-teacher conferences for a dozen solid years, you'd probably think or say just what she does. But that's really my strongest memory of my CIA graduation, the only graduation of mine that my parents can attend: "That guy's looking for a tip." And it is VERY funny to me - then and now.

Summer 1965 - A Fork in the Road

I spend so much energy on the Waldorf

and the possibility of a start with DiBragga and Spitler (meat packers) that I don't have a summer job. The third week in June I pack up a suitcase and my kitchen toolbox, pick up my girlfriend Ernie and her sister Ellen, and we head up to Martha's Vineyard. All three of us will look for jobs, and if it turns out that nothing happens, well, we'll have a nice weekend and head back home.

We stay with my friend Norm Vunk and a house full of guys in Oak Bluffs, and within 48 hours all three of us have jobs in Edgartown: Ernie and I at the Harbor View Hotel, Ellen at the coffee shop at the center of town.

Ern and I move into the Women's and Men's Helps' Dorms, respectively, at the Harbor View, and Ellen finds a place in Edgartown.

Ellen misses her boyfriend and leaves after only two or three weeks. Ernie stays until close to the last week in August, and I head for home right before Labor Day.

Why would I leave *before* Labor Day, which is pretty much everybody's commitment who has a key job at any island operation? Two weeks before, my mother gets a message to me through the hotel front desk to call her. She reads a letter of 'conditional acceptance' to me from the University of Denver. Dean Curtis comes through! It's all very exciting, but now I have to quickly decide between two life-changing things that I've pursued for many months: college at the third best school in the country for Hotel and Restaurant Management, or a two-year culinary apprenticeship at the world-renowned Waldorf-Astoria Hotel. It's the first time in my life that I stand at a major fork in the road. I figure I can always work in a kitchen, but this shot at DU, after all the rejections from other schools, is never, ever going to be offered to me again. I have to take the DU option. But DU wants me out there the second week in September, and I have too much to do, including the drive out there in my little middle-aged VW Bug. So I leave the Vineyard on Friday of Labor Day weekend. I feel bad about leaving Chef Willie Webber at the Harbor View but I don't have much of a choice.

On the way home, I stop at the Mermaid Tavern (Restaurant Associates), in Stratford, Connecticut, where I hope to find Joel Kunkel at his job as their pastry chef. I do, and while he's whipping up ten quarts of meringue, we make plans to meet up in Denver. Although to be more accurate, he does suggest, in what I come to know as his standard perv growl, "Hey, let's drive out together and stop at some o' them Mexican whore houses down in Chihuahua."

Life in a Mexican jail flashes before my eyes, and I say, "Nah, I'll see you out there."

September 1965 - Go West, Young Man

About ten days after I leave the island, I deliver my lifelong Teaneck pal, Richie Pink, who makes the drive out west with me, to a plane at Denver's Stapleton Airport, where I see him off toward his next assigned air force base in California. Registration for classes will start two days later, on Monday.

The morning after I see Richie off, it is time to check into the dorm at DU. The letter of instruction from the university says that the dorm check-in people are available as early as 9 a.m. I am assigned to an apartment dorm. This is a pretty cool concept in 1965. It means that instead of a traditional dorm room, it is a two-bedroom apartment, including a bathroom, kitchen and living room, right in the middle of the campus. It is a male dorm, but at very specific times we are allowed to have female guests. And vice versa for the women's apartment dorms.

Always an early riser, I check out of the motel on East Colfax Ave. and arrive at the parking lot behind several apartment dorms on campus. As I'm rolling into the parking lot, I spot, among a handful of other cars, Joel Kunkel's blue '63 Oldsmobile. I pull up next to it and discover that he's asleep in the front seat. I wake him up, and he tells me that he has spent the night there. We decide to go out for breakfast. As we take off for a coffee shop, he asks me what dorm I'm in. I pull out my letter and read that I'm in Skyline Hall. He says, "Me too. What room are you in?" I read off the room number and he says, "Open up the glove compartment and read my letter." I can't believe it: we're in the same room!

How can this be? Neither one of us knew anyone at DU to even request such a thing. I don't know I'm even going to the school until late August, about three weeks prior to checking into the dorm. And yet here we are, introduced by Al Hills two years prior in Connecticut; nothing more than casual acquaintances over this period, now about to be sleeping in the same bedroom in Denver, Colorado!

It is even more remarkable, given that any of the schools to which I apply during the preceding nine months could accept my application—which might change where I end up—but none do. I find out about Denver very late in the previous spring and decide to give it a shot. Joel, accepted with a scholarship at Cornell but on academic probation (an unusual juxtaposition), is insulted by the offer, and chooses DU, which also gives him scholarship money. Kunk and I could have easily gone our separate ways, but somehow end up as unplanned roommates 1,800 miles from where we met.

October 1965 - The Great Escape

Kunk and I are part of a small group of East coast boys at DU. We are enjoying each other's company and our newfound paradise, Denver, Colorado. It's all about the CIA and that junior college in upstate New York; the connections that we have to each other. All of us are from the Northeast, all have mutual friends back home that lead to our meeting up in Denver, and except for 'The Tomato,' we are all majoring in Hotel and Restaurant Management and living in the apartment dorms in the middle of DU's campus. And soon after we arrive, we all have nicknames, ergo, the Tomato. We are our own little gang, becoming very good friends over the years at DU, adopting others to be part of the group as the months and years go by.

Also at DU during my years there are Lynne and Maurie Morris, and Lois Elting, all of whom I grow up with, as they are the children of my parents' circle of best friends. None of this is planned, it just happens that all of us end up on the same campus 1,800 miles from home.

One night Kunk borrows my car (I don't remember why), and the next morning tells me he stole a fire extinguisher from an apartment building where he's been at a party. This, I would come to find out, is not out of character for him. For no apparent reason, he delights in removing stuff from people or places. And since my boyhood bedroom had one or two street signs, etc., presented to me by my father and/or his friends, I am quite at home with the whole thing. So the fire extinguisher remains on the rear seat floor of the Bug for a couple of weeks. Out of sight, out of mind.

It is not unusual during our first few months at DU to go to a bar called La Pitcher (*La Pishay*) for what is affectionately known as 'FAC' - Friday Afternoon Club. So we're at this joint and nothing much is giving us a reason to stay. We pile into my VW to leave: Scoty, the Yam, Tomato, and me. Right out of the parking lot, we have to slow for a red light. While we wait for the light to turn green, a car full of Mexicans in a '56 Chevy station wagon pulls up next to us. They're about our age—early 20s.

Now as background I should tell you that, being from the Northeast, we don't have a clue about Mexicans. Remember, it's 1965, and other than in about five western states, they are unknown to most Americans – and in Tomato's case, Canadians. There are no gangs, guns, drive-bys, low riders, etc. They're just, well, Mexicans.

We look at them, they look at us, and that's about it. But behind my seat in the car are two things that together will create some unexpected dramedy: the Tomato and a fully loaded fire extinguisher.

This cherub-faced guy, David John Eyre, who we call Tomato, and who everybody loves, is one innocent-acting, innocent-looking, but impulsive and unpredictable dude. So out of nowhere he manages to squeeze around me, and through my open window gives these Mexicans a BLAST of white powder chemical into the front shotgun window of their Chevy wagon. They are so shocked that they end up all laughing their asses off. Like any comedian, the Tomato thrills to their response and now gives them another blast, *a long one*. The Chevy is now completely filled with a fog of white powder, as the light turns green. Did I mention that we white boys also decide to laugh? Well, we do. And at some point, in that other car, its suddenly white powder-haired inhabitants decide that it isn't so funny anymore. But of course, I don't know this as we pull away from the light.

Pretty soon I can see in the rearview mirror that they are making some very aggressive moves to try to catch up to us. The race is on. It is an enormous challenge and fun playing cat and mouse in two vehicles that aren't built for speed or agility. We break out onto an uncrowded road that takes us along the Platte River. I've got the VW floored and we're going maybe 45, when I spot a large dirt and gravel parking area in what appears to be a construction company yard. I hang a hard left, as the Tomato's telling me to let him out of the car; he's been "beat up before, and it's OK."

"No!" I tell him, "You're crazy. We're never leaving you alone."

I assume that we'll make a stand in the dirt parking lot. But as we leave the asphalt road and swing hard into the lot, I don't foresee that the gravel surface and our velocity will propel us into a huge 360, leaving in our wake a monster cloud of brown dust and dirt, adding to the white powder mess in the Chevy. As we pull out of the arc, I realize we can just keep driving. We don't need to jump out and brawl with these guys; they've been temporarily blinded again.

Besides, it's not about fighting these idiots; it's about the fun of out-maneuvering and out-smarting them in a fully weighed-down, tired VW. We race out and go back the way we came, along the river, and when we get to a north/south main drag (I believe Santa Fe), we're on a pretty long hill, headed north. They begin to gain on us, and just at the moment when they're about to overtake us and force us to the curb, I see a side street coming up on our right. I wait till I'm sure they've gotten in front of us, and suddenly leave Santa Fe with a hard right onto the side street. They overshoot the street and can't follow us.

Now I'm looking for a way out of this totally unfamiliar neighborhood, going up and down streets, and BOOM, there they are. They're back on us. I'm scrambling now, looking for a way out, when I spot a construction site, an excavation—a big hole in the ground—with carved dirt drive ramp down into it. I take the ramp, and power right through earth-moving machinery in operation all around us. Just when I think we're trapped down in this giant hole (about two stories below street level), I see another dirt ramp on the diagonally opposite side of the excavation, which takes us back to street level. The Mexicans somehow follow.

We take a few turns through the blocks in this neighborhood, and I decide to drive down an alley. The Mexicans are gaining on us, and from the intensity of their moves, clearly have lost their sense of humor. Up ahead, there's a problem: a Pepsi truck making a delivery is blocking the alley. I keep heading right for it and manage to squeeze the Bug between a telephone pole and the Pepsi truck. That's it. They're stuck. We never see the Chevy wagon again. Lots of laughter.

That night when we get home, I give crap to Kunk for stealing that stupid, useless fire extinguisher. We laugh, and then he tells me he's all disappointed in us, that we should have just jumped out of the car and fought with the Mexicans. This is a major difference between us: I love a good laugh, and while he does too, he'd just as soon break noses. Fighting is one of his hobbies.

Summer 1966 - Making My Bones

There are two occasions when I make my bones in the restaurant business. In the Mafia you don't have to do this twice, but my deals are 14 years and almost 3,000 miles apart, in very different companies, so I have to prove myself once, and then again later: the summer of 1966 with Restaurant Associates (R.A.) for the opening of Fountain Cafe in the middle of NYC's Central Park, and in late August 1980, at Harrah's-Tahoe, during the Harvey's Casino bombing across the street (U.S. Hwy 50). I stumble into each situation with an opportunity to be tested by the best.

In late March of our freshman year, from my apartment dorm room shared with Joel Kunkel in Denver, I decide to write to R.A. to ask for a summer job in New York. After all, family friend Buddy Adler has gotten out of Penn State's hotel and restaurant program a few years earlier and is flourishing at the company. Also. during my time at CIA, my mother shows me a long *New Yorker* profile on Joe Baum, R.A.'s president. By some incredible luck, I am one of four seniors chosen to work the CIA booth at the Chicago

Restaurant Show in May 1965. While I'm there, I get to see and hear Mr. Baum's keynote address. I am seated in the first row because I'm with Mrs. Roth, the founder of CIA. I manage to get a hard copy of the speech. It's all very inspiring. I keep it for the rest of my life. That ought to tell you how inspiring it is.

One of the very nice things my mother does, after it's clear I'm going to be in the restaurant business, is that she begins saving menus from interesting places for me. And she takes me for drinks to expensive joints, most notably, R.A.'s the Four Seasons, where the food would be too costly, but I get to check out the restaurant via time spent having a couple of drinks. I never forget that first view of the Four Seasons. Through these experiences I'm being drawn toward the high-end quality and inventiveness that is Restaurant Associates. There is no restaurant group anywhere in the world that has its eclectic collection of Manhattan restaurants during the 1960s.

Based on my letter and resume, the R.A. personnel manager writes back and tells me that they'll commit to a summer job in Manhattan, but that they won't know what they'll offer me until I show up at their offices. I don't know what to do, but time is on my side since it's only mid-April. I know that I can have Kunk's sauté job at Denver's high-end Le Profil for the whole summer, or go back home and work for R.A.

After I get the letter from R.A., I write to Jacob Rosenthal, the new president of CIA, and ask his advice about the summer job. I tell him that I have a choice to make, between a sauté job at Le Profil in Denver (even sending the menu to him) or a promised but undisclosed job somewhere in NYC with R.A. I spend two or three sentences explaining Le Profil, its high-end reputation in Denver, its quality level, etc.

A week and a half later I receive Mr. Rosenthal's response. Simple and beautiful in its wisdom and logic: 'Go to work for R.A. Regardless of how good it is, the mere fact that you had to spend so much time explaining the restaurant in Denver means you will have to do so every time in the future when you present your resume to someone. If R.A. appears on your resume, it will need no explaining. Everyone who reads it will know that you worked for the best restaurant group in the country' (which is undisputed at the time).

By now it is May. I write back and thank Mr. Rosenthal for his help, then write R.A. and accept their offer. At the time I don't know it but going with R.A. becomes one of the most meaningful decisions of my working life.

When I arrive in the city, I am anxious to start working at R.A. I contact Joel Schaefer, the personnel guy who promised me a job. A few days later we have a very brief conversation in his office. He tells me I am to meet with a vice president. I ask why a V.P. and am told that they want to discuss a unique summer job opportunity. It's a kind of experiment, a seasonal outdoor European-styled cafe in the middle of Central Park.

Meeting George Lang

I'm taken to George Lang's office, which he shares with a secretary, and there's space at a vacant desk for another person. This is 1966, and there are still a whole bunch of industry people who really don't know anything about CIA—the school is still in its early stages—and Lang is apparently one of them.

He begins rapid fire questions in an intimidating manner with his Hungarian accent: "All I know is that you're 21 years old and you want to work in a restaurant. Tell me about yourself. And what is this school you went to?" I describe CIA.

Lang asks, "Is it for short order cooks?"

"No," I say, somewhat offended, but realize he is baiting me.

Another question from Lang, "Well, what kind of cooking do they teach there?

I tell him, "Everything: American, classical . . ."

"Classical?" he fires back. "Give me a recipe for a classical dish, anything."

I tell him, "OK, I'll do Lobster Americaine." The truth is, I've never made this dish; I've only seen it demoed once in the spring of my senior year at CIA. But I'm not going to be cowed by this condescending European/New York food snob. So I launch into what I remember from the demo.

When I'm finished Lang looks at me and says, "Very good! Except you gave me a perfect recipe for Lobster Pompadour."

He knows I am nervous, and lets it go. Somehow, he hires me anyway . . . maybe just to have me around to remind himself of how smart he is. Or maybe it's because as I read in his memoir many years later, *Nobody Knows the Truffles I've Seen*, that when he auditions with his violin (and is accepted) for the Dallas Symphony, ". . . I played the entire section in D minor, although even our stagehands knew it was written in D major."

And because I have a less-than-self-confident interview, he decides to give me a lesser position than they originally plan. He explains that we will spend some time putting the finishing touches on planning the opening, then get into the actual restaurant space, put the place together, and open it. And I will be "the number two" kitchen steward, assisting a more experienced guy. Lang tells me I'll be working seven days a week after the place opens . . . unless it rains. Since it's an outdoor operation, they'll pay me a set salary, regardless of the weather. It won't be my first seven-day gig, and I'm well aware of Buddy Adler's 'apprenticeship' at R.A., so I readily agree to the terms: $90 a week.

After about two weeks working at the vacant desk in Lang's office, a few feet away from him, I really begin to like and admire the guy, and begin an amazing journey of discovery and learning at his side. I have tremendous respect for his 'man for all seasons' persona. I am in awe of the little things I pick up just being around him.

This is the guy who is the very first to instruct waiters and waitresses at R.A.'s Tower Suite to greet each party with, 'Good evening, my name is ---------, and I'll be your butler tonight.' Later, in restaurants of lesser formality, it turns into, 'Hi, I'm (name) and I'll be your server tonight,' and is ubiquitous throughout the U.S., and sickeningly overused. But in the beginning, it is brilliant. This is also the guy who, based upon his musical background, creates the word use of 'intermezzo' for a palate-refreshing break in a fine dining meal, and who introduces America to the 'fine dining' Sunday brunch. He becomes one of the consulting editors for the groundbreaking Time-Life "Foods of the World" series of cookbooks (1960s). To really know him, you should read his remarkable story; at the very least, Google him, and you will read about this genius: a man who twice escapes the Nazis, gets to the U.S., plays violin in the Dallas Symphony Orchestra, is a saucier at a famous Dallas hotel (I forget which one), and along the way learns to speak English.

But then he moves to New York, and somehow gets a job running big parties at the Waldorf-Astoria and serves food to kings and presidents. He writes about art in the N.Y. Times Sunday Magazine. He speaks five languages fluently, using the English language in a truly remarkable manner, particularly for a non-native speaker. He is even asked to write the forward for one of the editions of "Le Repertoire de la Cuisine," a classic compendium which has been published since 1914.

He becomes a V.P. for Joe Baum at R.A., and in his later years re-invents and re-opens a classic Hungarian restaurant (Gundel) half-way around the world in Budapest. He definitely has a worthwhile story to tell. And while nobody would call him a particularly humble man, relative to what he's seen and done in his lifetime, he's not a bragger either.

Lang is clearly one of the truly fascinating characters I meet in my travels on this earth. He is a most remarkable man, a latter-day gastronomic version of Thomas Jefferson with a Hungarian accent, a powerful inventive force and a bookend to Joe Baum's creativity when they work together at R.A.

Months later, when I go to visit with him during Christmas break 1966, he isn't seated at a normal desk like everybody else in the new R.A. offices. No, he's seated at an original 18th century half-circular Hunt Table. The message is, *'I've got a level of sophistication and esthetic taste that requires this piece; I can't abide anything less.'*

I am working right in his office, sharing the spare desk with the guy who will be the restaurant director, my boss

Tony Gordon, a Brit, who has been working at R.A.'s Paul Revere's Tavern as Buddy Adler's assistant director. Tony's a very nice guy in his first job as an R.A. director, and also his first 'opening' in that role. We're learning together. We spend our days doing a lot of the administrative tasks that are part of getting a restaurant ready "on paper." We're at R.A.'s 57th Street corporate offices, and in the relatively short time I am there, I meet the bosses, the secretaries, and many people in-between. I work with them and I eat with them at the employee lunchroom. This is a huge advantage for me in many ways. My best buddy there is Mr. Lang's secretary, Florence Rothmel, who shows me the ropes and becomes like a big sister. She could be a stand-up Jewish comedienne and keeps me amused commenting on all things/people R.A. . . . when Lang is not around.

A few times Mr. Lang eats lunch at his desk while reading Time magazine or some other publication. The whole operation, the eating and *the reading from cover to cover*, takes about ten minutes max. The guy is unreal. And it's not even in his native language!

As time for the restaurant (the Fountain Cafe) to open gets closer, the pace picks up, and we are working in the office on Saturdays—mostly because Mr. Lang takes sick with the mumps (not good for a guy in his 40s), and R.A. President Joe Baum and Operations V.P. Alan Lewis (Cornell classmates) must get involved, filling in for him. It is great for me because I am getting exposed to these restaurant legends.

There Are Four Guys . . .

George Lang, Joe Baum, Alan Lewis, and Fred Rufe, who will change my life in one very, very long hot NYC summer. They are near the top of their collective game in the food business, although they'll pile up even higher achievements in the next decade or two. Three of the four are graduates of Cornell's famed School of Hotel Administration, Lang being the non-college guy, unquestionably the one with the highest intelligence, the miraculous anomaly.

Just imagine if you were a psych major and got to spend time with Freud, Jung, Binet, and Skinner; or maybe you're a young professional golfer and you could spend your 22nd summer with Hogan, Palmer, Nicklaus, and Tiger Woods. That's what it is like for me with these four guys. You can say, '*Why does their background matter? Why include this sort of detail in your story?*'

Answer: Because my career, my life, would have been far less, far different without that one summer when I met them and worked with them. These badass R.A. guys liked me. They didn't ask me about my grades in school, they only cared about how hard I worked and what I accomplished.

Who They Are:

Joe Baum

In my lifetime Joe Baum is the Steve Jobs of the restaurant industry, a brilliant, creative genius who doesn't merely invent restaurants, but whose impact on the entire retail food world eclipses anyone or anything before or since his active years. I don't know that all these words about Baum are of my invention. They seem too good to come from me; maybe I read some of them somewhere and combined them with my own thoughts: *Like Jobs, he is alone in his genius. And like Jobs, he can be a very tough, demanding, and volatile man. He can go off like a MAJOR volcano, but what a mind! Both men pair their technical knowledge with esthetics: neither is a superior "engineer" on the technical side, but by combining both, they place themselves above and beyond anyone else. That is the essence of their genius. Both connect imagination to technology.*

So many things that happen or are seen in today's restaurants, we take for granted, but many were created and/or popularized by Joe Baum. The man virtually invented the theme restaurant.

Both Baum and Jobs get voted out of the dynasty that each creates. And each regains his footing and later goes on to far bigger successes. When Joe Baum is removed from Restaurant Associates, he is ultimately hired to consult with the Port Authority to create and operate all restaurants in the World Trade Center. The project is years in the making. And Baum is so keenly aware of the details of esthetics that when he sees architectural renderings of the exterior window treatments for what will become the Windows on the World restaurant, he convinces all involved to re-design the major elements of window framing (AS THE BUILDING IS GOING UP!) to allow for better views and a more pleasing look—from both inside and outside.

No matter what project he is heading up, no matter which company he is with, he doesn't just create restaurants and menus counting on his own formidable expertise and taste; he uses menu advisors, who are the reigning NY Times food critics of their day. He hires lighting consultants and designers for everything from ashtrays to themed/logoed gift cufflinks (for important guests and R.A.'s senior management). No detail is spared. And for a short time in my young life I get to work with him and his Cornell- and European-trained generals, colonels, and lieutenants. I am one LUCKY kid, and fortunately, he treats me well.

Alan Lewis

This guy is an operator's operator, a field general, a guy who acts as Baum's down-in-the-trenches muscle. He is an animal, a very, very tough guy, who pulls no punches, spares no one his abuse if errors have been made, and who has as foul a mouth as anyone in the NYC restaurant world. All that said, he is a guy I admire, and in some ways can't help but unconsciously emulate (except for the abuse part). He's Baum's buddy from Cornell. He dresses well, has artistic taste, really knows food, and it's easy to look at him and think, 'Someday I want to be that guy.' But he IS an animal.

You won't find much to read about him in Google, because he is the guy in the background, the blocking fullback who makes somebody else look good, but trust me, once the doors open, operationally, he makes it all happen.

Once in his early years, right after graduating Cornell, he was a rookie managing a restaurant in France. The smartass chef asked him to taste the Coq au Vin. Lewis did, and took a big risk, bluffing, and questioned why he didn't use blood for a liaison (a very classical approach, mostly abandoned years before). The chef was speechless.

Years later, Lewis told a reporter, "I didn't want him to think he was dealing with some dumb Jew college boy from America."

After my second school vacation stint with R.A., I'm back in Denver and I mail a couple of impressive, very creative local menus from a well-run local company (the

Hungry Farmer, the Hungry Dutchman, to name a couple) owned by Tom Wilscam. Months later when I'm with Lewis in his office, I ask him if he got the menus. His reaction is something that stays with me always: "Yeah I got 'em. That son of a bitch!" And this is the real essence of Alan Lewis: he's a fierce competitor, and even if the guy's in a market 1,800 miles away, and in no way competing with R.A., he's still an S.O.B., simply because he had a good idea that Lewis didn't think of first. Years later I read something that Charles Revson (one of the brothers that founded and ran Revlon for many years) says, "Of course the other guy has a right to make a living but let him make it in some other business." And that, folks, pretty much sums up Alan Lewis' viewpoint.

Fred Rufe

What can one say about a man who successfully stutters his way through the college admission interview (Fred tells me this story himself), and past the famous but skeptical Dean Meek, founder of the world-renowned School of Hotel Administration at Cornell University; a man who not only survives Joe Baum's tirades and Alan Lewis being Alan Lewis, but does it in the NYC market, while himself being likable enough to have many of us who work for him think of him as—and sometimes call him—"Uncle Fred," and who can make you laugh out loud, or at least smile with his combination of a comical phrase and stuttertalk? He drives a white Caddy convertible in NYC! What a character! We love the man. All of us.

He is one of the operational pillars of R.A. And when I work for him, he is a group director, overseeing airport and freestanding restaurants on Long Island, along with the Fountain Cafe in NYC's Central Park.

Later, after the old Cornell gang leaves R.A., Fred becomes V.P. of all Marriott restaurants nationwide, then corporate F&B director for Hilton Worldwide. He is a great supporter of mine and remains a friend as I grow in the business over the years, until his passing in 1999.

Fred's stuttering and sense of humor are legendary enough throughout the company. One of the things that makes him so universally loved is his reaction to the world around him. A famous and absolutely true story about Freddy takes place during Christmas time at La Fonda.

R.A. opens La Fonda del Sol in 1960 or '61, one of the grand theme restaurants that Joe Baum creates. It's a beautiful large Brazilian-themed setting, so thoroughly researched that corporate executive chef Albert Stockli is sent to live down in that country for about six months to gain a strong knowledge of the cuisine and the culture. Baum, being Baum, sends off to Italy for a custom-designed, hand-crafted ceramic manger scene to place in the front of the restaurant during its first holiday season.

At the time, Rufe is the area director for a number of R.A.'s Manhattan theme restaurants, which means he oversees La Fonda. When the crate arrives from Italy, Fred is there to open it and set up the manger with a couple of busboys. But when they begin unpacking the various pieces, they find that the Baby Jesus piece has been broken in half.

Freddy of course becomes panicked. Not simply because the piece is broken, but also because he must now call the white-hot-tempered Joe Baum with this very bad news. The call is made, and Fred stutters through his story to Baum.

Baum says, "OK Fred, just calm down. All you have to do is go down to a construction site, find a load of bricks, and grab some of the burlap."

In these days, newly made bricks are shipped wrapped in burlap and straw to protect their edges. Baum continues, "You bring back the burlap and use it as a blanket to cover the broken piece when you set up the manger display. No one will ever know that it's broken." He even tells Fred where a new skyscraper is going up near La Fonda.

Rufe jumps into the Caddy and goes to the site, which, like all NYC buildings, starts in a huge hole below street level. It's in the December darkness of late rush hour (which is never just one hour in New York), and the site is empty of all workers. Fred rummages around and sure enough finds a bunch of bricks wrapped in burlap. Just as he is leaving with his find, he is tracked by the flashlight beam of one of 'New York City's Finest,' as cops are sometimes referred to in this era.

Now REAL PANIC sets in when the cop asks, "OK, buddy, what do you think you're doing?"

Freddy responds, "Nuthin', n-n-n-nuthin.' Baby Jesus, F-F-F-Fuckin' Baby Jesus. Gotta cover F-F-F- Fuckin' Baby Jesus. Blanket for Baby Jesus, right? Joe Baum, Joe Baum, right? Joe B-B-B-Baum sent me, right? Cover Baby Jesus."

Needless to say, Fred gets cuffed and taken away, until *the* Joe Baum (yes, a real person) can be reached, and asked to come down to the precinct to verify Fred's story and get him out of there. And of course, to add insult to injury, the white Caddy gets ticketed and towed for illegal parking.

Back to my story...The Fountain Café

I have no business being as close as I am to these men—the gods of NYC restaurants—during this summer, but unusual circumstances make it happen. When I work in Lang's office during the pre-opening weeks, Restaurant Director Tony Gordon takes me, like a younger brother, either to eat dinner at or visit several of the company's famous Manhattan operations. Everything is always comped.

We visit and dine at the Forum of the Twelve Caesars, La Fonda del Sol, Paul Revere's Tavern (where family friend Buddy Adler is the director), Tower Suite, Zum-Zum, Brasserie, Trattoria, and of course our future Central Park sister restaurant, Tavern on the Green.

This visiting is important, because we only have a finishing kitchen at Fountain Cafe, and we will be transferring (buying) prepped foods from several of the company units. So often we have meetings with the men from whom I'll be ordering food. And also I have a tour guide in Tony, who quickly helps me get immersed in the corporate culture. In some cases, during these visits I am given menus and restaurant-logoed cuff links and tie tacks.

After my first few weeks, helping to put the final touches on the restaurant's operating plans, etc., we are ready to open. You've seen it in countless movies made in New York: the lake with people rowing to nowhere on lazy summer days, the beautiful Bethesda Fountain adjacent to the water's edge, majestic old Central Park South hotels in the background of wide views of the park. This is where I will spend every day and a part of every night for the entire summer, into early September. Every full day and night except one. That one is just a morning, until 11 o'clock. Two thirds of a single day off, due to a steady rain all morning.

Fountain Cafe Moments I Can Never Forget

From pre-opening days of crew training, and into the chaos of this brand-new kitchen, spending 14-16 hours daily (seven days every week), plus or sometimes slightly minus, I get to know everybody very well. And they get to know me. And I learn a life lesson: How to Open a Restaurant.

Incredibly, in the beginning, every night after we close, I find myself in a small boat filled with plastic bags of restaurant garbage, rowing across the famous Central Park lake to the Boathouse. At the end of a typical 13-hour day, to then have to row a couple of round trips worth of garbage, adding another hour or hour-and-a-half of aerobic exercise, can't really be happening, but it is, and to me it's comical: I'm a galley slave like I've seen in the movies of my childhood in the 1950s—only a bronze-skinned, sweating Victor Mature isn't sitting alongside me plotting our escape while rowing. I'm pretty much in this alone. After several nights of rowing, someone in the company finds an old used trolling motor, and we now have the luxury of gasoline power to help get the garbage across the lake to the Boathouse Restaurant's dumpsters. But still, our waste will be transported via the rowboat for another two weeks. For political reasons, the City does not want motor vehicle traffic to enter the park's 72nd Street crossing, until R.A. finally gets the powers-that-be to grant limited access for a garbage truck in very early morning.

R.A. people are able to convince City officials of the need for access because they know how to schmooze them, and because it is obvious that we are far busier than either group anticipates. The City mandates that garbage must be picked up by 7 a.m. daily. But in order to make this happen, the restaurant's slop-filled 32-gallon Rubbermaid containers have to be hauled up two long flights of granite stairs by hand and delivered to the roadway above the restaurant. There is no other way. It is my least favorite time of the day, and it takes two guys, one on each handle, to get the multitude of containers up the stairs. Sometimes, instead of two of us, we find a way to take twice as many barrels per trip: we add a third guy to the job. We place two filled barrels at the bottom of the stairs, with me grabbing the inside handles of each, and two helpers each holding one of the outside handles. Needless to say, I don't have an ounce of fat on me this summer. Eventually I find a way to delegate this hauling task to others.

We have been open for two weeks, and from staff training days forward, there is a steady parade of R.A. execs from the 57th Street offices, plus restaurant directors and executive chefs from various famed Manhattan operations. Because this is a seasonal operation, there is no one permanently assigned. Only Tony Gordon is there to run the front of the house. Mostly it is this way because Baum, Lewis, and Lang never dream of the wild popularity this restaurant is beginning to achieve. So all the big bosses are coming in to lend a hand. There is a line for seating that seemingly never ends, a line that some days exists for 12 hours. Not that one must wait 12 hours to be seated, but that we can just never work it down—and service is NOT slow.

And in particular, there's a steady parade of the company's unit directors working the slide from day one. 'Working the slide' is terminology that is part of the R.A. culture. It means expediting orders in the kitchen. This occurs prior to electronic ordering systems, and although a form of it still exists in modern computer-driven kitchens, in the old days it is done using hand-written duplicate guest checks ('dupes'). The corporate guys start teaching me to do this job soon after the first several days beyond the opening, but they don't leave. They hang around in the kitchen kibitzing with each other and watching me. The best way I can describe this duty is that it is very much like being an air traffic controller. The job is easy for me to learn because I've got cooking experience, but it's brutally hot in this kitchen, and although we never have any human problems caused by the heat, early on there are one or two unanticipated heat-related food fatalities.

One of those is a 'Tiny Shrimp Salad on an Artichoke Bottom.' Because the salad's shrimp and celery contain water, if the liquid is not conscientiously squeezed out of the shrimp prior to mixing it with the mayonnaise and other ingredients, 'weeping' will occur from the intense ambient heat. The result is a droopy salad that can't possibly sit up on an artichoke bottom as originally intended.

On our second weekend's busy Saturday lunch, badass Alan Lewis is standing across from me, ten feet away. He's chatting with a couple of other execs but keeping his eyes on me and what I'm doing on the slide. He sees an order of the shrimp salad come up weepy and tells me to have the pantry guy re-do it. The guy does, but a few minutes later, it happens again, only this time I tell him to re-do it (squeeze out the shrimp) before Lewis can say anything. I think I'm OK, but Lewis yells to me, "Next time that guy gives you that fucked-up shrimp, I want you to throw it in his face."

I talk to the pantryman, Gene, making it clear about the importance of squeezing out the shrimp. Gene is a big

Dominican dude, maybe 6'2, 175. At the time, I'm 5'8, about 140. I get along with him just fine, but I've never thrown food at him either. Sure enough, as Lewis watches like a hungry eagle from across the pickup area, the next shrimp salad comes up all weepy in the blast furnace heat of the kitchen. I know what I have to do if I ever expect to have the respect of Alan Lewis; I whip the plate through the stainless-steel shelving separating me from the cooks, and the salad explodes all over Gene's chest. He looks at me in shock and of course anger. I tell him "Sorry, Gene, but no more shrimp salad like that. Go get a clean jacket." The guy is not happy. I turn around to see Lewis' reaction, hoping for approval, and all I see is his back heading through the kitchen door. He wants no part in the fireworks that may occur. I smile, knowing what that S.O.B. did to me. More than anything else, I guess because of who I am, I just have to laugh about this rite of passage. But I do learn a lot from this little piece of insanity.

A week later it's another Saturday lunch on the slide. There's a double sliding-door dessert reefer on the wall opposite where I'm stationed on the far side of the stainless table used for loading plates and their covers onto the waiters' trays. It's very busy and very hot in the kitchen. I love the pace, the rhythm, the whole eye-of-the-storm territory where I work. But the waiters are, for the most part, college boys—not loving it the way I do, not looking to make a career out of it like I am.

Suddenly a tug of war breaks out between two of the waiters—an American and a French kid (it's New York - there are all sorts of Europeans working in this joint). They are fighting over the one last piece of chocolate cake that a moment ago was resting at peace on its plate on the shelving of the previously mentioned dessert reefer. Each of these guys has a grip on an opposite edge of the plate, and as they both have an order for chocolate cake, they are having a real tug of war, because it is *THE LAST PIECE*, and they are *TWO IDIOTS*.

In the midst of the arguing and tugging, the American kid loses his grip and the Frenchie wins the cake. But he's so frustrated and the slice is so damaged by the brutal 100-plus degree heat in the kitchen that he throws the plate holding its now sagging prize against the kitchen wall. Up to this point, I'm watching this whole ridiculous, childish, stupid event as a casual observer, but when the guy throws the cake, I become incensed.

I lean across the stainless landing table between us, grab his shirt with both hands, pick him up off his feet, pulling him up and over the table with such force that the top of his head gives me a bloody nose. He doesn't think it's so funny, but inside my head I'm able to quickly see the irony, and therefore the humor in the event. After a few choice words into the kid's face, I get myself together and back to work.

If you were to try a move like that today, the lawyers would be lined up at the French kid's apartment. I guess you could say I have an abundance of passion for my work. Alan Lewis would have loved it.

Passion for Our Work

When I forcefully drag the French waiter across a stainless-steel table at the Fountain Cafe during the summer of 1966, I simply am doing what comes naturally to me. I never really think there is anything so unusual about it. These things are not planned. They happen in the heat (quite literally in most kitchens) of the moment because we take pride in what we do, and get frustrated, or worse, incensed with people who disrespect our food, our place of work, the paying guest, or the process in general. In today's world, the idea of grabbing someone by the front of his shirt and getting in his face is simply not done without severe consequences.

Back when I was younger, we all heard stories about people as we were coming up in the business. Stories like ...

... Joe Baum and Alan Lewis dropping in on the Mermaid Tavern maybe twenty minutes before brunch is to be served. They are not happy with the quality (freshness) of the rolls on the buffet line. Baum sends for the kitchen steward, the kid arrives to a greeting of the very same less-than-fresh rolls being pelted at him, pelted hard, by Baum and Lewis, president and vice president respectively, of the restaurant's parent company.

. . . my one-time boss, Freddy Martinez, who is so vexed with a couple of line cooks who just could not/would not comply with his instructions (three times) on how to fry a sunny-side egg during the first Sunday morning of the opening of the very first Village Inn Pancake House on East Colfax Avenue in Denver—with a long line wrapping around the building and down the side street—that at 1:30 p.m., after the rush, he forcibly grabs one of them by the shirt, drags him outside behind the kitchen, picks him up and stuffs him feet first into an empty galvanized steel garbage can, bitch slapping him across the face two or three times saying, "And that's how you fry an egg!"

. . . and there are so many more, but the funniest, for me, is when Joel Kunkel calls me laughing it up one day in the early 2000s, telling me about one of the cooks in his Mexican restaurant (in Steamboat Springs, Colorado) who also couldn't/wouldn't comply with his instructions on making a proper tamale, Kunk so pissed at the kid that he finally fires a tamale at him; the kid not liking that, calls the cops on Joel. And Joel a few days later having fun bragging to me, telling me, "Doc, I made the papers! You gotta see it. I gotta send it to you"

What? You don't believe me? Here:

Sunday, Jan. 3

4:22 a.m. Ambulance requested for 77-year-old female having difficulty breathing. Sleepy Bear Trailer Park.

2:10 p.m. Ambulance requested for 26-year-old male with broken arm. Steamboat Ski Area.

4:27 p.m. Suspicious incident reported. Possible graffitti subject walking down alley. Gone on officer's arrival. Alley between Ninth and 10th streets.

8:05 p.m. Assault reported. Reporting person was verbally assaulted and had a tamale thrown at him by co-worker. No crime, subject warned. El Rancho Cafe, 425 Lincoln Ave.

9:10 p.m. Ambulance requested for 34-year-old female with neck injury. Yampa Valley Regional Airport east entrance.

This is not the only time Joel gets upset with the kids in his crew, but the tamale thing is the funniest. The best verbal comes from another phone call he makes to me. Kunk has a way with words. So when another of his crew decides he's gonna actually get mouthy with Joel, disrespecting him, because now Kunk is getting a bit older, and this kid is a 20-something, Kunk tells the kid in no uncertain terms, "You don't know me well enough to talk to me that way. I'll take you outside and slap the dog shit out of you." This kid wisely decides to just quit.

.

OK, back to the summer of 1966:

On a Sunday, when we've only been open about two weeks, my father comes through for a quick visit. He's riding his ten-speed and stops while I'm in the dining area talking to Alan Lewis, who also just happens to be in for a quick Sunday a.m. visit of his own. *Mr. Lewis is not visiting me,* he's visiting the restaurant, but I'm the guy he talks with. At this point, in the restaurant's early existence, it's becoming a mystery as to who is actually running the place. Director Tony Gordon and the steward Eddie are both there only *sometimes*. I'm beginning to wonder about these two guys. On this morning, we're about three hours away from opening up, so nothing is particularly rushed. I introduce Lewis and my father to each other, and I leave to get on with my pre-opening tasks.

About a week later, after a killer weekend when it is clear that we are not keeping up with demand (running out of some components/ingredients, etc.), Mr. Lang shows up one afternoon. He pulls me aside for one of the several little metaphor/simile-filled coaching chats he gives me.

Although he has a notable Hungarian accent, it always amazes me how he can come up with these things in such expressive English. This one is about never running out of food. It is all very friendly, although he doesn't realize that this time Alan Lewis is approaching, just a few feet from us.

Lang saying, "Winnie, (it's always 'Winnie,' never Vinnie) this place is going to be very busy, busier than we thought it would be. You have to have enough food here to serve everybody. Think of your entire family coming to visit. Imagine it's St. Patrick's Day or Easter and everybody is coming for a big feast." Lang is doing his best not to talk to me like I'm a complete imbecile—maybe just a slow nephew—and yet, he likes me!

Lewis, ever the cut-to-the-chase, street-smart animal, interrupts, "George, what the fuck are you talking about? I met this kid's father the other day. He's a Jew like the rest of us."

Lewis looks at me, "Right?"

And I answer, "*Right.*"

And then Lang, a bit surprised, immediately switches to Passover and a couple of other 'big food' Jewish holidays, satisfying Alan Lewis with the illustration, and giving me a more humorous and unforgettable recollection of this little 'lesson' than he ever intended.

A few days later, it's 6:30 on a weekday morning. I'm always the first one in, and this day I find out the walk-in reefer is dead. I have never been told how to deal with such a situation or who to call. I wait till 7:30, and by some miracle find Alan Lewis in his office. I start by telling him, "Mr. Lewis, we have a problem." And I explain about the dead walk-in.

He calmly responds, "OK, write this down: Call Dee's Refrigeration at (number). They're in Brooklyn. Tell them to get over there immediately."

"Ok, thanks, Mr. Lewis," I answer.

"Oh, and Vinnie, one more thing . . ."

"Yes, Mr. Lewis?"

"*We* don't have a problem, *you do*." (and he hangs up on me.)

Once again, Alan Lewis, the tough-love teacher, giving an important 'life lesson for a restaurant guy.'

At about the three-week plus point, after the not-so-soft opening, R.A. is going to host a press conference and celebration party for this newest of their string of approximately 36 restaurants in the city. Mayor John Lindsay, many other dignitaries, and media people will be arriving for a celebratory brunch. The Fountain Cafe is truly the talk of the town in the summer of 1966.

After closing the night before the event, I stick around to mop the entire place spotless, and then take a seat to begin cutting several crates (yes, back then fruit is packed in wooden crates) of oranges in half, then using an old-fashioned electric juicer to make pitchers of fresh squeezed juice for the brunch that would serve maybe 100 guests. My boss Tony Gordon has been doing some other tasks to ready the place, and by the time we're finished at 4:30 a.m., we get into his car and head for my parents' apartment. I've worked for 21-1/2 hours that day, because after the regular business, we have to get the place ready for the 10 a.m. party. It's a quick 14-block drive from Central Park's Boathouse parking area to my parents' apartment. I cat nap at each of about four stoplights before we get there. I sleep for 2-1/2 hours and go back to work. Tony sleeps at my parents' a few more hours, then goes out to Queens in the morning to shower and change clothes at his place. He arrives at work a couple of hours after me. But his heart is not in this, and a week or so later, as I recall, he disappears. *Just disappears!*

The mayor's party is a huge success, and the beginning of a series of changes that cement my place with the big boys at R.A. I've made my bones, and the rest of the summer I am their golden boy. All kinds of management people come and go because this is just a summertime 'tent show.' Some of them directly supervise me and some just fill in where they are needed for a shift or two or three. But I'm the only one who is there every day, never wimping out, because: a) I love it, and b) this is the life, the career path I choose. And I am constantly aware of Buddy Alder's rise in the company, and how he does it: long hours and hard work.

Right after Tony's disappearance, my boss, the head steward, a nice enough person but a slow-talking, slow-thinking dude, misses work for the second consecutive day.

Because there is no longer a manager at the restaurant, it's another early morning phone call with V.P. Alan Lewis.

I ask him, "Mr. Lewis, you know Eddie the steward? Well, he said he had a dental appointment yesterday, and he was gone all day. Now today, he hasn't shown up either."

Lewis wastes no time, "Fire him."

I'm thinking, maybe Lewis has forgotten the structure. I explain, "Mr. Lewis, I can't fire him, he's my boss."

"Fire him!" he says.

"Mr. Lewis," I say with a tone that clearly is reserved for an unspoken, "Have you lost your mind?"

"OK," Lewis says, "call him on the phone at home and tell him to call personnel. *They* can fire him!"

And bam, Lewis hangs up. Again.

So now I am pretty much without a leader at the restaurant, front or back of the house. I have just celebrated my 22nd birthday, and there is no permanent leadership for me at this joint: the director disappears, wilting under the pressure, and days later, my direct supervisor, the head steward, is fired (*by personnel*, of course). Because they never expect to be so busy, the corporate guys are sending in a parade of chefs, managers, and directors from all sorts of places that R.A. operates. This lasts for maybe ten days, until finally they settle on one chef, Lem Veale (yes, a chef named Veale), and promote front-of-the-house host Buddy Smith (a Nat King Cole look-a-like) to maitre d'. Both are great and

I'm relieved to have effective leadership at the restaurant, although I really don't report to either one.

One day George Lang and I are standing on the Central Park roadway bridge that sits over the kitchens of the restaurant, a vantage point from which we can see the entire seating area of the café, just adjacent to the beautiful Bethesda Fountain. It's a blazing hot day and we're looking down at the unending line of people who for some crazy reason will stand for long periods sweltering in the NYC heat and humidity waiting for a seat. Suddenly he's got a flash, "Winnie, I want you to go down to a place called Azuma. It's a Japanese store." He recites the exact Manhattan street address for the place from memory (what doesn't this guy know?), and I write it down.

Lang continues, "Go there tomorrow afternoon, after the lunch rush, and buy two dozen full-sized paper parasols. We have a charge account there. I want them to be loaned to people who are standing in line, you know (*I do?*), to shield them from the sun."

And of course, 24 hours later, the parasols become an instant hit, another reason why New Yorkers love Fountain Cafe and the little details that make R.A., R.A. But those details, without Baum or Lang, simply wouldn't be there.

There is a truck driver named Dominick who is assigned to pick up all the food that comes from the various R.A. units around town which produce product for us to re-heat for service. He's a tough little 5'4" pot-bellied Sicilian (maybe

Joe Pesci's size), a union guy who reports to me early every morning. I give him a list of stops, and he then takes off in his R.A. refrigerated box truck for the day's food pick-ups, which he brings back to me.

The guy sees how hard I'm working and maybe takes pity on me; we get along great. We are linked to each other all summer long and become tight. Along with some other driving duties, he picks up for me at Tavern on the Green, Zum-Zum, Trattoria, the Four Seasons, Charlie Brown's, and maybe two or three other joints, sometimes twice a day.

The kitchen steward at one of these 'units' (as they are called within R.A.) is jamming me up every chance he gets. I have no idea why (we haven't even met at this point), it's maybe just the way things are at R.A., or in the City, or both. Or maybe because I'm a rookie. One morning Dom has had enough of this guy's mouth, and just hauls off and decks the guy, one shot to the jaw, lays him out, just like Joe Pesci does in "My Cousin Vinny" years later. I appreciate Dom's '*support*.' Not a word of it is ever mentioned. We are in New York. Stuff happens.

Another day Lang and a secretary come up for a visit, and he wants to use my office for a quick session of dictating a few notes to her. But my office is nothing more than a steel folding chair and a wooden tomato lug filled with invoices, credit memos, an electronic calculator, and a pad of receiving clerk's daily reports. Wherever I can find enough room to sit in the chaos of the back of the house storage area that is not supposed to serve a zillion covers a day—and is only a summertime restaurant—I usually grab an upturned melon crate and use it for a desk. George Lang is nothing if not flexible and does the same. After all, this is a man who, by his sheer wits, survives more than one concentration camp existence in the 1940s. Giving the one folding chair to the secretary, he sits down on a couple of sacks of potatoes. But as he's about to start, he says, "Winnie, would you please get an apple for me." I bring it, and after he shines it up, he says, "Winnie, watch this." The secretary and I watch as he holds the apple with both of his thumbs in the dimple at the stem, and splits it clean, as if it were cut with a knife. Try it. It happens fast, right before our eyes, like the trick of some tent show magician. The secretary and I look at each other with awe, amazement, and maybe a little spooky fear, while Lang gets that big, charming smile of his going.

During a weekday lunchtime after we're open about five weeks and it is obvious that the place is a screaming popular success with New Yorkers, Joe Baum and Freddy Rufe come for a visit, bringing along a Fountain Cafe flag. Leave it to Joe Baum to notice an empty flagpole on the park pathway immediately adjacent to the restaurant—and to have a Fountain Cafe flag created instantly. Once again, it's the details that separate R.A. from the rest of the crowd. Once again, Baum and/or Lang are the dreamers. Instant dreamers.

Mr. Rufe enlists my aid to help them hoist up this new flag. It's about 1 p.m. and while Mr. Baum is holding the grommeted edge of the flag, Rufe is supposed to attach the snap hooks from the hoisting rope to the grommets. My job is to raise the flag once it's attached.

But Freddy, who is almost *always* nervous around Joe Baum, attaches the grommets so that the flag is upside-down, and Baum quickly sees this and begins his jump onto Uncle Fred, "Fred, it's fuckin upside down. What the fuck are you doing?"

As Freddy is nervously fumbling around reversing the snap hooks, Baum is telling him in a strong, steady commanding tone, "Calm down, Fred, just calm down." Just for a moment, it feels like The Three Stooges. I have to turn away slightly, so they can't see me smiling.

As he's finishing, Fred looks up and sees, at least a hundred yards away, Maitre d' Buddy Smith escorting the world-renowned author and food writer James Beard to a table, and he immediately starts nervously *'talking'* to Buddy, as if Buddy can hear his directions, as if he can whisper into Buddy's ear from a distance the length of a football field. Baum and I are transfixed. We silently watch Buddy Smith and listen to Freddy, *"OK Smith, OK Smith, It's f-f-f-fuckin James Beard, right? Fuckin James Beard, right? Smith, Smith, Jesus fuckin Christ, fuckin James Beard. Take care of him, right, Smith? Right? That's it, pull out the chair, Smith, pull out the ch-ch-ch-chair, right? Smith, take care of him, right? Take care of him."*

This is a classic everyday Freddy Rufe moment. It's always a combination of hilarious stuttering, filled with teachable little episodes, punctuated with rhetorical *"Right? Right?"* and more *"rights";* and all the words coming at close to auctioneer speed. He is a unique character: warm, detail-oriented, Cornell-educated restaurateur, who becomes a special friend to me, an uncle in the restaurant business, an uncle because nobody says "mentor" in the 1960s.

He comps the champagne at my first wedding (Tavern on the Green) for maybe 150 people. Years later we will have great reunions, either in Chicago at the NRA (National Restaurant Association) Show, at CIA's Annual Meeting for Members of the Corporation, or at the Symposium on American Cuisine series. Nothing planned, we just run into each other at these events. We try to grab a meal together, and he gives me caring 'uncle-like' advice, "Vinnie, Vuh-vuh-vuh, Vinnie, you gotta start buying farms, right? Buy farms. Fuckin farms, f-f-f-farms, f-f-f fuckin farms. Great investment. I've got farms, farms in Pennsylvania. You gotta buy farms, right?"

And perhaps noticing my somewhat dry skin from living in Nevada, he coaches, "Vinnie, you gotta start using baby oil on your face at night, right, baby oil. Keeps you young, keeps you young, right? Right?"

As the summer is winding down . . . they realize that I'll be returning to school and will need to be replaced for most of September and early October. Eventually I'm training three guys to replace me, because nobody is that insane to work day and night, seven days a week.

One of these guys is a smooth-talking character whom I meet when we both attend that junior college upstate, before moving on to CIA. He, like the other two, begins learning my job, or pieces of it. He's an obvious BS'er, who comes to work dressed in a sharkskin suit and tie, kinda looking like a garment district sales guy. Every day he removes the suit jacket and slips into a white lab coat which he wears over his suit pants and dress shirt. He arrives carrying an attache case. A wanna-be executive.

My friend Nancy White (the head hostess) and I watch his arrival every afternoon with some amusement. After several days, we can't resist sneaking into his attache case to find out what could possibly be in there. I've been doing this job all summer long, and the only thing I ever bring with me are the clothes on my back and my father's ten-speed (my ride on most days). What would a kitchen steward need with an attache case? One that's an actor, that's who. It's a theatrical prop. Inside it we find one item: a hairbrush (for a guy who appears to be rapidly losing his hair).

Mr. Rufe visits one afternoon and pulls me aside. He asks me if I want to transfer from DU to Cornell, that Joe Baum can make it happen for me.

My God, these guys really like me! I listen respectfully (and with genuine humility and gratitude) to this life-changing offer, but in my heart I know two things: I could never hack it academically at an Ivy League school, and I don't want to be with a bunch of arrogant, snobby rich kids. I want to be with my boys - Scoty, the Kunk, the Tomato, the Yam, Stevie D., and the rest - and I love Denver and the West.

I politely turn him down.

"But-b-b-but Vinnie," says Uncle Fred, "Cornell is the best hotel and restaurant school in the whole fuckin' country, right? Why do you want to go to that cowboy school out in Denver? Vinnie, Cornell will place you on a different social strata, a different social strata, right?"

I avoid telling him about my less-than-stellar academic history, which is an embarrassment. I just say that I can't leave my friends. He's OK with it, and graciously leaves the door open.

Right around this time period he takes a walk around the back of the house with me. We walk into a tiny room where shelving holds the cooks' whites, which are delivered a couple of times a week from the linen service. It can get pretty disorderly after several days of guys rummaging through, searching for their correct size. On this particular day it's in disarray, several uniforms on the floor.

He's not angry (I never, ever see him angry), but he's ready to teach, "Vinnie, holy shit! Look at this. You've got f-f-fuckin' laundry walkers here, fuckin' laundry walkers. Jesus Christ, fuckin' laundry walkers. Vinnie, you gotta keep this stuff up on the shelves, right? Up on the shelves. Laundry walkers, right? Laundry walkers!"

Again, I have to turn away so he doesn't see me holding back laughter at his schtick (God, he is funny!).

During my last week, he shows up with a bonus check (unheard of at R.A. for a summer kid), and a beautiful thank you letter (which I still have). He is a thoughtful, sweet man.

September 1966 - Back to School: Denver and Central Park

Time for Joel and me to head back to Denver for our sophomore year. We meet at my parents' apartment in the city where another guy named Michael Simon joins us, and we head out across the G.W. Bridge, west on route four through Teaneck, and onto the Garden State Parkway southbound. We're in a roaring late summer rain in three separate cars, and Simon takes off like a bat out of hell, probably going 80 mph. We let him go, and never see the guy until classes start at DU. Kunk and I may be crazy, but we're not stupid. Without the benefit of conversation, we quickly develop a signal of holding up fingers, to tell each other when we've found a good radio station and settle in for the long drive to Denver.

We pull into Chicago in mid-afternoon of the second day out. Kunk tracks down a CIA acquaintance, a guy named Teddy Curran. Not your normal CIA grad, but a local kid seems to be into the action, wherever, however it comes. We find him at his cooking job at the prestigious Ambassador

East Hotel, and he takes us to his mother's dance studio, where there are a couple of guest beds for us to sleep on later that night.

The three of us go out and have dinner and a couple of beers. Long before we've had our second beer, I know this Teddy guy is a few cards short of a complete deck. We get back to the dance studio, park on the street out front, and just as Teddy is unlocking the front door, a Chicago cop car pulls up, then another. A sergeant questions Teddy's motives as we're opening the door, the cops acting as if we're breaking in. Instead of calmly explaining that it's his mother's place and he's using a key to let us in, Teddy explodes into a string of insulting expletives toward the cops. Chicago cops.

And then everything you've ever seen on clips of the 1960s cops in Chicago plays out right in front of Kunk and me—Teddy getting thrown to the sidewalk, cursing the cops, the cop sergeant repeatedly kicking him in the ribs, announcing for all to hear, "This is the Curran kid. He's a little mick son of a bitch." Luckily for all of us, it goes no further than a quick beating.

The next morning Teddy comes by on his way to work, unlocks the door so we can leave. We have some breakfast, Teddy acting like last night was just business as usual in his 'hood. We say thanks, and Kunk and I get the hell out of there.

On our third night out, we sleep in Kunk's car at a rest area in Nebraska. When we wake up, we shave and brush our teeth in the men's room and get back into our respective cars to drive until we can find a breakfast joint. While we are eating, we begin to look over a map to figure out how to proceed.

You need to know that during my years at the University of Denver (DU), the transcontinental highway system is still being constructed. These roads, known as the Interstate Defense Routes (the highways with an "I" followed by a number), are being built in unconnected sections across and up and down the country (even route numbers, east/west; odd for north/south). Eventually they will be all connected, but while they are being built, we drive on the completed portions a few miles here and a few miles there. Supposedly these roads were conceptualized by President Eisenhower during the 50s, based on his experiences with roadways in Europe during WW II. They actually take a couple decades to complete. They are essentially designed for emergency military traffic, and their surface is originally constructed to handle the wear and tear of tank treads. One in every five miles of this road must be straight. These straight sections can be used as airstrips in times of war or other emergencies.

But they take a long time to build. Every time during the college years when we drive home to the East coast or back to Denver, a little more of the road is completed, the sections connected, forming what becomes I-70 (parallel to U.S. 40, the older road), or further north, I-80.

As we are eating our breakfast in Nebraska (I-80) and looking at the map, it becomes unclear as to which of two possible routes dropping southward to Denver would be the quickest. We disagree. Over and over, each of us looks at the map, but the result is always disagreement. We aren't mad at each other. We simply disagree. We pay our tab and get into our cars. Without another word, when we arrive at the crucial fork in the road, we each head off in a different direction. It's about 8:30 a.m.

So having come through all kinds of geography, weather, and traffic situations (most notably the side trip on the crowded streets of downtown Chicago) in two cars, without losing each other, we are apart, driving across Nebraska, bound for two different roads which will drop us southward toward Denver. I drive and drive and drive, stop for lunch, and drive some more.

At 3:20 in the afternoon, just before I need to leave I-80 to head south out of Nebraska toward Denver, I can't believe it, but there's Joel in his blue Oldsmobile on a frontage road. Our cars are perfectly parallel, headed west, less than a quarter of a mile apart. He is due north of me, merging onto the interstate, and we're just looking at each other, both smiling at the insanity of it all. Once he gets onto the road, we pull over onto the shoulder, have a reunion and a good laugh.

I still think about that day once in a while, always in disbelief.

Spring 1967 - "I Got an Idea"

Because I am admitted to DU on "conditional acceptance," there is a strict requirement that I keep my grades at a certain level. I am naïve about what classes to schedule in the beginning so as to create a positive cushion to offset the tougher classes. It all catches up with me at the close of winter quarter of my second year, and they tell me to leave.

I try hard to succeed in the academic life, but it is a case of *the mind is willing, but the flesh is weak.* In my situation, I am serious about school vs. the younger Teaneck Vinnie, but all those years of wasting my time left me without a foundation of study skills and actual knowledge. This won't be the 3.0 GPA I assumed would be so reachable, when I thought about going to college toward the end of my CIA days. I mistakenly figure I'm grown up now, and all it'll take to succeed in college is effort. Then there's my total lack of awareness of my A.D.D., nor is there any treatment for it.

So I return to live with my parents in their apartment in Manhattan and begin working again for Restaurant Associates.

I'm working for a really nice guy named Ralph Tolve, a Fordham economics grad, who oversees all of R.A.'s fast food operations throughout NYC. He's perfect for the job because fast food is all about the numbers. When it gets close to summer, I am slated to return to the Fountain Café for its second season of operation.

Ralph has me doing some very ordinary things and some interesting things, always in Central Park. I learn a lot that schools just don't teach, especially in the area of retail accountability, souvenir sales analysis, park food and drink cart management, etc. Ralph encourages me to get interested in his area, and as much as I admire the guy and like working for him, my goals are aimed at tablecloth restaurants.

During this time I see the old bosses only infrequently, but one day in particular stands out. We meet at the Boathouse in Central Park—Joe and Ruth Baum, Fred Rufe, Ralph, and me. I don't recall the reason we are there, but whatever it is requires that we take an extended walk through the park in drizzling rain. The big black umbrellas come out and off we go, Uncle Fred adding his usual levity remarking in his patented rapid stutter that we looked as if we were a Central Park funeral procession, given the black raincoats and umbrellas.

One of the subjects—unrelated to our location at the time—that Ralph brings up is that his division of the company is on the verge of taking on a contract for food service at the Flushing Meadows Park area (former site of the 1964-65 New York World's Fair). The plan is to use mobile trucks moving through the various sections of the park.

Ralph wonders out loud how he will attract people to the trucks, as truck food, other than ice cream, is a very new concept. Without skipping a beat, vet Baum says, "I got an idea. We'll get a tape recording of an Army bugler blowing mess call, and the driver can just push a button and play it."

I think at the time, *so this is how it is* (Joe Baum creating on the fly). And then a few minutes later, it happens again, Joe Baum saying, "I got an idea." And another innovation— I forget the details—is born in my presence. Only now Baum catches my 22 years-young eyes staring at him in awe. By this time, the rain has stopped and the sun begins to shine on our little group. Baum puts his arm around my shoulder and directs me a bit away from the others so he can say a few fatherly words in private, "You know, Vinnie, creativity isn't something just a few of us are born with. Everyone has the ability to be creative, you just have to have the courage to voice your ideas." It feels good that this Cornell-educated restaurant industry giant puts his arm around me in such a caring manner, but of equal importance is the message I get that day: 'You too can be creative.' He helps me to see that anyone (even me) can imagine possibilities where there seem to be none. It is a watershed moment for me and leads me to a number of successes in my future.

Summer 1967 - From Garlic Toast to Blackened Redfish

In late May DU accepts my appeal for reinstatement and I return for summer school in June.

When my future wife Lily and I are first together at DU, we eat about once every two weeks at a place on University Ave. called Steak Master. It's right down the alley from my apartment and is patterned after Tad's, a chain of East coast $1.29 steak joints built for the masses. You walk up to a cafeteria-styled line and tell the guy standing at the flat top broiler what cut of meat you want. If you're lucky, he'll ask you how you want it. And if God is looking down on you with particular favor that day, he might give you a miracle, and the meat will actually be cooked to your preferred degree of doneness.

They offer a chemically tenderized, very thin steak, served with a baked potato and a garlic-butter grilled chunk of Texas toast. You pay at the end of the line, and a few moments later, they bring the food over to where you are seated. To help the dining process you need to have a fully loaded bottle of Heinz Ketchup on your chosen table.

At some point there is a new guy cooking at Steak Master, a very heavy guy with a twangy accent. He's polite and friendly. About the third time we see him there, he comes over to the table after we are given our dinners. He looks at me and asks, "How's your steak, sir?"

I haven't even cut into it yet, so I test it with my index finger—the way I'd do if I were standing at a broiler cooking—and tell him it's fine. He picks up on this move of mine, and says, "Oh, you too?"

I tell him, "Yeah." And we have a brief conversation about where I've cooked. He goes back to his station. Over several months, we are friendly and always have a nice visit.

When I return from working all spring with R.A., and eventually eat at Steak Master, the cook looks like a different person. He has lost a bunch of weight, well over a hundred pounds. He has time to talk and sits down with me while I eat. When I ask how he lost the weight, the guy tells me that he's taking 17 pills a day, prescribed by a doctor who has a weight control practice. Then he tells me his back story:

As a child in rural Louisiana, he is the youngest of 13 children. He eats normally but can't keep food down. As a consequence, he is quite skinny. All his siblings eat normally and are of normal weight.

When he is six, his grandfather hitches up a mule to a buckboard wagon and takes the boy into the swamps to a witch doctor. The witch doctor cooks up a potion in a black kettle over an outdoor fire. The boy drinks it out of a wooden spoon. It is bitter tasting, Paul remembers, "like grapefruit."

After he and his grandfather return home that evening, he begins to hold down his meals. He never overeats but begins to gain weight—so much weight that soon after I meet him, he goes to see a doctor who specializes in eliminating obesity. The Denver obesity doctor prescribes the 17-pill-a-day regimen for Paul. At the end of the first day of taking the weight loss pills, he throws up and the same bitter taste that he experiences at the bayou witch doctor's is in his mouth. Now the weight just seems to fly off his body.

We remain friends, but at some point, as I'm finishing up my last academic quarters of school, he disappears. I am told he left town. This is about 1968 or 1969.

Flash forward to 1978. I'm sitting in my office at the Hitching Post Inn in Cheyenne, Wyoming, opening the mail, and Institutions Magazine is in the pile. This is a very well known, famous trade magazine in the restaurant business. Who is on the cover, dressed in giant blue jean overalls, alongside a bayou creek holding a big net full of crawdads? You guessed it: my friend Paul (larger than ever), Paul Prudhomme. I cannot believe my eyes. How does this guy go from Steak Master's $1.29 meal to becoming the executive chef for Ella Brennan at Commander's Palace in New Orleans—one of the very finest restaurants in North America? And in the process, he creates a national craze: blackened redfish, and soon after, a nationally marketed line of Cajun spices. And since I know this 'Miss Ella,' and have been to her home in New Orleans, interviewed with her, and eaten in the restaurant, the whole "horse race called restaurant business," as George Lang calls it in the recommendation letter he writes for me, is becoming more and more crazy, and one whose people seem to travel in a smaller and smaller universe.

I finally run into Paul in 1983 at the Symposium on American Cuisine in New Orleans, where he is a featured speaker, and years later at John Ascuaga's Nugget in Sparks, Nevada, where I am executive V.P. of F&B, and where he is working a trade show in our convention area. He is his usual very cordial warm self, and we have a nice visit. As several old food friends do, he gives me a personalized copy of his most recent cookbook.

Joel Kunkel - The DU Years and a Bit Beyond

There were a number of times I could have gone to jail because of Joel's antics, although as he is fond of saying (with intentional poor grammar), "Maybe you wasn't playin' the fiddle, but you sure was tappin' your foot to the music."

Once on a cross-country haul, he pulls over for the night, and is sleeping across the front seat. Joel has a Colt 45 - 1911. A state trooper wakes him by tapping on the driver's side window. Kunk, who, as you may remember, sleeps very well, hears a noise, and as he moves to get into an upright position—not knowing it's a trooper—instinctively jams the .45's muzzle against the door, beside which the cop is waiting. Joel knows the .45 will rip right through the door and blow back whoever woke him. He looks up and sees the cop, who in the darkness of early morning has no idea there's a gun pointed at him. Kunk immediately does his best to bury the weapon, and then tells the cop he was just cutting a few z's, and the guy leaves none the wiser. Another narrow escape. Our lives were filled with them.

July 1967 - Bring Me a Surprise

One afternoon in early July, Kunk shows up at my apartment on S. Josephine St., and Lily and I ask him to stay for supper. I throw a glaze together for the chicken I'm putting into the oven and give Lily cooking instructions. Kunk will make a salad when we return. We need to go to Target to shop for a rifle that Lily has been talked into giving me for my birthday, talked into by Joel, so that I can go deer hunting with him.

Her last words as we are leaving are, "Bring me a surprise." At this point in our relationship, she is still reasonably trusting. Trusting of me alone at this point in my 'development' is not smart. Trusting of me with Joel Kunkel along is like asking two television cartoon cats not to plot against the mouse with which they share space.

We go look at guns at Target, then get down to the serious business of Lily's surprise. In no time at all, I find a rubber tarantula with realistic hair all over its body and legs. Then I pick up a cheap 'Made in Japan' little tin cap pistol and a box of caps.

We plot things out on the ride home, stopping off at a grocery to buy ingredients for Kunk's salad. Arriving at home, the aroma of the peach-glazed chicken fills the apartment, and I'm able to pull it from the oven just at the right moment. Kunk goes to work on the salad, and Lily remembers to ask, "Hey, where's my surprise?"

I grab the small paper bag holding the cap pistol and caps, telling her to close her eyes. She obeys, and I give her the bag to open. We have some fun playing with the cap pistol, and pretty soon it's time to eat. I get the chicken and vegetables and set them up on a platter, ready in the kitchen. Kunk tells us to sit down; he's ready with the salad. He comes over to Lily, and with the large salad bowl in his left hand, proceeds to 'French' (as a well-trained CIA graduate would do) the salad into her individual bowl with his right.

Lily has probably never been served like this, and she watches intently as Kunk, holding a fork and tablespoon in his right hand, doles out two perfect mini portions of salad into her little bowl. Delivery number three, however, contains the hairy rubber tarantula amidst the greens. Have I mentioned that Lily is deathly afraid of any of nature's creatures beyond cats and dogs?

Slow motion: First comes the scream accompanied by shock and fear. And then as only Lily can do so well: anger; anger fueled by the fact that she knows she's been had by these two crude goons who are now in major hysterics, trying between the laughter to tell her that this was the REAL surprise. She leaps backward, up out of her chair, which makes a great crashing noise behind her. This noise awakens the primitive anger response, which in turn reminds her that she must punish those who have preyed upon her naiveté and sensibilities. She picks up the heavy, old-fashioned, 1950s-styled chrome-plated dinette chair and flings it at us with the full force of her considerable strength as we're trying to escape from the table. This, of course, only makes us laugh even more.

We finally get her calmed down and have a really good dinner. After she gets control of her emotions, Lily has the ability to laugh at herself. Well, to be truthful, not every time, but most of the time. Sometimes she just tolerates my behavior. More about this later.

Right around this time, in July 1967, I get a phone call at 7 o'clock one morning from Lily's father. He calls looking for her because he can't reach her at *her* place. The gist of the conversation, although friendly in tone, is, "Lily needs to stay at her own apartment. I'm from Spain, and I'm old fashioned. If you want to live together, get married."

So we make plans to get married during the Christmas break. And we do.

April 4, 1968

Just as I'm rolling up outside the DU Business School to take my evening statistics class, I hear the news on the radio: *Martin Luther King's been shot dead in Memphis.* Having experienced the JFK assassination and sensitive to the racial tension of the times, I don't consider this to be a big shock. I know that King has been trying to bring about a peaceful settlement to things on the streets, but sadly it may not be in the cards. I feel that nothing good can come from this act, and of course, that soon will be the case.

June 6, 1968

I wake up to go to class and hear the news that Bobby Kennedy's been shot in the head in L.A. last night. I go to the HRM Library, where many of us spend down time between classes. Department Chair Doc Wilson comes in, and as he's grabbing a cup of coffee, asks if I'd heard about RFK. I tell him, "Yeah," and we discuss RFK's condition, and Doc tells me, "It doesn't matter if he lives. He's going to be a vegetable, no matter what." Kennedy dies that day.

By this time, having either seen famous people getting murdered on TV, and/or hearing about others on the news, watching televised big city race riots, the last five years in American public life have yielded a body count that, along with the war in 'Nam, leaves a wet blanket of depression on the national spirit. There is a loss of innocence that for me will never quite allow us to return to 'what was.' The golden age of America is clearly the decade of the 50s, and sadly, we cannot go back. I know it in my gut in 1968, and unfortunately, it turns out to become our reality as time moves forward. If a country can be spiritually depressed,

1968 is the year for the U.S. to have a whole bunch of reasons to feel this way. Until 2020.

A Summer Day in 1968 - The Shoots, a Smart-ass Porcupine, and the Flying Monopoly Game (and table)

It's July 1968 and Stevie Densham and I are waiting to go into Marine OTS and Army Basic Training, respectively. I've been hearing about 'The Shoots' for some time. All I can really gather is that it's a great place to go tubing on the South Platte. I go down to East Colfax Avenue with old Teaneck friend, Tony Savarese, and buy a couple of nice big truck tire tubes for $2 each. But for some reason, Tony isn't going to ride the river (a working brain, maybe?).

That afternoon, after getting some vague directions about how to get to Deckers, which is 40-50 minutes south of Denver, Stevie and I head down there on a Saturday afternoon. We've committed to being back to Adele's apartment for dinner with Lily and her, and then we'll play bridge or a Monopoly game. This commitment shouldn't be a problem, really, we're just going tubing (something we've never done before).

We get down to the general area where we think we're supposed to be and are driving on a dirt and gravel road running alongside the river. But it just doesn't have the look or feel of a place to go tubing. I tell Stevie to drive the car along the river, and sort of trail me while I get in the water and hop onto one of the tubes and paddle my way to what I hope will be the right section of the stream. Yes, 'stream,' because that's what it looks and feels like—a 40-foot wide stream, about 18 inches deep. Not very exciting. The water is moving so slowly that I am forced to paddle. I manage to get into a current, but it's pulling me off to the far-left side of the stream. Stevie has my VW creeping along, following my slow progress. The stream and the dirt road seem to be drawing closer to one another.

Something is happening now, a different feel to the water. I'm finally gathering some momentum. The water is getting deeper, and the stream is narrowing. I'm not paddling anymore, and the current takes me to a large grouping of rocks, still on the left side of the river; yes, maybe it really is becoming a true river. I grab onto an outcropping of the rock to stop my progress. I have the tube stopped in an area under the outcropping, which has been carved out by a zillion years of the South Platte running against granite. I get as still as I can and listen to what sounds like a dull roar of water. I yell to Stevie who is still on the dirt road, but now considerably more elevated than a few minutes ago, and now about 50 total yards away. I motion to my ear with a cupped hand and yell, "This muss' be the place." He doesn't hear me so I give him the 'come on down' arm motion, and I make sure he's pulled over and getting out of the car. I can't wait. I'm ready, and I'm going.

I push off the rock as hard as I can, so that I'll be in the middle of the "shoots" (whatever *they* are) when I get to them. It doesn't occur to me that I might have been hearing a 67-foot waterfall, 300 yards downstream. I'm a week or two away from my 24th birthday, and caution is not a lady with whom I dance very often. The water moves me along quite quickly now as I enter an area momentarily darkened by rocks on both sides. And suddenly I see it all: bright sunlight and white water narrowing into a six- to eight-foot-wide roaring e-ticket experience between rock formations that reach up about 20 feet towards the sky. It stands to reason that what was a few minutes ago the width of 40 feet is going to be an adventure when it narrows to six to eight feet. Here we goooooooohhh . . . There are a bunch of Mexican 20-somethings drinking and sunning on the rocks, some diving or jumping off into the river further downstream where the widening water allows a pretty good chance of survival. I survey this scene in about 2-3 seconds, because I am suddenly and very forcefully whipped around, with my back heading downstream. I CAN'T SEE WHERE I'M GOING. Some sixth sense tells me to look over my left shoulder, because I can "feel" the closeness of the rocks. My peripheral vision picks up a dark form, and I instantly lean to my right. I go flying under a real scary "melon squashing" outcropping. The power of the water in this small space is awesome, but soon after going through the shoots, it slows to a section of rapids, and then becomes a fairly normal fast-running small river. The near miss is as close as I come to death for many years to come (the very real proximity to sudden death doesn't hit me until weeks before my 68th birthday, when I read a book called, "Off the Wall: Death in Yosemite," and I realize that it had to be God truly protecting me that day).

Stevie follows, and I'm able to watch him whip through, face first, all the way. We ride the water just past the shoots a time or two more, and then we load up the car and continue down the dirt and gravel road along the river toward Denver. Everything is more or less on schedule for the evening's activities.

We're riding along in great spirits, minding our own business, when I spot a porcupine adjacent to the ditch on the right side of the road. It's a big one, and he's clairvoyant. He's got me figured out, and hurries for the ditch. I gun it and tell Stevie to door-pop him. We time our moves, Stevie and me, just perfectly. Stevie whacks him with the shotgun door, and he tumbles head over paws, three full revolutions right through the ditch, and lands on the far berm. He gets up, and I swear, just like a human, he kind of knocks himself on the side of his head with his right paw and takes a good look at us. We're laughing our ass in the car, and he knows he's got to pull himself together and beat feet. We jump out and chase him with a couple of canoe paddles, but he spots a tree, and quickly scampers up, finding a comfortable place in a substantial notch.

Now the fun starts. I race back to the car for my Wrist Rocket slingshot, but it's not there. I suppose we can just leave. I mean we've already had great tubing, and on a personal basis, some outrageous fun treeing a porcupine, something that no city boy from Teaneck and Manhattan can claim. But he's up there in the tree waiting for our next move. And just by his mere existence in the tree, he kind of throws down a gauntlet of sorts. So we begin throwing stones at him. Nobody will ever accuse me of having a good arm, but Stevie is an athlete. We go to work bombarding this little bastard, and then he starts to taunt us. That's right, he taunts us. And that's why we are going to be late for dinner. Because every time one of us lets loose with a rock, Mr. P. is standing in the notch, holding the tree trunk with one paw, and playing peek-a-boo. He sticks his head out from behind the trunk and plays us. We fling every stone we can find, and then graduate to big rocks. Every single time we throw, just before a well-aimed rock would seemingly find its mark, he ducks back behind the tree trunk, and the missile goes whizzing by. This whole stop lasts about 20 minutes, with that smartass little ball of quills outlasting us. He probably has a good laugh with his four-legged pals down by the river this night.

We get back to Denver about an hour later than promised. Lily is a bit annoyed, but who wouldn't be?

After I shower the river off, I change into some clean dry clothes, and we head over to Adele's for our burgers and a game. It's the usual: fun, laughter, plenty of rapid humor and repartee out of the brilliant Stevie, along with cokes, chips, and Monopoly.

An hour into the game, it's clear to me that I'm poised to slaughter the three of them. The normally ultra-successful Stevie is uncharacteristically going down. His money is disappearing. But I don't want my friend, my buddy, relegated to the sofa while I grind down the girls, and I don't want the evening to end too early. So I begin a quiet under-the-table transfer of money to Stevie.

This 'bailout,' as it called during the time I write this part of my story, goes on unnoticed for maybe 15-20 minutes. Adele, bless her heart (as they say in the South), is really nice, but not the sharpest kid in the region—or in the room, for that matter. Lily, on the other hand, is nobody's fool for very long. She is watching Stevie improbably circle the board over and over, and in spite of being continually clobbered for rent on her hotel-filled properties on the orange row of St. James, Tennessee, and New York, he doesn't run out of cash. She finally smells a rat. And she's already been aggravated by our late arrival due to the tubing and the crafty Mr. P.

This stuff that Lily does when she explodes always revisits me in slow motion; I see every detail of her movements. But in the real-time of the moment, it is more like a tornado and there is nothing slow motion about it. This is not the normal everyday inanimate tornado, but a tornado that is part human and has the ability to seek out that which caused its irritation . . . and respond accordingly.

She leaps up out of her chair, screaming at the both of us, her hands putting a death grip on the edge of the metal card table frame. Adele of course is somewhat confused but is going to catch up with this pretty soon. Just give her time. Now comes the slo-mo part of this: Lily's up and yelling and squeezing the edge of the table, and Stevie and I are clearly aware that some sort of explosion is in process—after all, we lit the fuse, didn't we? We're up and both moving sideways trying to get out of the vector of the blast. The table is up in the air now, about chest-high in Lily's grip, and it's leaving her hands, taking off with a serious velocity toward its targets. Us. Monopoly money is scattering across the little apartment living room like a Wall Street confetti parade. Dice, houses, hotel, and the Monopoly shoe, along with its friends the hat, the dog, et al, are all becoming an indoor rain, part of the tornado. The table and its contents land short of our position, with Stevie and me, particularly me, surviving another of Lily's squalls. It's all fun and laughs. Nobody takes any of it seriously, because we all know that Lily started her life at DU as a drama major. We know it, and she knows we know it, and that's a fact. Peace soon returns and we go home, ready to live and laugh yet another day.

August 1968

I'm about to go into basic training at Fort Bragg, North Carolina, and the guy at the U.S. Army Reserves in Denver does me a big favor and sets up my travel so that I have a stopover in New York. It's maybe 24 hours, but in that time my mother gives me a great piece of advice that comes in very handy several weeks later, "Never let them (southerners) know that you're from New York. Tell them you're from Denver. They won't even know where Denver is." Unbelievably, that's *exactly* what happens when some psychopathic drill sergeant, having ordered me to drop and give him 50, gets right down on the ground with me, and six inches from my face asks:

The DI asks, "Where you from, boy?"

I'm pumping out the 50, and answer, "Denver, drill sergeant."

"Denver? Where's Denver?" he asks.

Still pumping, I respond, "Colorado, drill sergeant."

"Coll-or-RADO?" he questions, suspicious and confused. "Where's that?"

Continuing to pump, I say, "You know, near New Mexico and Utah, drill sergeant."

Suspicious now, he presses me, "You sure you ain't one a them New York boys, or Philly boys, or Baltimore boys?"

"No, drill sergeant," I answer, as I'm getting up. He goes away, looking for a more appropriate victim to torture.

Fall 1968

Sometimes in a novel the author brings his characters together in a situation that doesn't ring true. You know that it's all fiction, so you suspend disbelief and go on reading. But these connections and events are for real:

In 1968 Kunk falls into some demotivating circumstances at DU and decides to drop out. He goes to work for R.A. (Restaurant Associates) in Connecticut and is soon offered an opportunity to become an executive chef of a new hotel that their Midwest subsidiary, Al Green Enterprises, is about to operate. The hotel is the Sheraton Ann Arbor.

R.A. provides him with another CIA graduate who is to be his sous chef—a guy I barely know, who is a year ahead of me at the school. His name is Walt Hayne, nicknamed Burke. Joel doesn't know him until they meet in Ann Arbor.

Burke goes into the Navy several months after graduation. In this era, you and a friend could join "on the buddy system," and be guaranteed the opportunity to go through basic training together. His buddy is another 1964 CIA grad named Doug Zader, nicknamed Moose. I know

Moose from school, and because we both work on Martha's Vineyard in the summer of 1964. We don't work in the same kitchen, but the island is relatively small, and CIA grads have a grapevine. We all know each other's whereabouts on the island. We are just acquaintances.

Moose ends up in San Diego after his Navy discharge. He soon gets a call from Burke, offering a job in Ann Arbor with a stranger named Kunkel. Moose takes the job.

Of all the college towns in the U.S., Merilee is going to grad school at the U. of Michigan in Ann Arbor, where my best friend is relocating from Connecticut, via Denver. It is inevitable that they all get to know each other. And they do. That whole "Six Degrees of Kevin Bacon" stuff occurs in my own life long before it is given a name by college research profs and the media.

After I have completed basic training and am working in an Army kitchen at Fort Bragg, I get a message to call collect to a number right away. I recognized the area code to be Ann Arbor's. You just don't get phone calls in the military (no such thing as cell phones in 1968). It is unheard of. Luckily, there is a phone booth close to the mess hall. I call the number, and once I get past the operator, there is the unmistakable voice of my former roommate, my running mate, Joel Kunkel, asking in a medium 'pervert' growl, "Hey Vinnie, you got a sister?"

I know something's coming from him, but answer, "Yeah."

And in a more pronounced growl he says, "I got her too!" For a second, I'm caught off guard. I recover with, "You son of a (expletives deleted) bitch. You called me all the way down here, faking an emergency with the Army to tell me that?"

"Aw, I was only kiddin,' he says. "I haven't touched her. I thought you could use a break from the Army."

That was the Kunk: A crazy combination of bad-to-the-bone anti-social aggression, but at the same time full of real affection and fun . . . if . . . he liked you.

Four years later, in March 1972, I have just been hired for my first Food and Beverage job, at Stouffer's Denver Inn. I actually apply for catering manager, because I have it in my head that I want to go into that business for myself some day in Denver. But the G.M., Jim Cohee, already has hired a catering manager, Barbara Barrows, and he sees some things on my resume that say "F&B manager" to him. We are to open this brand-new property in May. One of my first priorities is to hire an executive chef. I have no luck with those resumes I receive in Denver, and at some point, I talk with Joel about the situation. He recommends Burke, but after we track him down, it turns out that he has just bought a restaurant in Massachusetts. Back to square one. Then Joel says, "What about Moose?"

I answer with, "I'm not sure that Moose can handle this job. I really have never seen him work in a kitchen and haven't even seen him at all since the summer of 1964 at the

Vineyard." But Kunk assures me that Moose would be fine. We find Moose in Michigan. He's married a girl in Ann Arbor, and has settled in there.

After flying out and interviewing, Moose gets hired to be the executive chef. He fits in perfectly and stays in the job for five years. We soon become very close friends for the rest of our lives, all because of his connection to Joel, through Burke in Ann Arbor four years before, which really has its foundation in our CIA/ Martha's Vineyard/ Restaurant Associates connections from the early 60s.

Later on the job that year I will also meet Charlene, who will become my wife in 1975.

Summer 1969

DU graduation will probably be a nice event on a warm August day, but I am doing my two-week active duty with the Army Reserves at Camp McCoy in Wisconsin, so I miss getting my diploma in the traditional manner.

After I arrive home, Lily and I pack up, say our goodbyes to those few friends that are still in town, and head for NYC. Someday I want to come back to Denver to settle down, but for now, I need to get back to the city to learn the restaurant business. I have a job waiting for me with R.A. I don't know specifically what it will be, but during my last Christmas break I visit with the personnel guys, and they are happy to commit to a back-of-the-house (management) job somewhere in Manhattan.

We arrive home, say "Hi" to our families, find an apartment we can afford in Sunnyside (the Queens), pay off the 'super' with $75 in cash to get to the head of the waiting list, then race up to the Vineyard to meet friends for Labor Day weekend. That weekend, with "the Yam" and Patty Hutchins, will be the last time I smile for a while.

What I don't know when I'm so happily celebrating with my wife, my friends, and my freshly minted college diploma on Martha's Vineyard, is that all the guys who are my godfathers, my rabbis, when I work at R.A.—and who I visit during my previous Christmas vacation—are no longer there when I report to personnel on the Tuesday after Labor Day. *Whaaaat*?

And these new dudes in personnel couldn't care less about what I was promised eight months ago during Christmas. I'm headed for Newark Airport to run a coffee shop.

I'm shocked and say, "But I was promised a back-of-the-house job in the city. And I rented an apartment in the Queens."

And this stranger, this personnel prick says to me, "You'll figure it out. That's what we have for you."

So we get an apartment in Fords, New Jersey, buy some very slightly damaged furniture, and begin to settle in. I'm not happy with the new R.A. and how they screw me out of what is promised by the previous regime, but I do what I'm told and go to work in their facilities at Newark Airport.

It's known informally as R.A.'s basic training camp: a rough environment with heavy union activity, typical airport crime of every sort, violence, a hardened employee culture, and a director who usually guns down as many as three triple scotches before the daily 9 a.m. cost control meeting (and he's not a happy drunk).

I do meet a handful of good people there, and I'm surviving, but after a few months, who do I bump into but Alan Lewis. We see each other in the airport snack bar where he's grabbing a hot dog before his flight takes off.

There's no "Hi," no "Nice to see you"—it's classic Alan Lewis:

"What the fuck are you doing here? he asks, barely understandable, because his mouth is occupied by a good half of the hot dog.

I tell him what happened with R.A. and my promised job. He's now a corporate V.P. with Longchamps, a famous old NYC restaurant chain, and hands me his card, saying, "Call me next week."

I call, and eventually meet him at his office. He's got Al Ferraro, another former R.A. guy, with him. They offer me a cost controller position at Luchow's, a renowned German restaurant in the city, but numbers are not my thing.

Two weeks later they call with a back-of-the-house opportunity at Madison Square Garden. That's more like it.

Winter 1970 - Getting to the Garden

The Steer Palace is located at Madison Square Garden in #2 Penn Plaza, above Penn Station. Marty Sussmane runs the place. That's Sussmane, not Sussman. And I have no intention of asking this guy why it's Sussmane—he's just too big and bad—but he does love me, so it would probably be OK.

The place is a large three-level restaurant with several different rooms, all decorated differently, all of it with an overriding turn of the century (1890-1900s) plush, gaslight-era feel. The top floor houses the main kitchen and three dining rooms. There's a saloon located on the middle floor, and offices, a food prep area, and receiving are on the ground floor.

I arrive, after Alan Lewis pulls me out of Newark Airport during the winter of 1970. It's a great fit for me. I have many opportunities to see Mohammed Ali fights and NHL hockey, because old DU friend Keith Magnuson is playing for the Blackhawks and gives me tickets whenever they are playing the Rangers. And I get to experience some unforgettable things during this period. I learn great lessons about high volume food operations and teamwork that I will carry with me for the rest of my life. And I see crazy NYC stuff both in the restaurant and out on the streets.

Toots

Right around the beginning of my second year at Steer Palace, the IRS padlocks the mega famous New York spot, Toot's Shor, (also the name of its owner). Toots owes over a quarter of a mill to the feds, which in 1971 is a considerable sum.

A couple of weeks after the closure hits the front page of the local rags, I get a phone call from our corporate purchasing office. I am told that I'll be getting a delivery of food and booze, and that I'm to absorb it into my inventory (an interesting accounting procedure that transcends my independent study in F&B Cost Control with Doc Keister at DU). In fact, it is a pretty large delivery, and I am impressed that these guys who I work for—along with Toots—can pull off such a move. After all, they somehow manage to move several pallets of beef, frozen super jumbo shrimp (five to the pound!!!), and aged whiskey, which is padlocked under the watchful (?) eyes of the IRS and/or the ATF boys at Toots Shor on 54th St.

Steer Palace is twenty blocks south. Notice to IRS/ATF: *Now you see it, now you don't.* A geographical magic trick: only in New York. This won't be the last time I find myself 'doing my job' in a way that is *making the bosses happy; the feds . . . not so much.* This "non-event" with the Toots inventory, for all the world, never really happens.

April Fool's Day 1971

Bruno Schiavetta is the executive chef at Steer Palace. I meet Bruno in the early winter of 1970 when I go to work there as back-of-the-house manager. He is very good at his job, very smart, physically tough, yet has a stuttering problem when he gets the least bit excited. There are two kinds of stutterers: the kind like Freddy Rufe, who just talk 60 miles an hour, and the words sometimes just can't keep up with the brain—so things get kind of schmushed-up in the mouth like a NY subway train disgorging too many people for the width of its doors at rush hour; and then there are the poor souls whose utterances just drag on and on, going through some really sad word wrestling match inside the mouth, with lips, tongue, and brain working, but not together, in a struggle to make a meaningful sound. (See "My Cousin Vinny"—the courtroom scene—when a new lawyer for the defense is brought in.) Bruno, like Freddy, is the 60-mph kind.

He's born and raised in the Philadelphia area, but at the age of nine, while most European families begin leaving the Continent (c.1937) in a very big hurry, Bruno's parents decide to leave the safety of the USA and *return* to their homeland. He stays there for 10 or 12 years, where I guess he spends time working on a strange accent... and other strange things.

Strange things like locking his beloved dog in the trunk of his car when he and his family arrive at wherever it is they are headed to on various Sunday drives. Or like walking over to a Steer Palace shaved ice machine during a lull in the business of expediting in the 400-seat steak house's main kitchen where we work, and forming baseball-sized ice balls, which he throws with body-bruising velocity at dishwashers and waiters (never at his cooks) who are maybe 30-40 feet away. This is just for fun. Well . . . *Bruno's fun.* Then there is the time he picks up the head dishwasher, Choo-Choo, by the waist and turns him upside-down, dunking his head into a pot sink of filthy, disgusting water, and proceeds, with his free hand, to viciously scrub the guy's head with a pot brush. (You have to have worked in restaurants to know what a pot brush is, but I can't think of a domesticated animal that you'd use one on without feeling guilty for being so cruel.) After the scrubbing, he then gives Choo-Choo a few raps on the head with the WOODEN body of the brush, just for good measure. And remember, *this is just for fun.* For real. Or on my very first day of work at Steer Palace, after finding out that my boss, Marty, uses me—the new kid, who HAD to be believed—to play a wicked practical joke on him, Bruno becomes incensed and picks me up off a chair by my white cabby cap and hair, my entire body goes airborne for a moment, then drops me back into the chair. And when Marty (who is present) protests, Bruno proceeds to tear my cap into pieces with his bare hands and then stomp out an angry dance on it. I lose some hair this day, but it is all in fun. And the truth be told, when there is work to be done, this restaurant is a collection of maybe the most capable high-volume crew I ever am part of, and we're all very fond of each other. But when we have a bit of down time, anything can happen. And that means punishing physical pain, or practical jokes, and one way or the other, lots of laughs.

I've been working with Bruno for 12 or 13 months when he comes to me for a favor. We are pretty good friends at work, so of course I say, "Sure."

He explains that he has ordered a brand-new Pontiac to take with him on a long summertime visit to Italy. He's actually going to SHIP A CAR TO ITALY (there's that thing about reversing direction, from the U.S.A. to Italy again—it must be genetic). The cool thing to do, in this era, is go to Italy or Germany for vacation and buy a car at the local price, then ship it home to the U.S.A. Italy? Maybe an Alfa Romeo. Drive it everywhere, have a great time. But *bring* a car over to Europe??? Insane. And not just any car, but a big American Pontiac.

Bruno asks if I can call the salesman every once in a while, to check on the delivery status, "Caw-caws you know when I get n-n-nervous, I st-start to stutter."

I tell him, "Yeah, sure, Bruno. Give me the guy's name and phone number."

I make one or two calls to Bruno's salesman over a few weeks, and report back that everything's fine, and tell Bruno, "You'll have the car in time to put on the very same boat that will take you to *the other side." Bruno's happy and grateful for my help. And it is then that I realize that April Fool's Day is coming. I get absolutely gleeful.

So I make arrangements for Lily (not a stranger to my schemes) to have her friend at work out in Metuchen, N.J., call Bruno at Steer Palace on April 1, at precisely 10 a.m. She's to tell him that she's calling from Pontiac headquarters in Detroit, that she's happy to inform him that he has just ordered the 50,000th Pontiac that year. She'll already know the dealership's name out in the Queens and also the salesman's name. She'll tell Bruno he's WON IT—as a gift from PONTIAC. She'll need to keep him on the phone getting his contact information, etc., and tell him he'll be getting a letter soon.

Well, the big day arrives. And Bruno, who is standing a few feet from me on the ground floor of the multi-storied restaurant, gets a page to come up to the main kitchen, where he's received a phone call. Now I tell my pal Ralphie, Bruno's sous chef, what I've done. I tell Ralphie to sit at my desk and look like he's doing some work. I go hide on the floor underneath a bunch of shelving holding canned goods. I hide because I know that if Bruno sees my face, the game will end—and maybe he'll try to kill me. And I'll be laughing so hard I won't be able to defend myself.

We wait a few long minutes. We hear the elevator door open. I am hugging the concrete floor as if grenades are headed my way. The footsteps are getting very close to Ralphie.

Bruno is yelling, "R-r-r-r-ralphie!! I w-w-w-won a f-f-f-fuckin car!!!"

From my hiding place I can't see Bruno or Ralph, but it gets VERY QUIET VERY FAST. Before I even have time to develop any concern, I hear Bruno demand from Ralphie, "Where's that f-f-f-fuckin Vinnie?"

And right then and there I know it's all over. Ralphie would never give me up. He is a tough P.R. from 105th Street and 5th. But maybe he loses control of his facial muscles and smiles just a little bit when Bruno comes running toward him at my desk. I'm hugging the ground like a winning lottery ticket, and he leaves. I've escaped. And if I stay away long enough to find 325-lb. Marty, I'll have him laughing like hell, and when Bruno finds us, I'll have protection. And that's just what happens. It is the BEST April Fool's Day ever. Thank you, Lily.

*For those who have never been around a bunch of New York area Italians, either family or friends, 'back in Italy' is referred to as 'the other side' during the years of my youth. Maybe it still is, but I've been away from there for decades, so I don't know.

A Springtime Day 1971

There's a big, strong, fiftyish Swedish guy named Bennie at the Steer Palace. Even though he's officially the dining room's captain (fourth in command of the front of the house), Bennie dresses up like a wannabee maitre d' every day. He wears a tux and fancy frilly-fronted shirt, the de rigueur cuff links, etc. Everyone else in front of the house management wears a suit and tie when working the floor.

Bennie is one of those guys that is pretty serious about things, but this restaurant is a haven for jokesters that happen to be very good at what they do when it's time to feed people. In the down times it can be kinda crazy—not every day, by any means, but here and there. So we have reason to laugh at Bennie, because he remains very serious in the midst of the craziness. He saw some nasty, scary stuff during WW II, and maybe it prevents him from ever getting around to having a good laugh. He's really a nice guy, so nobody takes issue with the fact that he's not one of the jokesters. His family hid Jewish people during the war, so even though he's a bit quirky, we all like him very much.

New York is a city of foreign tongues. They are an ever-present sound on the street, in the subway, in restaurants. If it's not the actual foreign language that you hear, then it's English with a foreign accent. And Captain Bennie's English has its own mixture of a Swedish sound and some words that no Swede or American ever says—or hears.

One morning, as we are getting ready for the normal lunch period, Bennie is busy directing a couple of bus boys to rearrange the Poker Room to accommodate a group that will be eating there. After the meal, the group will watch a live presentation by a guy making a product pitch. It's a party of about 20, and we've hired a projectionist from Willoughby's, the well-known camera store up the street. We've used them many times before when we need AV equipment or a guy to run a speaker's film for a business meeting. This is way before the days of computer-driven presentations, so it's done with a film projector and a white movie screen at the far end of the room. Of course, as is the case today, films or video presentations are best shown in total darkness.

For some reason, Marty, our G.M., leaves the building, so Bennie is in charge of the dining room.

We pump out the meal with ease, and the rest of the restaurant's lunch is business as usual. After running the slide (expediting food orders), I go back downstairs to work in my office. Around 2 p.m. I return to the main kitchen to get a Coke, and I hear a commotion.

It's Captain Bennie, who I run into at the confluence of the kitchen and the dining room. He's got a stranger in his grip. He's pretty much dragging this guy, his formidable right hand squeezing the dude's left shoulder and his sport coat. They are moving past me from the carpeting onto the quarry tile world of the back of the house. He's furiously half talking in his Swedlish to his captive, and half to anyone who'll listen, "You mudden fuckin son of a bitch, I'll fuckin kill you."

I ask, "Bennie, what the hell is going on here?"

Bennie tells me, "This mudden fuckair from Willoughby's took a shit right in the Poker Room when the lights were out!" Benny is crazy with rage and continues dragging the guy towards the pot sinks where he begins filling a mop bucket with steaming hot water. He makes the guy hold the bucket, and still gripping his left shoulder, grabs a mop with his left hand, and they head back for the Poker Room, Bennie still yelling at the terrified projectionist, "Mudden fuckair, I'll kill you!"

If you know me even a little bit—even now, as an old grandpa—you know I have long ago dismissed the idea of getting a Coke and am following about three feet behind Bennie and the Willoughby's guy. I'm not about to miss this e–ticket ride (Google this if you don't know what it means). I remember it today as well as the night Lily, Hyman, Carl Datz, and I watch the live broadcast of Neil Armstrong taking his first steps on the moon.

But it's a fair piece from the kitchen through the main dining room to the Poker Room. And Captain Bennie, in his fancy frilled tux shirt and the rest of his ensemble, is still raging at this guy. People who are finishing up late lunch conversations begin suddenly looking up from their tables.

"Jesus Christ, Bennie," I urge in a low, but commanding voice, trying to quiet the bad, barely understandable-to-strangers language, "take it easy, there are still people eating here."

Bennie acquiesces, making a growling noise, quieting down until we arrive at the Poker Room, where once again he begins ranting at the guy; and now, is intermittently instructing (in Swedlish?) the art of cleaning up human poop from a carpet with a mop and hot water—something I can't imagine is even remotely possible to accomplish. But I want to get the back story, so I interrupt the process long enough to find out from Bennie that, "While this mudden fuckair was showing the fuckin' movie, he went behind the (red velvet) draping" (that covers much of the Poker Room's walls) "and shit, like a fucking animal" (looking at his captive). "Didn't you? You fuckin' animal!" The guy is terrified and not speaking.

I watch the mopping for a minute, amazed that anyone would poop there, but more amazed that anyone, *anyone*, would think that a mop would be the appropriate tool for removing poop from a carpet. And then, regrettably, I go back to finish up the daily desk work that awaits me in my office.

Only in New York.

A couple of months later I'm ready to get back to Denver, so we do. But less than a year after our return, Lily and I are divorced. We remain friends but move on with our lives.

Adrift 1972 – 1979: "Doctor"

My Denver nickname comes from a very unlikely and unique source. I fall into the job at the Royal Platte River Yacht Club (formerly the Red Ram, down in Larimer Square) because Joel, who is cooking there during this period, is scheduled for knee surgery. I get to take his place for a couple of months while he recovers, and while I continue searching for a more appropriate situation. The guys who have recently bought the business are out of Atlanta, and because they'll be absentee owners, they of course install a manager whom they know from their home base. The manager, Jeff, brings along a bartender from the Peach State, and pretty soon a talented Atlanta-based band, Wheatridge, shows up as well.

The bartender is Nolan Maddox, a very nice guy with a heavy southern accent. Nolan has very weird, rounded shoulders, and is the nephew of an infamous uncle: Lester Maddox, the chicken-restaurant-owning segregationist and former Georgia Governor, who is frequently in the news, mostly for his bizarre behavior (I suggest you Google him) and his non-compliance with the progress of integration.

Uncle Lester is so infamous that his name actually appears
in the lyrics of a great Randy Newman song:

"Last night I saw Lester Maddox on a TV show
With some smart ass New York Jew
And the Jew laughed at Lester Maddox
And the audience laughed at Lester Maddox too
Well he may be a fool but he's our fool
If they think they're better than him they're wrong
So I went to the park and I took some paper along
And that's where I made this song"

Anyway, Nolan has this thing of calling a few of us
"Doctor." Then Manager Jeff joins in. As in Doctor Oakes,
Doctor Kunkel, etc. Nolan pronounces the word "Doltor,"
and for some reason it sticks on me alone. Kunk likes it and
begins calling me Doctor. Eventually many of my Denver
friends from this period, both male and female, begin calling
me Doctor, Doctor Oakes, The Doctor, or Doc.

A few years later, in the first half of 1976, I'm working
in Room Service for grocery money at Stouffer's (Moose is
still the chef there). I'm again waiting for something
appropriate to pop up. Everybody knows me in this joint as
I was its first F&B manager in 1972. But there's a new kid
in Room Service, whose mom was a waitress for me, and
he's just been released from the slammer. Nice kid, who gets
locked up for a year resulting from a DUI where a death

occurred. He's a character, Dennis is. He's about half crazy with the joy of being free and out of prison, and every day—*I mean every day*—that I come into work in the afternoon to relieve him from the early shift, as soon as he sees me, he breaks into the Harry Nilsson song, and *dances* around the room service area of the kitchen:

"Doctor, ain't there nothin' I can take,
I say, Doctor, to relieve this belly ache?
I say, Doctor, ain't there nothin' I can take,
I say, Doctor, to relieve this belly ache?"
"Now let me get this straight ",
Put the lime in the coconut, you drank them both up

Etc, etc.

And so it goes: one crazy after another. It's part of what draws Kunk and me deeper and deeper into the business. We love telling each other stories of the crazy nut cases we meet on the job (many of them lovable), and if it's possible, we go out of our way to introduce each other to them.

Spring 1974

While most of the craziness, fun, or life-threatening occurrences take place in cars, one amusing memory has me sitting in a golf cart.

Because I buy a condo on a golf course in Denver, and given the fact that Moose loves golf, it seems reasonable that I should start playing again. One day we take Bruce Harms along for a round. Charlene also joins us, just for the ride. The condo development is called Strawberry One; the course is Heather Ridge. The use of carts is required on this course.

We have a pretty uneventful round until we are about three holes from finishing up. Charlene and Bruce are across the fairway, about 40-50 yards away from us. Moose takes an iron shot that is particularly displeasing to him. As a matter of fact, he is so displeased that he throws his iron as hard as he can. At 6'3, and about 245 at the time, Moose can put a lot of hang time onto a five iron. From our spot just left of the center of the fairway, the club takes off into a long sweeping arc and with the help of a light breeze, finds the exterior wall of a condo bordering the course. We are quite far away from the wall of the home but hear with clarity the clanging of the iron as it makes contact.

Before we have time to react, a man steps out from the condo's patio, which prior to this moment is concealed from our view. He looks down at the iron on the grass, and then looks at us. There can be no question in this guy's mind about the cause of this offense to his home. We are over to the condo in a flash, and as fast as words can come—a special talent that he has always possessed—Moose apologizes, and in a self-deprecating manner, is shaking his head, telling the guy, "I just can't believe that thing flew out of my hand like that. I am SO embarrassed."

The guy just gives us a flat, blank stare, and we quickly drive off.

As soon as we get over the next hill, and are out of the guy's view, Moose stops the cart.

I ask him, "What the hell are you doing?"

Moose says, "That asshole is gonna call the clubhouse and tell them to look for a guy in a yellow sweater. I'll just take this off and hide it in my bag."

Moose is very proud of how smart and cagey he is. He is smiling. I am sitting next to him in the cart, impressed with his fast thinking. We finish off the next couple of holes and head for the clubhouse.

When we arrive, the pro comes out of the clubhouse, making a beeline for us. Moose is a frequent golfer, and the pro knows him. "Hey," the pro says, "I got a phone call about you guys, and if you ever pull a stunt like that, you won't be playing golf here again."

Moose doesn't try to play this guy. He apologizes, and we head for the parking lot where we meet up with Bruce and Charlene. We quickly load up the car and leave.

"How the hell did we get caught, Moose?" I ask him. "I thought taking that sweater off would take care of us."

Moose, somewhat defeated, says, "Yeah, well, I guess I forgot about the number on the back of the cart."

May 1974

A whole pile of connections begins to occur in May 1974, starting with a phone call from Marty Sussmane, who explains he is now working for Al Ferraro at a Rockville, Maryland, area chain of 34 steak restaurants called Emerson's Limited. Ferraro (R.A. and Longchamps connection) is V.P. of Ops, Marty is an area director of some Maryland stores, and Arnie Pincus (two years ahead of me at Teaneck High School, of a restaurant family in Teaneck) is Marty's counterpart in N.J. The company is run by two high-flying Jewish boys, the president a Hungarian immigrant, the executive V.P. a sharp-shooting American. One big happy family. 'Mishpocheh,' as they say in Yiddish.

The timing couldn't be better: I'm real tired of dealing with owner and founder Jim Mola at the Village Inn Pancake House corporate offices. The Emerson's guys want to talk to me about "Assistant to the V.P. of Purchasing," which sounds like a title for a really good secretary but is actually the number two job in corporate purchasing and commissary ops down in Alexandria, Virginia.

So within a week or two, I'm flying out to their corporate offices, where I see Marty for a moment, Al Ferraro for maybe twenty minutes, the two guys running the show for maybe another twenty minutes, and then the guy I'd be working for, the V.P. of purchasing, Don Schwartz.

Somebody takes me to lunch, and I'm then driven to the office of an industrial head-shrinker named, I swear, Dr. Freud. The guy interviews me to make sure that I'm not going to do anything above and beyond what the typical crazies in the restaurant industry perpetrate, and then takes me to a small room where I have to take a battery of brain-twisting IQ and personality tests.

At this time in my life, I'm okay with the process of most IQ and personality tests. Not that I ace them, but I move through pretty fast. I just have to concentrate and plow through on this day.

But I begin noticing that the time is getting closer and closer to my scheduled flight out of National Airport for the return to Denver. And just about this time the good doctor and his receptionist begin, within earshot, to have a conversation about me. I'm trying to do the tests and not be distracted by the conversation. I'm trying not to look at the time, because it's a Friday afternoon and traffic in D.C. is notorious. Can I make it back to National in time to get the plane? And suddenly I realize this guy Freud is intentionally messing with my head; it's all a setup to see if I can handle pressure. The conversation about me becomes a significant distraction, and it angers me, but there's no way I'm gonna let this clown win, so I just concentrate my way through.

I do just barely make my flight. After the weekend, they call and offer the job to me. I had just bought my first home several weeks earlier—a brand new two-bedroom condo on the same nice golf course in Denver that Moose would almost get us 86'd from. I arrange to lease it though a management company, pack up, and leave after the mover's truck is loaded.

When I get to this job, they all treat me like family—and after all, I am always very close to Marty when we work together at Madison Square Garden, Ferraro and I are associated at R.A. and Longchamps in our past, and now this. The job starts the first week in June 1974. I'm to assist my boss in negotiating contracts, do some buying, and learn how to run a meat fabricating operation, which serves the 34 restaurants from D.C. up through Connecticut. The commissary in Alexandria, where we work, has a meat freezer with a one-million-pound capacity. As soon as I can, I begin every workday spending an hour on the fabricating line learning meat cutting. One afternoon during my second week, Don Schwartz, my boss, is complaining about the fact that he's got a meeting the next day with Senator Feldman, and blah, blah, blah. I don't know who this senator is, but it's D.C., so I just figure it's business as usual.

"Why don't you want to see him, Don?" I ask.

Don says, "Well, I'm busy, and besides, he's gonna want us to buy liquor from him."

Late during the next morning, and probably just as a courtesy, Don calls me into his office to meet the Senator, and I can't believe my eyes. This is no stranger, and he's *no* Senator: It's the former mayor of Teaneck, New Jersey— Matty Feldman. I went to school with two of his three kids, and my father was the campaign manager for a family friend (Brad Menkes), who was a member of the town council and ran against "Hizzonor" for the mayor's seat. I don't personally know Matty in Teaneck, but we are certainly connected geographically and socially via family, friends, and others.

We are introduced by Don and immediately launch into a few minutes of "Jewish geography," an old ethnic characterization for what becomes known as networking in the 1980s. Afterwards I return to my office. But it's not over.

Later, after the 'Senator' leaves, and by the way, I am inwardly cracking up every time Don refers to Matty this way: 'Senator.' Senator, my ass. This guy is a *state* senator from N.J., not a real Washington, D.C. senator. I'm not sure if Don is trying to make himself feel powerful or if he's kissing-up to Matty. Matty's business card says "President" of the New Jersey State Senate, so he *is* important, but in New Jersey. The next day Don calls me to his office and explains that since I "know" Senator Feldman, he thinks it would be best if I become the primary contact. *Primary contact for what, Don? I'm wondering.* And here is a good place to point out, as is mentioned years later by a TV interviewee who is referring to Chris Christie's "Bridge Gate" scandal, "Politics in New Jersey is not ideological; it's transactional. It's all about making deals. Deals about development, deals about education, deals about whatever." And I'm about to be *'dealing'* with a New Jersey politician.

Well, it turns out that a meeting is set up between Matty and me for the following week, up at his liquor distributorship in N.J. Somebody high up in my company, the organization that I've been with for all of *three weeks*, decides it would be a good idea if our seven stores in N.J. would begin buying their booze from Matty's distributorship, and they also feel that Matty should show his appreciation by giving us a 7% cash kickback each month. Who better to handle this than a 29-year old kid who's been with you for all of 15 workdays? I don't find out any of this "juicy" stuff until a few hours before I'm about to jump into the car to begin driving up north. Apparently, Dr. Freud says nice things about me.

So, the following weekend, I stay with old friend George Ackerman and his wife Rosemary at their rental house down the shore at Seaside Heights. On Monday morning I drive up to Teaneck to have a briefing breakfast with Arnie Pincus at the old Cedar Lane Grill. (This is the diner in Teaneck all my friends and I go to during high school as a late-night rendezvous after dates, etc.) The Pincus family knows Matty very, very well: both through their own Rt. 4 restaurant, the Steak Pit, and socially.

I am nervous about this errand. There isn't going to be any grey area with regard to my success or failure. I either swing the deal, or the guy, who is old enough to be my father, and who I really don't know, becomes highly offended and God knows what happens after that. But Arnie assures me to relax, that the guy is going to fall right into it. He knows that Matty has been doing something very similar with another company for years.

This becomes a scene right out of the movies. I arrive at 11 a.m. to a warehouse area down by the docks. If I remember correctly, it's in the vicinity of Hoboken, one of those little ultra-tough waterfront places in Jersey. Matty welcomes me and we shoot the breeze for a while. There's more Jewish geography. We're surrounded by photos of Matty the young boxer and Matty the politician—with everybody from JFK, Adlai Stevenson, on down. He asks me if I'd mind if his son Danny comes along to join us for lunch. No, of course not. (The kid, I'm thinking, is the least of my problems). I don't know him. He's maybe four years younger than me, but I know his sisters, so we all connect: one happy little party of three from Teaneck.

We go to a dark waterfront joint for lunch, a saloon with a dining area, the kind of place where Popeye would eat, if there really is a Popeye, and if they have spinach salad on the menu, which trust me, this place does not. We have a nice meaningless conversation before and during lunch. I'm beginning to take perverse joy in the fact that I haven't made the first move: I'm going to force Matty to start the conversation. The meal is drawing to a close, and we're maybe a minute or two from getting the "Will there be anything else?' from the waitress.

Finally, he looks at me and stops with the BS. "You know, Vinnie, I didn't fly all the way down to Washington, D.C., for my health."

"No, I didn't think you did. We want 7%," I answer.

"7%? What are you talking about?" he asks.

I tell him, "Matty, you know exactly what I'm talking about: 7% back to us, in cash, every month, based on the prior month's sales to all of our Jersey stores."

Matty gives me his best incredulous look, and says, "Vinnie, I can't do that. I, I can't."

"Oh, come on, Matty," I say, "You're doing it right now with other people, and I happen to know you've been doing it for years."

He comes right back with, "OK, how about 6?"

That's it. It happens *that fast*. I tell him I need approval to finalize the number, because it is not what I proposed. I need to borrow a phone. We get back to the office and Danny scoots. Matty opens a closet door opposite his desk and grabs a 'safe' phone which is wired to a wall inside the closet (this is spooky stuff, but I'm acting like I do this two or three times a week). I'm standing half inside the closet (*ridiculous!*) and call Don Schwartz.

I start with, "Hey, Don, I'm talking to our friend. You know that number we talked about?"

"Yeah," he says.

I tell him, "Well, it's one less. Will that be OK?"

Don says, "Yeah."

"See you tomorrow," I say. "Bye."

We arrange the mechanics of the drop: a brown paper bag will be handed off at Newark Airport monthly.

And oh, yeah, we also arrange the actual purchase system for his products!

(…To be continued in two years or so…)

So now I go back to Alexandria, and of course they love me. They love me because guess where the cash will be going?

Meanwhile, Charlene arrives from driving across the country, and we get a waitress job for her at the Emerson's in Alexandria. But three weeks later, Don now mentions that he wants me to go up to the Seagram's Building on Park Avenue and get a similar deal from them that I arranged with Matty. Charlene's not crazy about the whole D.C. life and being away from her son from her former marriage, Jimmy; I'm not thrilled with D.C. either, not to mention that it appears I've signed up to be a bag man. And I really want Jimmy to be with us too. I really love the little guy. So we quickly make plans to return to Denver.

September 1974

Moments of craziness occur in this life, like the time I get the job at Shakey's Pizza. Well, that's not the entire story, but that's how it starts:

I'm on a two-week menu writing job at the Denver's Royal Platte River Yacht Club for Kunk, which allows me to have a guaranteed income of $200 a week, so that I can return there from D.C. The job allows me to have some cash in my pocket while I live for free at Moose's house and look for a *real* job.

We're wrapping up the menu job when I find a bellhop gig at the Ramada on Quebec Street, out by the old Stapleton Airport. I have to lie on the job application. I do the opposite of what most 'resume liars' would do: I don't mention CIA or DU, just simply a half-truth that I was a truck driver in the Army. About two or three days before that, Kunk tells me about this kiosk that has just opened up a few blocks from the Yacht Club.

"It's called the Shakey-Go-Round, and they are selling pizza slices out of it," he tells me. I walk up the street and look it over. As I'm checking the place out, there's a cute little blonde there taking pictures of the place. We talk a bit, and I find out that she works for Shakey's Corporate, which I also learn is in Englewood, a Denver suburb. I tell her about my background and that I'm looking for a job in purchasing.

To my surprise, she asks me for my phone number and tells me there might be something brewing with the purchasing job at Shakey's.

I go back to the Yacht Club to meet Joel for dinner. It's the last night of my two-week job there, so we'll have a little celebration, a night of craziness, and I don't get home to Moose's place until 1:30 a.m. I set the alarm for 5:30, and when I wake up, I know that the horrible black polyester uniform slacks they give me at the Ramada need hemming. They're about six inches too long for me. I go out to the car where I find them in a wrinkled pile in the back seat. I grab some filament strapping tape that I have from packing all my boxes for the mover in D.C. and go into Moose's kitchen where there are no scissors, but I do locate a dull scalloped edge steak knife. The knife is not cutting the pants, it's shredding them at the estimated hemline. There's no way I'm going to sew the hem—that's why I have the tape from the car. I somehow manage to fold the spongy pants legs under and do my best to secure a hem with the tape. It's pretty fragile, but only I know this.

I get to work by 6:30 and find a kid named Bob who's going to break me in. He teaches me how to drive the hotel van to and from the airport, how to sort a breadbasket full of hotel room keys (yes, at this time hotel doors are unlocked with *real* keys), how to greet a guest and take bags up to a room. The morning drags on, with occasional work tips from Bob. At about 10:30, he takes me over to the hotel's coffee shop, introduces me to the hostess, and teaches me how to order a meal, a meal *that I have to pay for.* Paying for food where I work, for somebody with my history, is foreign territory for me, and I am not pleased. But it's not time to eat yet.

Next, Bob takes me outside on what is turning out to be an unseasonably cool, overcast, and windy day. He takes me to the muddy base of the giant Ramada sign and shows me how to slide clear plastic sheets with letters and numbers painted on them (about 14" x 8") into tracks so that they will form a backlit advertising message, something like "Today's Special Lunch $3.45." Then he leaves.

I'm standing in the mud, which is sucking on my black leather shoes every time I attempt to take a step, and I'm holding this giant aluminum pole straight up in the air like a pole vaulter. The pole is maybe 20 feet long and has a humongous suction cup on the end of it, which is *supposed* to hold the rectangular plastic letters/numbers. There's a chain attached to the suction cup, and when I slide the letter across the horizontal track built into the sign, I'm supposed to pull the chain, which will release the letter from the pole and cup. The wind is really kicking up, and the giant pole is swaying in my hands as I try to position it close enough to the track to tell/sell all the world our $3.45 lunch specials; but even the bucket of water I've been given to facilitate the adhesion of the suction cup to the plastic letters is not cooperating. The letters are sticking in the track, actually jamming up, and the wind begins to blow the letters right off the suction cup when I'm trying to approach the track and guide in the letters. I've got the pole way up high over my head, and as the wind is taking the plastic letters off the suction cup, they're landing with a splat in the mud below on nearly every attempt. Then I have to use the bucket of water to wash them off and start again. I'm getting upset with this whole stupid business. And be reminded: I only have four hours of sleep behind some serious partying with Dr. Kunkel.

Somebody comes outside and tells me I can take my lunch break. There's no way I'm going to pay these people for my lunch. Just as I'm standing in the lobby, trying to figure out where in the hotel's vicinity I'm going to have lunch, the front desk clerk tells me she has a message for me. It's from Carolyn, Moose's wife. I walk over to use a pay phone to call Carolyn. She tells me that somebody from Shakey's Pizza has called, and she gives me a number. I call and it turns out they want to talk to me. I decide I'm going to get that job at Shakey's, and even if I don't, I can't deal with this place. I go looking for Bob, thinking I'll be polite, offer some excuse, and return the altered uniform slacks in a day or two. When I finally find Bob, I see that he's out in the parking lot, *while on the clock*, working on his engine. This is too much for me. I walk over to my car, take the black pants off, get in, and drive over to where Auto Repair 101 is taking place. I'm five-six feet away but Bob is oblivious to me. I roll down the shotgun window, ball up the slacks, yell "HEY BOB!" When he looks up from his engine, I throw the slacks in his face, and tell him, "Give my regards to Broadway," and zoom off.

I'm feeling pretty good, and then I realize that I have to get into Moose's house out in suburbia, in broad daylight, wearing only my underpants, along with a white shirt and a bellhop's bow tie. The only way to pull this off with any scrap of dignity is to behave as if it's a perfectly normal thing to do. So I park in front of his house, get out of the car, and (somewhat) calmly head up the front walk to his door, and by some miracle, I get away with it. And the next day I go to Shakey's, interview, and a few days later, get the job—Corporate Director of Purchasing for 485 restaurants. I only stay about 13 months, but when I do get out of there, *this time, I'm wearing my pants.*

September 1976 - A Whole Pile of Connections – Part 2

Right around the time I'm trying to sell my condo at Strawberry One (late summer 1976), I get a phone call from a person identifying himself as the Federal D.A. (we'll call him Berman, because I really can't remember his name) from the state of New Jersey. He's calling from Newark and would like to talk to me . . . in person. He asks if I'll come to Newark, based on his verbal request, or if I'd like a subpoena. I'm quickly thinking, *are you kidding me? 'Not for nothin' (as they say back in NJ/NYC) am I Al Oakes' kid.*

"What's this about?" I ask.

"It involves Emerson's Limited," Berman answers.

Then I ask him, "Can you tell me more?"

He says, "It's centered around purchasing practices."

"What's it got to do with me?" I wonder out loud.

We're playing verbal tennis, it seems. And then Berman verifies, "You worked there in purchasing, right?"

"Yeah," I respond.

Berman finally is taking this somewhere, "Your name was mentioned in connection with an investigation that's going on in New Jersey."

I need to know more. And so I ask, "What kind of investigation?"

"An S.E.C. investigation," he claims.

OK, I'm thinking, one more volley, "Can you be more specific?"

And here it comes Berman's serve, "Emerson's Limited was traded on the stock exchange. There was a standard year-end audit taking place, and one of the auditors looked up at the top rack of the freezer at a pallet full of cases of meat marked "Filet Mignon." He wanted to see what the steaks looked like, and when they pulled them down and opened up the cases on the pallet, they were all filled with hamburger meat. One thing led to another, and it was clear, after further investigation, that this was no accident; and there are questions about liquor purchasing."

And we're coming to the end of the set, with him asking me, "So, will you come based on what I just told you, or do you want a subpoena?"

"I want the subpoena," I answer.

Within an hour there's a knock on my door, and a federal marshal runs me through the drill and hands the subpoena to me. I must sign for it, of course.

First, they call me on the phone and ask a few very preliminary questions to verify my days of employment with

Emerson's and that sort of thing. I quickly call my father and explain what is going on, and most of what had gone on with the whole Matty Feldman experience. As I would expect, "Alzie" tells me, "Well you know, you gotta protect Matty."

"Yeah, of course," I tell him. We don't discuss the consequences of not protecting Matty, it's just a given that I need to 'do the right thing.'

The phone interview with the D.A. is nothing heavy. Then a few days later, they send a twenty-something kid out to interview me in person. He's a federal investigator working for Berman, the D.A. who originally phones me. We meet at the Village Inn Pancake House at Cinderella City Shopping Center. We'll call him Asher (because *his* name also escapes me).

Asher is a nice guy and as we go through his questions, it's becoming clear that they have a pretty good idea of the basic highlights and subsequent results of my visit with Matty. They just need me to connect all the dots, show them the mechanics of how it was all set up. But at this point, I'm just doing more listening than talking. Maybe two weeks later I get the call: go to the airport and be ready to fly to Newark for a day or two. There'll be a voucher coming in the mail. I'm to purchase the actual ticket but they already have reserved a seat for me.

I fly to Newark and Berman and I talk most of the next morning. He's asking me questions, but I'm not really forthcoming. He's forced to give me the info I need in order to know how to proceed. By virtue of his questions, he's telling me more and more of what they know. And all of it is beginning to show me that somebody at Emerson's and/or Matty is setting me up to be the chump, the guy who will be punished for this activity from which I haven't made a dime. I'm being totally calm because I know I'm holding the trump card. Berman leaves the room, telling me that it's time for lunch. He's clearly frustrated and begins using phrases like, "we don't want to see you get jammed up." Neither do I. But I have to play this out.

He sends Asher to take me to lunch, which consists of hot dogs down on the street in front of the federal courthouse in Newark. We're on the courthouse steps, and I know it's game time: I have to make my move on these guys. I've seen how it all works many times in the movies and on TV shows.

"Hey, Asher," I ask, "just hypothetically, what if when we go back upstairs, I start to remember some of the things I've forgotten . . . Could I walk away from all this untouched?

"Well, I can't say for sure, but I think we could work something out," he says, and continuing, "Hey, by the way, Ted Levine says hello."

"Ted Levine?" I ask, trying to hide my concern. "What's he got to do with all this?"

Asher says, "Oh, he's a lawyer with the Enforcement Division of the S.E.C."

Another insane coincidence in my life.

"Oh, great," I'm thinking. I grow up with Teddy Levine, go to Teaneck schools with him all my life. We're friendly when we're young, but I pop him with a right to the side of his face in ninth grade. He is considerably bigger than me, but one night I get tired of his condescension. We end up rolling around on the concrete of Garrison Avenue, but Marty Buxton quickly breaks it up. Lucky for me, it ends with the one shot. But now I have visions of him getting even with me. And I'm now wondering, *"Who else from Teaneck is going to show up in this tale?"*

I take a chance and say, "Yeah, OK. I think I'm starting to remember, but I gotta be sure that I can walk away before I really have a clear recall."

We go back to Berman, and Asher gets with him alone for a few minutes. I'm alone with time to think, and I know, without a doubt, somebody has told them a whole bunch and tied it all to me. When Berman returns to the interview room, and after he assures me we've got a deal, I begin to open up. I begin on that day when Matty visits us in Alexandria and take them right through what I can remember. I include information about the mechanics of the transfer of cash, which was to take place at Newark Airport each month via brown paper bag, etc. And then I pull the trump card: I tell them I can't make the deal without the phone call from Matty's closet, and that without the approval of my boss, Don Schwartz, it can't happen. The meaning I'm conveying is that I am just a messenger, an errand boy. And it is true.

Berman is unsure. He's one smart, smart guy, as evidenced by a feature article about his crime-fighting successes in New York Magazine months after I deal with him. He mentions to me multiple times, in no uncertain terms, that "my situation sense tells me there's more to this story than you're telling me."

"Nope, that's all of it," I answer (each time he asks).

He seems convinced that he knows better, but he's fishing. I know it, and best of all, I know he knows I know it. There's really no point in continuing. I've given them what they need. They send me back to Denver, telling me that the grand jury will be convening within two weeks or so.

Sure enough, I get the call and go back out to Newark. In the morning I sit with Berman and we go over all that I have told him, once again getting the "my situation sense" probing, but I'm not moving on it. I have nothing to tell him. Mid-morning, we head into the grand jury room. While I'm waiting outside, I spot Matty's kid, Danny, but we're far away from each other, and I really have nothing to say to him. I get called in, where I answer a few questions for maybe ten minutes, and am excused.

In the morning I fly back to Denver.

Weeks later they pinch Matty precisely on the day he's Acting Governor of N.J. (because the real Governor is in Japan, and since Matty is President of the State Senate, he's Acting Gov.). It is a calculated move to get maximum positive publicity for Berman and maximum negative press for Feldman. Berman so much as tells me this.

After the grand jury visit, I go back to work for Jim Miller. He's a prince about the whole thing, never mentions it. Family friend Mel Elting calls my father and tells him he sees my name in a front-page piece in the Wall Street Journal. I never do get to read the article. In the end I walk away while the others pay fines, lose the whole chain of 34 stores, and I imagine, end their careers.

May 1977

Jim Miller is a self-made millionaire, at a time when having a couple of million dollars is special. When he gets out of the Marine Corps, he works and rounds up enough money to buy and operate an eight-stool diner in Cut Bank, Montana. He's a hell of a nice guy, real down to earth, with a great sense of humor.

When we meet, he owns twenty-eight Kentucky Fried Chicken stores, five Wendy's, and a smattering of other fast-food investments. I work with him on and off doing restaurant project work over a couple of years. He's mostly interested in breaking into the pizza business, and he's thinking about two very different concepts: one being deep pan pizza, and the other a little six-inch pie that can be served within one minute of being ordered; and it's priced to compete with the hamburger guys. The concept is that pizza can truly compete in the fast-food arena. At the time, the basic six-inch cheese pizza is priced at about $1.50.

It's pretty ordinary for restaurant industry people to head to Chicago where every May the giant National Restaurant Association Convention takes place. If you are buying or selling new equipment or on the hunt for new ideas, you simply have to be there. Jim wants to be there for all of those reasons.

Not only is Jim a restaurant owner, he's also a silent partner in a Denver firm that manufactures and sells pizza warming ovens. He has two partners in the warming oven business. One of them is a guy named Ron Roderick, who Jim fondly calls "Rotten Ronnie." Jim and Roderick cook up a scheme to get into the kitchen of the most revered deep pan pizza joint in America, Pizza Uno in Chicago. I know nothing of this 'intel gathering plan' until right before we're about to leave for the Chicago show.

Ron has an appointment at Uno, to show their corporate ops guy one of the warming ovens. So, we get to Chicago and Jim and I walk through the front of the restaurant and ask to be taken to the meeting in the kitchen. Rotten Ronnie has pulled up in a rented pickup truck behind the restaurant and is unloading one of his ovens, getting it set up in the kitchen. My job is to drift away from the meeting between Jim, Ron, and the ops guy, so that I can absorb anything and everything having to do with the production of the pizza.

It's a scene worthy of an SNL skit: Rotten Ronnie heading into a major "BS" song and dance sales pitch, Jim blocking the Uno guy's view of me spying on two old ladies who are prepping deep pan pizzas, baking them off, and boxing them up. Roderick's plan is made funny—at least to me—because deep pan pizzas take much longer to bake off than regular ones, and Rotten Ronnie has to awkwardly extend his sales pitch to accommodate the timing – something he really doesn't understand or think through on the flight from Denver to Chicago.

The three of us corporate sleuths exit through the back door of the kitchen and pile into the pickup where I am furiously scribbling down everything I can remember about the production process.

Actually Jim already has a remarkably good recipe replication for the Uno product, which he features in a small pizza joint in Littleton, Colorado. But ultimately the numbers for the concept just don't make sense to me, given the Denver area restaurant market at the time, and I tell him so. He drops the concept, and due to some pretty serious cash flow problems, eventually has to abandon the "pizza as fast food" idea. Too bad, because the fast-food product was alive and well in a test operation in suburban Detroit.

Summer 1977 - Smuggler's Blues

It's time for my monthly haircut, and as usual I'm getting it done by Marcia Saylor, Mary's sister (Joel's ex-live-in girlfriend). But as I walk into the shop—and she happens to be alone this time—our eyes meet, and she is coming at me with a very strange look on her face.

"Marcia, what's wrong?" I ask, and instantly she falls into my arms.

She's sobbing in my arms now, and tells me, It's Jerry (Mary's boyfriend). Somebody shot him in the back of the head as he sat at his desk in his house. Mary found him when she got home. He's dead. It had to be somebody he knew, somebody he was dealing to. His gun was on his desk, loaded and unused.

This isn't a hit, but a rip-off. You have to listen to the words of Glenn Frye's, "Smuggler's Blues." You'll get the whole scene, right down to the location of *this* murder: Boulder, Colorado. Only this is no song for poor Mary. It's the real deal. It's life in the fast lane, or on the adjacent service road, where we all live at the time. I'm just thankful she isn't home when it happens. Sadly, over the years, several people I know will lose their lives to drugs.

Winter 1978

Jim Miller and DU friend Tom Ricca help
me land a job with Paul Smith at the Hitching Post in
Cheyenne, Wyoming. Charlene takes one look around town
and can't stand the thought of living there because it reminds
her of her Kansas upbringing, so we settle on Fort Collins,
Colorado. It's a 90-mile round trip commute, but way better
than the alternative. Working in Cheyenne, and at the
"Hitch" in particular, is a surreal experience, especially
during Cheyenne Frontier Days—ten long days and nights
of crazy high-volume business to support a world-class
rodeo.

But also surreal because upon arriving there, I do a
complete inventory of product in the food and beverage
areas. This is pretty standard if you're taking over and you're
the person who's going to be responsible for the numbers.
During the interview process I meet the owner's son, Paul
Smith, to whom I'll be reporting, and the C.F.O., who I'm
told is treated as a member of the Smith family. After the
inventory, I turn in my numbers to establish a baseline
financial picture for 'cost of goods sold.' Immediately upon
my sending the numbers to the family, the C.F.O. can't be

located. He's disappeared and can't be found for several days. Oh, and BTW, when they do finally talk with the guy, he's got amnesia. Can't remember a thing. The family loves this guy and consults with medical people. They feel horrible that he's 'taken ill.' But based on the inventory numbers I turn in, they also get their accounting firm involved, and an audit takes place. Bottom line (I couldn't resist) of all this: the C.F.O. has tagged them for a quarter of a mill . . . but he can't remember anything. *Yeah, sure.*

But because they do consider this guy a family member, he is sent away for treatment, but he will never return to the business.

Jim Miller calls again and wants me to do some product development work for him with his KFC group, so I leave the Hitch, knowing that Jim's project is just for a few months.

Early Fall 1979 - Escaping ShyWhy and Finding a Home

As my temporary consulting job with
Jim Miller in ShyWhy (four-year-old daughter Allie
coins this term) is winding down in early fall, I am scanning
the Denver Post for a job. I'm really unsure of what I want.
The only thing that seems clear to me is that I've outgrown
the Denver market. I want something fresh, a new challenge.
Within a two-week period, I see a couple of jobs that interest
me. One is a corporate meat buyer position with Sheraton
Hotels, the other an "Assistant Food Department Manager"
with Harrah's Hotel and Casino in Reno, Nevada. I haven't
been anybody's assistant in a while, but a job is a job.

Both jobs are appealing, maybe the Sheraton a bit more
so. The only things I know about Harrah's are: Every once
in a while, I see their big semi running on I-25, with wall-to-
wall signage for Harrah's Auto Collection on the trailer. I
guess they move cars around to auto shows in that trailer. I
also know that my parents' Teaneck friends, the Kohlmans,
stay at Harrah's-Tahoe on a vacation, and my parents visit
them there once during a driving vacation through the West.
And I know that Moose goes to Harrah's-Tahoe on vacation

with Carolyn a couple of years ago and relieves them of several of the finest hotel bath towels I have ever used. That's it—a fancy trailer truck, my parents' quick visit, and great towels.

I wait, and hearing nothing after three weeks, I finally put both jobs out of my mind. Then Sheraton calls and I get an interview set up. A few days later, Charlene calls me at my Jim Miller temp job in ShyWhy and tells me that a guy named Joe Strini calls from Harrah's, saying that if I'm the same Vinnie Oakes who went to CIA, that the job is mine. He leaves a number. I call back and of course, it's Joe Strini, former CIA classmate and acquaintance. He explains that the job is to be his assistant, overseeing food operations for Harrah's-Reno: restaurants, snack bars, employee feeding, banquets, the showroom, etc. It takes him a while, but he sets me up for an interview trip out to Reno.

In the meantime, I interview with Sheraton a couple of weeks later, but never hear back from them. Three days after the Sheraton interview I'm flying to Reno.

They keep me in Reno for two days, interviewing with several different people: Joe Strini, Harrah's-Reno Food Manager; Corporate Employee Relations Director Dave Cacci; Corporate Exec. Chef Julius Weiss; two Reno casino shift managers, Bill Jones and another; Corporate F&B Director R.J. Lukas; Corporate V.P. of F&B Joe Fanelli; Reno Personnel Manager Mary Ann Perkins; Reno ER Counselor Bill Zelinski, and two or three others.

I would be working for Joe Strini, with R.J. Lukas and Joe Fanelli above him in the hierarchy. There are only two Harrah's Hotel-Casinos at this time: Reno and Tahoe.

When I meet with Fanelli, he looks at a faux leather photo album I carry to interviews. It contains pretty much my entire work history in the form of letters of recommendation, certificates, and diplomas, etc. He stops at one particular letter, looks up at me, and says, "So you know F-F-F Freddy, huh?" And bingo! It's the 'Cornell connection,' that years before, Freddy Rufe told me would be so important if I were to go to school there. *Yes, it is! Even if I didn't go to the school.* Fanelli and Uncle Fred, it turns out, were classmates at Cornell.

During the two days of interviews, there is some talk in my presence, where Strini brings up to Joe Fanelli and R.J. the fact that no decision can be made until Rome is consulted and is in agreement. *Rome? They gotta call someone in Rome about me? Holy crap, just who am I getting involved with here? And this kind of scrutiny and approval just for a casino assistant food manager job? Well, it is for the whole giant department, but still . . .*

Clearly these are careful people, in a careful company.

In late afternoon of the second and final day of interviews, Strini takes me to a Harrah's-Reno United Way cocktail party for employees. He introduces me to a number of Harrah's management people, both corporate and from the Reno property.

This is an annual affair which celebrates the conclusion of the Reno property's fundraising effort on behalf of United Way. The food is lavish, almost no expense spared. The culmination of the event is a drawing of ten winning employee names from a large revolving drum. To be eligible for the prizes, an employee must pledge at least one day's pay to the United Way. Of course, they start announcing winners at the bottom: the smallest prizes, $100, gradually getting into the thousands, with the grand prize being a brand new 1980 Honda Prelude (and it's there in the room—like on a TV quiz show). Somebody wins a thousand, then another wins $5,000, and finally they call out the name of the Honda winner. He's not at the party. He's in the back, working in a kitchen. And in a few minutes, they bring out this little Filipino man, a guy who, moments before, is elbow deep in the muck of a pot sink, and they hand the keys to him. I wonder to myself if the poor guy even possesses a driver's license. Right then and there, as I'm stuffing myself with chilled jumbo shrimp and roasted lamb riblets, I know I want to be part of this company. But it's not that simple.

First, I must get home and wait for their phone call. Sounds easy. After all, I have a plane ticket that is sitting up in my Harrah's hotel room. I say goodbye to Joe Strini and leave the cocktail party. I figure I'll just have a little fun on this Friday night and get on my scheduled flight for Denver tomorrow. I walk across Virginia Street to the Reno Hilton and begin playing roulette with a "system" that I dream up on the spot. I start with $5 worth of quarters. In 1979 you can play quarter roulette and quarter craps in certain Reno/Tahoe *"clubs,"* as casinos are called by locals at the time. I start with only $5, because all I have on me is about $40, most of which I need for payment of airport parking where my car is in Denver, and for gas money to get me from Denver to Fort Collins (home). I take my time and run the quarters up to $12.

Now that I'm a proven success (not a genius, but *I must be* smarter than the roulette crew at the Hilton, anyway), I decide to try the system at Harrah's. Wow, it appears I'm smarter than them as well. I start drinking. Why not? They're all but pouring the free drinks down my throat. Oh, and did I mention that I've never played a casino table game as an adult prior to this? I'm hot. I take the $5 up to $200 and I don't notice it, but I'm starting to draw the attention of the pit supervisors.

Strini comes by for a while, borrows some money from me (which I will never see again), and promptly loses all of it, maybe $20. He's plowed and leaves for home. I don't need the $20, I'm doing fine. After all, I've got a system. I'm clever. "Another drink?" the cocktail waitress asks.

"Sh-shurrr," I answer.

They start to work me, changing up dealers frequently, who in turn change up the rhythm of the wheel. The piles of chips start getting lower. Every once in a while, I hit them for a big win via a zero/double zeros tactic, but I'm trending downward. And they're in no hurry. I realize what's going on but I've been drinking their free booze and I start 'chasing' the losses, convinced that things will come around my way on the next spin of the wheel.

I play from 5:30 p.m. till about 11 p.m. Not bad for starting with $5. All that is fine if I'm *actually* clever, and leave with my original $40, but soon enough, that is gone also. *How will I bail my car out of the Denver Airport parking lot? Hell, how will I even get to the Reno airport without cab fare? Where would the needed gas money come from to buy enough in Denver for the 60-mile drive to Fort Collins?*

Why am I even telling this embarrassing story to you? Because if you're reading this you are a member of my family, somebody I just plain love, or somebody who bought my story, and I want you to know there is no way to beat a casino in the long run. If you walk into a casino with some money, understand you may have a fun time and you may find it entertaining, but you should know going in you won't be leaving with your money, at least not over the long haul. You may even leave with winnings for 'the trip,' but you'll be back, and the inevitable will occur. And that's OK, I suppose, if you're willing to buy your entertainment in that way. Just don't gamble more than you can afford to lose, because you *will* lose.

Eventually I am grateful that: a) there are no ATM's yet in casinos (or I would have lost way more than $40); b) I learn a valuable lesson; and c) I am and have always been a big chicken—as opposed to my father—when it comes to betting, so I don't suffer from an overly optimistic attitude about gambling.

The next day I use my wits and have major help from God finding spare change and a few singles here and there (in my luggage, in my car at the Denver Airport) and manage to get from Reno to my house in Fort Collins, Colorado, on schedule.

It takes Harrah's a whole month to finally say "yes" to hiring me. It turns out that they have more guys to interview, and among other things, Rome Andriotti (*a person!*) has to be consulted and give his approval. One of the hang-ups being that Rome hasn't had a face-to-face with me, apparently something that is de rigueur for candidates.

Late November 1979

When they finally say "yes," Harrah's, at least according to Strini, requires my presence almost immediately, a 'wait and hurry up' scenario. I suspect he's lying, but who cares? It's Thanksgiving week, so I take care of a little business, make initial arrangements for the family move (which Harrah's will pay for), have our holiday meal, and prepare to leave on the next day. I pack what I can into my VW Bug, grab a quarter pounder meal to go at McDonald's, and head out of Fort Collins at 4 p.m.

A heavy Colorado snowstorm greets me as I get into the mountains. It's one of those horizontal blowing, blinding snows, but I'm on a mission and make it to the western slope where I find a motel, rest for a few hours, and continue on to a motel in Elko the next day, and finally into Reno a day and a half after starting out.

Strini wants me to find a place to live before I begin to work, "get it out of the way," he says. I find nothing affordable in the Reno area. I'm looking at houses and they're way more than what I'm used to in Fort Collins, whether it's a rental or for sale. So I decide—since I already know that someday I want to work at the crown jewel

(Harrah's–Tahoe), like maybe after 18 months or so—why not live in Carson City, from which I can commute to either property? I find an apartment to rent in Carson and decide to drive up and see this place called Lake Tahoe.

As the car tops Spooner Summit, I am greeted with a magnificent view of the lake, an experience I'll never forget. I drive a short distance on Highway 50 and turn back for Reno without seeing Harrah's.

After a week or so I call my mother, telling her I don't know how long I'm going to last with these people, but I'm going to make the most of it while I'm here. I tell her it seems to me 'the beautiful people' all work here, and standards of all kinds are very high, as in 'I may not be good enough for them.'

During these first several days, Joe Fanelli invites me to lunch at the locally esteemed Prospectors' Club, a private collection of rooms located within Harrah's-Reno. He's taking me there because its oversight belongs to the food department, and without him bringing me in, I can't just take a seat and order a meal. It's a typical "members only" men's lunch club with rooms for card games, pool tables, and special events. And of course, you have to be "a somebody" to be a member. We just sit down to eat when Harrah's President Lloyd Dyer stops by the table. He's about the only person, other than Rome, who I didn't meet during my job interviews. He's a very distinguished-looking sixtyish gentleman, so I am a bit surprised—although pleasantly—

when the first thing out of his mouth is, "It's about goddamn time we hired an American" (for a high-end food job). I'm gonna like this guy!

Although our apartment in Carson City won't be ready for a couple of weeks, I can now go to work. Strini puts me with his food shift supervisors to learn how the department operates and how it interfaces with most of the others. He also has me meeting and chatting with a number of management people at varying levels, from many different departments.

But there's way more to learning about the department: there's the corporate culture. And while there are certainly many things in common between Reno and Tahoe (the only two Harrah's in existence when I start with the company), they are two very different places.

This becomes important, because after working fourteen days straight (might as well just work every day: nothing else to do till I can move into an apartment and get the family out from Colorado), R.J. tells me I need to meet him up at the lake on the following day, a Friday, because they want to talk to me about transferring up there. The food department manager has been fired, and I'm to meet R.J. at Tahoe's executive offices at 1 p.m. where he and Joe Fanelli will talk to me about a promotion and a transfer to the lake *(already?!?)*.

I drive up to Tahoe in late morning, and after cresting Spooner Summit on Highway 50, I am again blown away by the view of the lake. This time I slow the car and try to take it all in. It is a scene unlike anything I've ever experienced: the bluest of any blue water in my recollection, the sheer stretch of its length, which is too much for my eyes to actually take in from the roadway, all of it framed by snow-capped mountain tops rising to the sky. Such beauty!

When I get to Harrah's, I park my car and walk in through the Pony Express entrance. Relative to where I've worked in my past, it's huge, the casino floor stretching to infinity before my eyes. I am stunned by its immensity and a bit scared. I am not a Don Knotts kind of guy, but if I were, my knees would be knocking.

I immediately tell myself I need more casino experience before I take on something this big, not to mention the Mobil Guide Five Star/AAA Five Diamond ratings that the property has just received. I don't feel I'm ready for this job. I want the comfort and relative security of my previously imagined 18 months working with Joe Strini at the Reno property.

The Conversation

I get directed to a hallway of executive offices, where I find R.J. (age about 40) and Joe (age about 60) waiting for me. We talk. Joe tells me he knows that I'm new at all this, but he knows that I can do this job. R.J. doesn't say much, letting his boss Joe do the talking. It's not an interview; it's a conversation. I ask Joe what I'll be making, and he tells me a figure that's only a thousand more than I'm making as the assistant food manager at Reno, a smaller and less important property than Tahoe. And remember, I'm *moving up* to department manager. So in my mind, it's a double promotion: position *and* property.

I look at Joe, this man I barely know, and say, "Do you think you're talking to a fool?" Joe stares at me, while R.J., clearly mortified, says, "Uh, Joe, I have to step out a minute."

Joe waits for R.J. to remove his considerable bulk (he's a power lifter) from the room.

Joe very calmly starts, "A minute ago, before your outburst, I was talking about my belief in you." And on he goes, talking me into taking the job with the promise of help from people who have been at the property for years, and a raise in six months. So how can I not agree? And late that afternoon, when I return to Reno, the family arrives from Colorado, joining me at the Holiday Hotel and Casino, where Harrah's has us temporarily housed.

The following Monday (December 17), Joe Fanelli has me meet up with Bob Stirling the minute I arrive for my first day at the lake. Bob has been at Harrah's–Tahoe since 1959. He's a walking encyclopedia and will hold my hand over the first six months or so, while I'm in the steepest section of the learning curve. He is selfless and thoroughly loyal to Harrah's, to Joe, and to me.

It may be difficult for you, the reader, to understand that when I begin at Harrah's, there are only two states that have legalized full-blown gaming (and to be accurate, New Jersey was not truly "full-blown"); that there are only two Harrah's properties, both in northern Nevada, 56 miles apart. And perhaps equally difficult to grasp in today's context would be the collection of facts, innovations, and idiosyncrasies that make up Harrah's culture when I arrive at the lake. This is an era when company veterans talk about "getting you Harrahrized." It's not like that now.

Christmas

We are getting settled into our apartment in Carson City, and my parents come up to join us for a few days. It's a fun and exciting time for all of us, and we have a nice Christmas having them along for this adventure.

The Harrah's Culture

This long "A to Z" (almost) list refers to what it is like at Harrah's-Tahoe in 1979 when I arrive. In the big picture, Reno and Tahoe share the same corporate culture, and yet each property clearly has its own very strong subculture. This list gives a certain amount of context to anything Harrah's that I talk about later in my stories.

Holiday Inns buys Harrah's on February 28, 1980. Over my time at the company, some of these cultural things simply fall by the wayside; others are eliminated by those who want to overpower the culture, creating a new look and feel to life there. It becomes a matter of who's going to control who. Will the community of proud employees continue down the road they've been traveling for many years, or will the new people "break" the culture, just for the sake of control? One thing is for sure: the policies and procedures that disappear take Harrah's from the Cadillac of casinos—and in the case of Harrah's-Tahoe, the highest-rated hotel-casino in the country for twelve consecutive years—to the Chevrolet of the gaming industry. It becomes, over time, all about shareholder returns, and one G.M.'s need for control, mostly based in his ego and insecurities, having never been a gaming guy, let alone a Tahoe guy before getting appointed to the job. But that all comes later . . .

Asset Tags - Perhaps not too unusual for large corporations, but in light of where I've worked, I find it a bit strange. Every time a new piece of equipment of any type arrives, an asset tag quickly follows in the company mail and arrives at the department manager's office. The tag must be affixed to the equipment and a form filled out, returned to engineering. Records of everything are kept.

Benefits - Lots of companies like to say that their employees are treated as well as guests. Mostly, they lie. In the case of Harrah's, the benefits, stated or subtle, are pretty amazing back in the good old days. Certainly, a lot of the 'benies' are initiated to combat possible unionization of the work force. Nonetheless, in my early years there, while Bill Harrah's people and culture still drive the feeling of the place, it is a great organization, both for the employee *and* the clientele. So here are just *some* of the benies when I start at Harrah's:

All "Group One" Managers have 100% coverage (no deductibles) on medical, dental, and vision insurance for selves and families—from day one. There are probably about two dozen Group One Managers and above at each of the properties. Once I transfer to Tahoe, I am one of those lucky few.

Board of Review - If an employee is written-up or terminated, that person has the right to a Board of Review. The board is made up of three people: an H.R. representative, a salaried supervisor from another department, and a representative from the claimant's work unit (these BOR reps are elected annually by their peers). This is another of H.R. V.P. Joe Spect's brilliant tactics to avoid unions. By giving an employee a way to be heard by three impartial people, and allowing witnesses for the 'defense,' we are supplanting the job of a shop steward and his union reps.

Birthdays - An extra day's pay or the day off with pay on one's birthday.

Breaks - 70 minutes of breaks in an eight-hour shift for most full-time hourly employees. The Pit gets 20 minutes of break time out of every hour worked.

Comping Privileges - A detailed computer print-out is issued daily, detailing who comped who, what, and where, and of course, the dollar amount spent. It could be drinks, restaurant meals, a hotel stay, gift shop purchases, a visit to the health club, etc.

There is another computer report sent out monthly which details the name, vertically on the far left, of every management person who has these privileges. Across the top of the page, each bar and restaurant is listed. The bar and restaurant columns are split vertically, showing whether a person has an Unlimited Comp, a Business Comp, or a Self-

Comp, or no comping at all in each of the locations. Not everyone who has comping privileges can comp in all venues. There is a clear hierarchy of spending locations allowed.

A self-comp essentially means no questions asked— provided you don't over-step—regarding who or why. A business comp means you are supposed to be using this expense for business purposes only. The level of comping *privileges* is of course depending on where you reside in the hierarchy of the place/corporation, where you are in the pecking order. An unlimited comp means no questions asked re: who, what, where, or how much is spent.

There are also specific designations if you are comping someone other than yourself. For example, you might hand a guest a comp slip for a specific meal or drinks at a specified restaurant or bar, including a date or date range.

In ten years, I never once get questioned about my comp expenses, but others, time and again, get tripped-up by this privilege and find themselves in hot water, and sometimes even end up looking for work. Stupid.

Drink Stamps - Salaried supervisors at certain levels and in certain departments are given a little rubber stamp encased in a two-inch long nickel-plated steel oval case, which they may use to comp drinks or food. The stamp has the supervisor's name, of course, and an assigned comp account number, along with his/her job title. For those who do not have one, it is a big deal. If you have one of these, you've arrived (at least that's the way people act). Because I am vitally involved with Food and Beverage, and am a Group One manager, I have a stamp from day one. Therefore, I never really have an appreciation of, or can relate to, the whole drooling thing that occurs sometimes when I pull it out and buy a round of drinks for employees at one of the bars. Or maybe it's just no big deal to me because I'm not much of a drinker. After a couple of years, I abandon the drink stamp, because it's a weird weight in my pants pocket; I just sign my name onto bar tabs or guest checks.

Drink Tokens (aka Drink Tokes) - These are huge rolls of glossy, color-coded, perforated tickets (like large movie theater tickets): one color for employees, another for guests/players. They are used to say "Thank You" to employees, or "Thanks" to a player; sometimes to say "Sorry" to a guest or player who has a gripe. There are also a couple of drink tokes attached by perforation to each employee's paycheck. For me and others in management, these are meaningless for personal use, as we have drink stamps or signing privileges, but they are an important tool for employee and guest relations. Eventually I become conflicted about their use because they encourage drinking by some people who shouldn't. And also, they are frequently used by Daily Rates (non-salaried employees) the same way cigarettes are used in the prison system, i.e., they are used to buy favors.

Eligibility for Major Benefits - Partial benefits after 90 days, the balance after six months; again, for Group One management, on day one.

Free Binaca for Employees - This one is geared strictly to avoid offending a player or guest with possible bad breath from an employee (although truth be known, every cage employee—casino cashiers—would use those tiny bottles of Binaca to help remove ballpoint ink stains from their white blouses/shirts). About two or three years after Holiday Corporation buys Harrah's, they put a few of us on a mission to discover opportunities to save money. I jump on an easy one—Binaca expense—and find that a total of $47,000 a year is spent by Tahoe alone on this item.

Harrahscope - A monthly corporate "feel good" glossy publication—professionally written, photographed and published—written for and about employees, and includes positive company news. It is mailed to each employee at his/her home. And it is 'Class A.'

PA's allowed to smoke while working - This always seems unbelievable to me, but the pit bosses—called pit administrators (PA's) and pit supervisors at Harrah's—are permitted to smoke while on duty. It's incongruous with a high-end environment, but I believe it's done to throw yet another union-busting benefit at them. Later this will change, and rightly so.

Service Award Parties/Retirement Parties - After five years of service at Harrah's, male employees receive a single-diamond embedded lapel pin; for females, it's a lavalier on a necklace. Just before each subsequent five-year anniversary we turn in our pin or lavalier and another diamond is embedded. A pin can hold five embedded diamonds for a 25-year employee, but *then* the employee is also given a gold ring with five diamonds. The anniversary employees are invited to a lavish cocktail party (heavy hors d'oeuvres) for all award recipients. All are honored and given their pins, lavaliers, or rings. Award parties are twice a year.

Retirement parties are similar. These occur if an employee has at least 15 years with the company and are big generous affairs with those employees who are being honored allowed to invite a fair number of personal guests.

Silver-plated flatware in the Employee Cafeteria.

Steak Day - Once a month in the Employee Cafeteria, when vein steaks (end cuts from the end of a strip loin, that contain a streak of gristle so can't be served to guests) are given to food employees for free, and at a very nominal cost to all others.

Three free meals a day for Food Department employees. I believe beverage employees get one free meal a day. All others pay a minimal amount for their food.

Warehouse Sales - In the early years, about every six months there are employee sales down at Harrah's-Reno warehouse. The stuff they sell is amazing, all of it priced to move. Some of it is used, some brand new: furniture from hotel rooms and offices, bedding, china, glass, flatware, carpeting, lighting, etc. We still use Villeroy & Boch 'Troubadour' pattern china at home. It is made in Belgium, and I buy it for next to nothing in fall 1980.

The Troubadour china pattern is used in the Forest Buffet on the 18th floor of Harrah's-Tahoe during my early years at the lake. It is an unmistakable signal to the dining public that they are eating in a place that's a cut above, a real classy buffet. But the cost of this china is outrageous. When Holiday Corporation buys Harrah's in February 1980, it's quickly marked for replacement. Clearly their leadership feels that the Tahoe property is overbuilt, and future construction projects will be designed and built with a broader, mass-market appeal . . . and a more modest budget.

Other Benies - Truly, there are so many that I don't remember all of them, or some are probably too inconsequential to mention. Big and small, these include the annual United Way parties, Harrah's Auto Collection free admission, annual employee cocktail parties and South Shore Room dinner shows, stock options and gifts for upper management, some forms of tuition reimbursement, make-up consultations for female employees, high-end educational seminars for selected management people, partial matching funds on charitable donations, et cetera. Add to all this, the big one, which comes along in about 1985: a 401K plan with a 1:1 match of up to 6% of one's annual salary or wages.

OK, back to the culture in general . . .

Bulletin Board 'Death Notices' - Harrah's-Tahoe is like a little city. It has an employee population of about 4,400 when I arrive. There is actually a procedure for announcing employee deaths: a horizontal half sheet of white paper holds the obit and is mounted over a larger rectangular piece of black construction paper, allowing a half inch black border. It's surprising how many funerals I attend at the lake. Maybe not so surprising when one factors in the average age of employees (young), the roads, the weather, the 24-hour availability of booze (and drugs), and the menu of dangerous outdoor activities in the region.

BUT . . . 'Nobody dies at Harrah's.' Although DOA at hospital is permissible. This is something I never hear about but am told years after I have left by a *very* reliable source: Within the four walls, stuff happens, but according to my source, *"only in the ambulance, or at the hospital does one actually die."* It's just one of many secrets that exist at the property, and only needs to be known by a very select few.

Butler Service - The suites on the 16th floor have butler service. These guys, dressed in 'tails,' run down to the room service kitchen to pick up food and beverage orders, but they are involved with other services, working out of the butlers' pantry on the 16th floor. They do whatever it takes, including concierge duties, or even drawing a bath—should a guest desire this service. They are part of my department, reporting to the room service manager.

Butter Roses in Room Service - An idea I pick up from a stay at the Fairmont Hotel in New Orleans when I go down there with Moose for the Symposium on American Cuisine. (Harrah's-Tahoe is a Five Star/Five Diamond Hotel. We need to do this!). It's all about being the very best you can be, and luckily, we have a pastry shop that takes pride in what they do (although some down there are not fully enamored with the necessary labor behind the butter rose concept). We don't serve pats of butter in the Summit Restaurant or in 16th floor suites once we install this change. We serve butter that looks just as if it is a rose. We also serve thousands of the roses at high-end banquets. This is the kind of thing that I don't have to ask permission for. Within reason I have enough autonomy to make these little improvements, and the creative freedom feels good.

Buying the Business - A term used when referring to cash pay-outs made to players to 'prime the pump'—usually in the form of one or two rolls of nickels for bus customers stepping off tour busses (weekdays only) from 67 cities in northern California. The term also refers to other incentives, mostly various couponing promotions around the club.

Over the years, as marketing and demographic changes evolve, Harrah's-Tahoe bus customer counts dwindle down from a high of 1,200-1,300 a day to maybe 400-600 while I am working there. And of course, the nickel slots disappear after a few years.

Calendars - Only Harrah's calendars allowed (they have no graphics, just the months, days and numbers; and they alternate the background colors every other year.) Uniformity and consistency are valued in this company. Anything displayed on a wall (art, etc.) has to be in a frame (more uniformity and consistency). When I arrive, it has to be a 'Harrah's frame,' built by our carpentry shop, but over the years, as with many peculiar mandates, this one loosens up.

Celebrity Guests and Players - You name the category, and you will see them at the south shore of Lake Tahoe: athletes, actors & actresses, singers, comedians, artists, celebrity lawyers, writers, politicians, big biz people, etc. Some hide behind disguises and/or fake names, others just try to blend in. One state governor who loves to use comical fake names when checking into the hotel—B. Lee, B. True, and a few others—is especially outlandish in his behavior, as are several guests in the entertainment field. Parties in our guest rooms occasionally get a bit wild.

Over the years, I meet many of these celebs, and just as life goes, they are a cross section of human personality types—from jerks to incredibly gracious, friendly people.

"Clubs" is an old term that is used by northern Nevada gaming veterans when I start work at the lake. It is a synonym for casinos, and several of the old, smaller places have the term in their name, such as "The Bank Club," "The

Nevada Club," etc.; also, earlier in time, "Harrah's Club." To this day, I still slip into using this term.

Coffee Klatsch - A strong part of the culture when I arrive, a coffee klatsch is a quick informal meeting to communicate immediately needed information. Often we call for a coffee klatsch to speak with a group of employees about some urgent matter or procedure change. These are not the same as a pre-shift meeting or 'line-up,' which occurs daily in many restaurants. These days, as I write this, the term that is used at the Food Bank (for the warehouse crew) is 'a stand-up.'

Corporate Jets - At the time Harrah's begins acquiring jets, as with many of the things Bill Harrah initiates, it is a gaming industry innovation. These are used for various purposes, such as ferrying showroom entertainers, players, and groups of management people in and out as the needs require. Of course, we have our own pilots and our own stewardesses (former waitresses who worked in my department), and (thank God) our own REAL food.

Daily Rates - When I start, non-salaried employees are paid a daily rate, i.e., a flat amount of money for a shift. These non-salaried employees are often referred to as "Daily Rates." Years later the basis becomes hourly.

Food Shift Supervisors - Every 24-hour casino operates three shifts: day, swing and graveyard. Harrah's org chart is set up so that the hotel casino has a V.P./G.M. over two or three A.G.M.s who split the departments up. But the operational god of the entire building during most of my years with the company is the shift manager. He reports to the G.M. and has total control over any important operational decisions for his eight-hour shift. Every department in the company replicates this structure, each one having shift supervisors who are responsible for major decisions for his/her eight-hour shift. When I arrive at the company the restaurants are set up under the same structure. There is a food shift supervisor who oversees everything of significance for eight hours. They write about their shift in a log book, which is shared with their peers. There are several built-in problems in trying to make restaurants function as if they are a casino. It takes me a couple of years to see the light, and in year number three, I am able to convince Rome and the others to switch to a system that will be much more effective: restaurant managers/maître d's (for white tablecloth restaurants) and assistant managers. Now we can hold people accountable for planning and executing for each of their assigned operations on a 24/7 basis—not for a mere eight hours, i.e. they "own" their restaurant. No more "putting out fires" for eight hours, without a care in the world for the following 16.

Free smokes in the pit - This part makes sense . . . for the players. You don't want a player to leave a table for any reason, so you bring things to him or her. And you comp those things . . . because he or she is playing. An inventory of cigarette packs is kept in every pit stand and given to players of value. Years later, most casinos adopt "No Smoking" policies.

"Friendliness and Courtesy" - is the mantra of Harrah's-Tahoe when I arrive and until Tom Yturbide leaves the company. Casinos within the same general levels of quality (one quickly learns) are all really the same. Oh, they may have different carpet patterns, different restaurant themes, styles, perhaps a giant fish tank behind the front desk, etc. But the truth is, they all buy the carpeting, the prime ribs, the cards, the felt table games layouts, the slot machines, and the stoves from the same handful of guys. So what differentiates one club from another in the eyes of the public? Pretty much two main things: *a perception of luck* in a given casino, and the *relationships formed with the staff.* 'Friendliness and Courtesy' are the initial drivers of those bonds between casino and guest. There are certainly other drivers of player loyalty, but those two main things are the foundation. Every single week of my early years at the property, we (department managers) are reminded of Friendliness & Courtesy in our Thursday management meetings. It's a 'drumbeat' *every single week.*

Glass Exchange 'On the Hill' - There are four large casinos in Stateline (not today's 'Vegas large,' but large for the time), as the area is officially named, and three smaller ones; but the Stateline/South Lake Tahoe area is referred to by many people, especially those who live down in the Carson Valley towns, as "The Hill," or also known as "South

Shore." And since many people tend to walk 'next door' or 'across the street' to try their luck at another casino, and because all the larger clubs have logoed glassware, we have a monthly exchange agreement with the three other clubs. Rookie bar backs (apprentice bartenders) are sent out pushing large carts on monthly runs to trade glassware. Even so, we lose thousands of glasses to souvenir seekers every month. I doubt very much that casinos these days use logoed glassware. That's because most are held by publicly traded corporations, and every penny expended must be justified.

Godiva Mints in the Summit - You don't serve cellophane wrapped mints when you're operating a room like this one. After I get my feet on the ground, I realize we need to make some minor improvements—just details really. I find where to buy Godiva in bulk—direct from the manufacturer in Pennsylvania—and we introduce Godiva mints wrapped in gold foil. These are dark chocolates filled with creamy mint centers. Very luxurious. On Thanksgiving, Christmas, and New Year's Day, I make it a point—even if I have the day off—to take a large bag of these mints around to all the restaurants, kitchens, and other production areas to give each employee one of these mints, along with a verbal "Merry Christmas" and "Thank You" for coming in to work on the holiday. A couple of times, when I do have the day off, I bring my very young son David along with me to experience this. I want him to know that a leader should be appreciative of those who have to work on holidays.

Guest Checks in Restaurants - Are always presented *face up* to the guest. One of the corporate cultural idiosyncrasies to get used to, this policy's rationale was, "Mr. Harrah is not ashamed of how much we charge our guests for food." Employees are taught to say this to guests, should the presentation be questioned. Yes, even after Bill Harrah has passed away.

H.A.C. (Harrah's Auto Collection) - A remarkable assemblage of some 1,200 cars on display in a pair of warehouses in Sparks, a town adjoining Reno. It is owned by Harrah's, but really it is Bill Harrah's curated personal collection. Employees go there for free. Everything, as with all of Harrah's during my early days there, is spotless, and the collection is overwhelming in its size and attention to detail. It is reputed to be the largest collection in the United States. There is a crew of full-time expert restoration guys who are always working on new acquisitions. Around 1984-85 three large auctions take place. These are designed to convert the cars into cash for the owner at the time, the Holiday Corporation (Holiday Inns). There is a public outcry, resulting in the formation of a foundation which operates a building to permanently house about 200 of the cars in Reno. The collection is re-named the William F. Harrah National Automobile Museum, and it quickly becomes the top-rated tourist attraction in the city.

"Hey Rome, feel . . . it's still warm" - A famous legend that circulates when new management people are being

'Harrahrized:' Rome is up for one of his Tuesday visits and spots a light bulb that is out. This is one of the Bill Harrah hallmarks of attention to detail carried on in the years following his death, and Rome is the principal 'keeper of the flame' when it comes to preserving that legacy. So Harrah's being Harrah's, a maintenance guy is dispatched to immediately change out the bulb, after which he comes down off his ladder and goes to show Rome what he's found, "Hey Rome, feel, it's still warm!"

We actually have one employee who is assigned to replace burned-out lights throughout Harrah's-Tahoe. It's that important. His nickname: 'Bulb.'

A year or so after I begin working at the lake, Tom Yturbide becomes the G.M., replacing Joe Francis who has been promoted to a corporate Sr. V.P. position. Tom and his wife Paula go up to the Forest Buffet on a busy Friday evening to eat dinner. I'm making a tour of the restaurants before I leave for the night, and I am somewhat horrified and yet pleasantly amazed to see a very tall ladder set up next to Tom and Paula's table. Apparently, he had spotted a darkened bulb right above their seats. He points it out, and everybody knows, you don't wait at Harrah's. You take care of *it*, whatever *it* is, right then and there; in this case, while they are at the buffet line getting their food. The cultural sense of urgency is one of those things that I learn from Bob Stirling when he is assigned to 'Harrahrize' me. And I totally buy in. Still do.

Hookers - They are around, but it's all *very, very discreet*, and nothing the company really wants to tolerate. They work out of a place in a nice residential area nearby called Round Hill. The club doesn't want them hanging around, making trouble. Prostitutes, if left to their own devices, will slip drugs into people's drinks and steal money from them in hotel rooms after they are passed out. So security chases the pros out of the place at night. It really is a 'clean' joint.

Keno Writers - In my early years, they are artfully using brushes and India ink to mark-up players' tickets. At the lake, the majority are Asian, many being from the Philippines. They are mesmerizing to watch, but in the mid-to-late eighties, all casinos begin converting to machine-generated Keno tickets, and another little piece of the charm of the old clubs is gone forever.

Last names for women (and men) in the Pit (dealers of table games) - At first this strikes me as unusual, as we don't refer to Food and Beverage women by their last names, let alone call them by that to their face. But one of my early-on 'cocktail after work' buddies is Ken Kettler, who at the time is the assistant pit department manager. Gradually I fall into step with Ken's lingo and understand why it is done: restaurants are separate entities, run almost as a chain of independent free-standing businesses, having differing menus, uniforms, themes, etc., but pit areas, numbered 1-6 or 7 at Tahoe, are indistinguishable from each other. The same goes for dealers' uniforms: they're all the same, regardless of which pit they work in. Only shift assignments separate these people: day, swing, or grave. And so, since the Pit Department has almost 1,000 dealers when I start at Tahoe, there could easily be five "Judys" on the same shift, dressed the same way. Hence, the use of last names. Cocktail waitresses are pretty much the same, but for some reason, in that department entire names (first and last) are usually used. Maybe it's because there aren't nearly as many cocktail servers as female games dealers.

The person who handles scheduling the entire Pit Department is known as the 'pencil.' This is a temporary assignment for up and coming P.A.'s (pit administrators: the public and non-Harrah's casinos would call them 'pit bosses'). Supervisory gaming people do this job for maybe six months, then rotate back onto the gaming floor. Another reason for last names: the pencil is probably not interested in writing the first names of every single person he or she must place into the schedule unless it's just an initial. During most of my years at Tahoe this job is done without the help of a computer for several hundred hourly employees plus salaried supervisors. They are on three different shifts, assigned to one of several games (craps, blackjack, pai gow poker, baccarat, mini baccarat, poker, roulette, big six wheel) depending on their knowledge, training, and experience. The scheduling job is not for those easily confused.

"Likes and Dislikes" - A few days before a given showroom entertainer is due to arrive, a single pink sheet of paper arrives in the company mail to those managers who need to know what his or her preferences are. The sheets are called "Likes and Dislikes." They describe an entertainer's favorite food, beverages, snacks, and personal living habits, so that our housekeeping crew (working with Adeline Murphy) assigned to the Entertainment Department and the butlers (who work for me) can do everything possible to make them feel at home. Purchasing finds a way to get Cuban cigars for Bill Cosby (even though this kind of purchase is not permitted by the U.S. government), Tootsie Pops for Frank Sinatra, and virtually anything a star may ask for. I still have some of these pink sheets. They are a unique look at the details that Bill Harrah wanted for his entertainers' comfort. We are often told that entertainers can get more money from other venues, but no other company treats them as well as Harrah's.

Lines - Unlike many restaurants in the U.S., be they freestanding or in hotels, Harrah's management does not view lines in a positive light, as in, "Hey, look at the line for the (insert restaurant name here, or the showroom), we must really be doing well!" I am quickly told, probably on my first day of work, walking around with Bob Stirling that if we have a line that's too long, "they'll go across the street or next door (to competing casinos) to eat, and they might not come back." This is not based on fear of losing a restaurant guest. No. It's about losing a *casino player* (gambler) . . . even if it's just the guy who plays a couple of Keno tickets while he's waiting for his french toast at the coffee shop.

After I'm at the job a few years, we get smarter, and *when we do have excessive lines*—usually on holiday weekends—we actually use stanchions and vinyl-covered ropes to form two parallel lines: one for guests of the casino and one for regular civilians. Depending on current demand factors and line lengths, we run a ratio system to seat the guests, e.g., we seat three casino guests for one civilian guest. We want to keep gamblers happy and get them back to the casino floor as quickly as possible.

Long Coffee Shop Menus - Using a similar rationale of keeping the lines short to retain guests, we keep menus long, with lots of variety, particularly those in casual restaurants, and of course the Forest Buffet. We don't want anyone 'going across the street,' because he/she can't find what he/she wants to eat at Harrah's.

During swing shift in our large coffee shop, the Sierra Restaurant, we even have a 'Chinese line' in the kitchen. So does the coffee shop at Harrah's-Reno. It's pretty standard stuff for the time, with 30-40 menu items offered, two Asian guys working the big woks.

One night during my first winter at Tahoe, Casino Manager (at the time) Russ McLennan comes in at 11 p.m., finds the food shift supervisor, and tells him, "I want a Chinese buffet for eight people in ten minutes." This of course is for one of Russ's comp parties. He gets it . . . in ten minutes. We don't say, "no" at Harrah's, and we don't make excuses. Ever.

"May Harrah's Buy You a Cocktail?" - While it isn't correct English, in my time there Harrah's *insists* that cocktail waitresses assigned to gaming areas ask players this question. If the 'girls' just cruise through, announcing, "Cocktails, cocktails?" which several are prone to do, they are written up. This behavior is fine in other clubs, but Harrah's wants to be a cut above. And it *always* is, at least for *most* of the years that I work there. It's not my doing. I simply am lucky enough to be part of the culture.

Military Time - This is really a smart way to avoid communication pitfalls in a 24-hour environment. It is abandoned by the guy who becomes our Sr. V.P./G.M. in 1989. He wants to make a political statement, and at the same time, intentionally dismantle the corporate culture, particularly that at the lake. His memo goes out, "… this is not a military camp …" He begins deconstructing the finest casino culture of all time, right before our eyes. Later, he also fires me for what I believe to be personal reasons.

Monthly "Bottom 10% (employees)" and action plan - Once a month, department managers have to fill out a report, naming the bottom 10% performers, along with a 30-day action plan to upgrade their status or remove them from employment. For me this means a list of the bottom 10 for every single operating area in my department. God help any department manager if one of his individuals should appear in the bottom 10 three months in a row. This element of managerial life disappears about 1985 or so, probably resulting from Rome's passing.

Name Badges - Only first names and hometowns are engraved into the Daily Rates' name badges. No nicknames allowed: Frank would be OK for a Francis, but not something like Bubba. Salaried supervisors and above get last names also but no hometown. Details, details: that's what makes the place a Five Star/Five Diamond property. That's what results in the place having a 43% market share for several years running, amongst the four large casinos at Tahoe.

The cocktail waitresses hate *their* name badges, which they refer to as "dog collars," a ¾-inch-wide rhinestone-decorated, black velvet neck band. Hanging from it is a round black Formica disk with engraved first name only. No hometown, no leash.

Nevers - These come from Bob Stirling during my first weeks of being "Harrahrized" by him. Everything I learn from him, countless little hints, hold me in good stead, no matter the subject or circumstance. He's like a walking, two-legged cheat sheet for me.

Never make a promise. You don't know if people above you might nix it; then you lose credibility.

Never make an excuse. Apologize, and say what you will do to fix the situation or "prevent recurrence." If it is a guest giving Bob a complaint, he has a very strict routine:

1. Apologize.
2. Listen to the guest's story, repeat back the issue(s).
3. Apologize again.
4. State what will be done to correct or satisfy the guest. And get it done.

Never call something a "problem." "We don't have problems at Harrah's. We have situations," says Bob.

Never say, "I don't know." Bob teaches, "Instead say, let me find out and get right back to you." "And get right back!" he says.

Never start a written sentence with the word "I." The use of this pronoun is highly discouraged, as is the possessive, "my," as in "my restaurant." It's not yours, it's ours. It's not "my cooks," as chefs are in the habit of saying. After the incomparable Susan Newbre begins supervising front-of-the-house operations in the restaurants, she tells rookie salaried supervisors in her humorous way, "They are not *your* crew. Slavery ended 120 years ago." This aspect of the Harrah's culture is designed to slow down ego creep, which can be a formidable task among casino management people. It's about creating a team. In my own business writing, I am keenly aware of using "I" at the beginning of a sentence, and I try to avoid it for the rest of my life.

Nineteen-Minute Room Service (24/7– 540 rooms) - At some point in the 1970s, Bill Harrah stays in a hotel in Ohio where they advertise 20-minute room service. When he gets back home, he announces that his hotels will have a 19-minute limit on room service orders. Interesting . . . and unheard of during this time.

Meticulous records are kept day-in and day-out for years. Time and motion consultants are brought in. They stay down in the room service kitchen for weeks, using stop watches to record the entire process. Ultimately, they discover that we are hitting the goal something like 94% of the time, a remarkable achievement . . . but not good enough. To speed things up, we even have a couple of the service elevators programmed to drop non-stop to the basement (where room service is located), so that waiting time is greatly reduced for servers needing to get up to the hotel rooms. This programmed drop occurs after a waiter steps off to deliver onto one of the guest room floors.

But when things fall apart, there is a domino effect. If a problem occurs, it's usually during the breakfast rush on a busy holiday weekend. And sometimes, no matter how much help is scheduled, when it goes south it really goes. And soon enough, the Day Book arrives on my desk (see below), with its, "Here we go again" questions/remarks in Rome's black fountain pen ink, along with Joe's (Fanelli) in blue ballpoint.

No dark eyeglasses - Mr. Harrah doesn't like photo-grey eyeglasses, the kind that turn dark under bright lights and lighten up in darker environments. If you want to own some, fine. *But not when you're working in my casino.*

No hanging of temporary signs from a ceiling in the back of the house (more or less in line with the prohibition on scotch tape).

No hiring of overweight people, those with facial hair (except a neatly trimmed moustache), no hair below the collar, nails must be neat and clean, and no five o'clock shadow. These things change over time, but at their strictest, these are the rules Harrah's old-timers remember. No former union members or anyone arrested for a felony. Period. There is actually a cheat sheet used by those who don't interview often, which lists about 20 questions that can pretty quickly determine if a candidate has a 'union mentality' without actually asking about union membership.

"No Photographs in the Casino Please" - And what the signs don't tell our guests is that if they are observed taking a photo anywhere in the casino, security will politely but firmly take their camera from them. The camera will then be taken to a dark room on the property, where the film will be removed, developed, and processed. The camera and prints will be returned to the owner on the spot, minus any photos (and negatives) that contain images of anyone in a casino environment.

This strictly enforced policy is to prevent publication of photos of persons who don't want to be seen in a casino environment: celebs, politicians, or perhaps gentlemen accompanied by their young 'nieces,' etc.

BUT, if they do want to be seen . . . there are camera girls working the showroom during dinner and cocktail show service, and for a price, they take a photo of our guests and bring an 8x10 glossy in a souvenir folder as the show is closing.

And of course, we have a full-time photographer ready to shoot a 'Grip and Grin.' The lucky winners (Grinning) of big slot payouts are photographed getting a handshake (the Grip) from someone in casino management (hopefully, also Grinning) right in front of the machine's big sign showing the flashing jackpot.

No scotch tape allowed. (Mr. Harrah doesn't like how sloppy it looks).

Only jumbo paperclips allowed anywhere in the club (the small ones have a tendency to fall off documents). Another thing I carry on for the rest of my life.

Papering the Room - Another of several unwritten rules, this one concerns a combination of entertainers' fragile egos and the visual impression of a successful casino showroom. If it looks like the South Shore Room's cover count, for either the dinner show or the cocktail show, will dip below a certain number on a given night, the casino shift manager will initiate the casino-wide distribution of a block of comp tickets to accomplish filling the magic number of seats to make the room 'feel good' for both the headlining entertainer as well as those people who actually are paying to see the show.

Phone Answering - Once, *and just once*, I answer my phone (on my desk; there is no such thing as a cell phone at this time) on the fourth ring. It's Joe Fanelli, and he's quick to remind me in a way only Joe can do, "I didn't realize we no longer answer the phones within three rings at Harrah's." Oh, he can "bust 'em off" when he is in the mood. This is his way of teaching, using a facetious or sarcastic turn of phrase, and it's very effective. Notwithstanding this treatment, I grow to have great affection for the guy... but it's a slow growth.

Pit School Interviews - "Are you happy with your height-to-weight ratio?" In my early days there are two jobs that are highly sought after: dealer (table games) and cocktail waitress. This is simply because, a) a good amount of cash can be made in these two jobs, and b) the IRS has yet to create a system to catch up with these people.

Relative to the rest of the country, for many decades Nevada is the only place where legal casino dealer jobs even exist. The amount of tax-free income (tips, aka tokes) that can be made is not common knowledge around the U.S.–and certainly nobody's informing the IRS of this fact.

This brings us to Harrah's Pit School, where the teaching quality is so good that other clubs take ex-Harrah's dealers with open arms, no tests, no demos. In the early years of my time at the lake, during every April a Pit School posting appears on 'the board,' actually *three glass-enclosed, locked* bulletin boards located around the club, where job postings are listed by the personnel department. And this Pit School posting is a happening that stirs up a lot of buzz around the property. Those in attendance at every single pit interview are the pit department manager or the assistant manager, a personnel department representative, the manager of the applicant's current department, and the applicant. Annually, there are a good 300-350 applicants for maybe 60 Pit School openings. If you are ugly, fat, kinda old, or are not highly recommended by your department manager, you ain't goin' anywhere. And when I say fat, I don't mean *fat,* I mean *somewhat overweight.* If you're heavy, as the interview is coming to a close, a question is asked, "Are you happy with your height to weight ratio?"

This question is pretty much a kiss of death. If you say "no," you're admitting that you're too heavy for them; a "yes" means your standards for your own appearance don't meet theirs, and you're not going to trim-down or *stay* trimmed-down once you get the job. The truth is, before the IRS 'pushes-in' (circa 1982-83), Harrah's dealers and cocktail waitresses, with few exceptions, are *very* good-looking, mostly youngish people—especially on swing shift (that's where the money is—and the partying).

And *always*, when the interviewee is leaving the room, all eyes are on his/her rear end. If it's too big, *forgeddaboudit!*

Pool Cars - Company pool cars are Cadillac Sevilles (prior to the Holiday [Inn] Corporation takeover).

Putting heavy emphasis and employees on the scale - There is a pretty fancy scale down at wardrobe, where employees pick up their uniforms after they are cleaned (by the company). This is no accident. There are large mirrors there, also no accident. Personal appearance is VERY important at Harrah's. And so, if you are a supervisor of a heavy employee, there may come a day, when after counseling and no positive change in that person's weight occurring, that you must meet the person at the scale in wardrobe. And put it in writing—a personal development plan.

Bob Stirling and I have to do this to an assistant restaurant manager during my first summer at the property. The young man, really a nice guy, has a shape that reminds me of a breeching whale. He is counseled again and again and eventually leaves the company to find a place with lower standards of personal appearance.

There is also a scale outside the board room in the 'bank building' in Reno. Until Harrah's Rock Street building is constructed to house corporate offices, this room, upstairs from a ground floor bank neighboring Harrah's-Reno, is where important company meetings take place. It is a place where allegedly, at the appointed start time of a meeting, Bill Harrah locks the door. You aren't going to be late for meetings at Harrah's, and you aren't going to be chubby when you *do* arrive.

Once, and *only once*, I'm headed for home after a day's work, walking past Joe Francis' favorite watering hole, the entrance to the Casino Cabaret. As I'm walking, I give him a *"Hi, Joe,"* and he remarks, *"Hey Vinnie you look like you're putting on some weight."* I might be up about eight pounds. Eight! Never again—not while Joe is still around. All of us the management group watch our weight during my early years at the club; and we don't wear "photo grey" glasses, either!

Restaurants & Kitchens –

> The NY Deli (eventually this unit and The Carousel Pancake House were converted to Friday's Station)

The Sierra Restaurant

The Carousel Pancake House

Friday's Station Steak House

The Employee Cafeteria

The Forest Restaurant

The Summit

Winner's Circle

The NY Deli

The Seafood Cove

The Snack Bar

Banquets

Room Service

16th Floor Butler Service

The Bake Shop

Veg Prep

The Butcher Shop

The Food Cart

Security Department - Security officers are unarmed. Sometimes they tackle rowdy people onto the casino floor and take them handcuffed down the steep stairs near the coat check booth. Often, the perps accidently fall down the stairs. If there is real trouble, Cleaning Manager Bud Coyner and Assistant Security Manager Phil Gilow are called to help. They are quite capable.

Harrah's corporate security management is headed by former J. Edgar Hoover underling Rex Schroeder and another FBI alum. Harrah's is not playing around. Years later when I go to work in Vegas, I am a bit surprised to see that all the security guys carry big, loaded weapons; many are 45's. Not up north in Reno or Tahoe.

Sixteenth Floor Suites - There are about 16 suites on the 16th floor, each one having two bedrooms and a center 'parlor.' And each one designed by San Francisco architect Henry Conversano (who designs the entire property, and who must personally approve any changes to the building—inside and out—in my early days there). Each one of these suites has a different interior design, all first class: a mountain cabin, an all-white suite, an African safari look, a very contemporary black and white, a Japanese suite, etc.

Half of them face the lake, the others look up at the mountains and Heavenly Valley ski area.

Slots - Slots are all color-coded to denomination and there are slot coupons for jackpot winners, free handy wipes for slot players, and of course complimentary drinks for steady play.

The deafening noise of mechanical slots in crowded areas such as the section over by the old snack bar (near the front of the building at the California/Nevada state line) is an environmental casino element that will also disappear forever during the mid-1980s. And with the change comes the growing need for a very different set of skills and knowledge in the daily work of slot mechanics and management of the games. These departments—slot repair and operations (the 'people' part of slots)—are handled under two separate management teams.

No area of casino operations changes faster and more often during my time at Tahoe than that of slots. Whether it's mechanical slots to chip-driven, coin-in devices to our own Harrah's slot tokens on dollar machines, to bill accepters, to club card tracking devices, to the size of jackpots, to statewide progressive machines, to national progressive machines, the speed and innovation are mind-boggling. And with good reason: this is not your grandpa's casino anymore. The days of the WW II vets coming home and wanting to have fun playing table games—craps in particular—are dwindling. We are in a culture of instant gratification. And that means SLOTS. *And the gratification largely belongs to the casinos. Instantly.*

South Shore Room Postcards - There are so many little touches that make Harrah's stand out from the other clubs during my time there, all of them falling under the banner of attention to detail. It's all very comfortable to me, and in some ways reminiscent of Restaurant Associates in the Joe Baum era. For instance, every time there is a change in the showroom headliner act, new photographic postcards (oversized – about 4"x10") are designed, printed, and placed around the entrance to the room, but especially on each of its tables. The cards are almost always unique in layout and design, never repeated. It is one of those special touches that is only done by Harrah's. Who else can afford it? No other casino company during this period can match this sort of constant and ubiquitous attention to detail. The cards are among the many free souvenirs for visitors (and many employees, including yours truly).

South Shore Room and Summit Sport Jackets - In my early days at Harrah's, a man can't get into the South Shore Room or Summit Restaurant (the fine dining experience on the top floor, facing Lake Tahoe) unless he's wearing a sport jacket. If he doesn't arrive with one on his shoulders, one of the showroom captains escorts the guest into a small room near the SSR entrance, where he chooses from a few dozen loaners. It is a different era. And while it certainly can be viewed as a classy thing to do, I am one of those who push to end the 'jackets only' policy, as I feel that people want to dress more casually for a *resort* experience.

When I visit my old CIA friend Rod Stoner for culinary recruiting trips at the world-renowned Greenbrier Hotel in White Sulfur Springs, West Virginia, there is a sign in the lobby that says, "Gentlemen will wear a jacket and tie in the lobby after six p.m." A grand 'old money' resort for sure, but also an 'uptight East coast/DC mentality.' I don't want that for Tahoe, and I do what I can to effect a change.

Stealing - As is the case with the list of interview questions which uncover a 'union mentality,' there is also a list of 2-3 dozen behaviors/indicators that help managers to identify possible thieves within the workforce.

The kind of stealing the list alerts managers to is almost always stealing from Harrah's: servers playing games with restaurant guest checks and charges, removing cash from a till, employees stealing food, dealers removing cash/chips from games, anyone with access to slot machines lifting cash, supervisory theft, illicit payroll recordkeeping, etc.

But there's a whole host of other kinds of theft, large and small, even minute in some cases. All of it results in the same thing: people lose their jobs and sometimes get 'hooked-up' (hand-cuffed . . . not what the term connotes when I write this) and taken away. There is a concerted effort to march cuffed-up employees who are caught in some sort of theft down the long corridor where many offices are, so maximum exposure hallway traffic occurs: *Go ahead and steal from us.*

Here's what it looks like when we catch you. And we will catch you. As for theft or attempted theft by guests and customers, they either get arrested or '86'd.'

The Box - Once a week a contract polygraph examiner named Hugh Lantz comes up from Reno and tests anyone who is under suspicion for any sort of malfeasance against Harrah's. Of course, nobody is forced to get wired up to 'the box,' but if you say, "no," then we say "no" also . . . no more job! About 1986 it becomes unlawful to use the device, and the party is over. It becomes much more challenging to prove that an employee is 'dirty.'

The "Day Book" is a report, usually about three pages in length, one for Reno, one for Tahoe (Tahoe's, of course, on pink copy paper). It is sent to Sr. Management and arrives every morning, covering the previous 24 hours. Standard on the report—by the shift—are gaming statistics for each of the areas (slots, table games, keno, poker, sports and race book), the drop, the win, the hold, hotel occupancy numbers, restaurant cover counts, security department 'incidents,' shift manager summaries, significant wins/losses in gaming (listing the players' names), and any unusual occurrences or large comps.

If I am lucky, I never receive a torn-out page with black fountain pen writing on it, often followed by two more remarks/questions in blue ballpoint. This means that I am expected to answer a question from Rome, followed by another from Joe Fanelli, with Rome or Joe writing, "Here we go again." Nothing makes me feel lower than "Here we go again," which refers to a negative situation that has repeated itself.

And this is where we come to:

"To prevent recurrence ..." - an oft-used and *required* phrase in answering to some negative occurrence in one's area of responsibility at Harrah's during my early years there. It could be an unacceptable number of room service orders exceeding 19 minutes, or restaurant wait times/lines too long, a stealing incident, an out-of-order piece of equipment affecting production/service, etc.

The response to a question or remark from Rome or Joe explains what happened and why, and "to prevent recurrence (blah, blah, blah) ..."—and *you'd better mean what you say.*

The Personnel Menu - a daily publication on a half sheet of paper (pink, of course) put out by the personnel department, listing all job vacancies by department. If the numbers within a given work unit get too high, somebody's not doing his/her job. There are consequences for high turnover and consequences for the sub-standard performance/results of the work unit's staff, but also for the supervisors and manager in that particular area. So great attention is paid to this little pink sheet that comes in the company mail five days a week.

The "Tahoe Star" is the largest yacht on Tahoe. The Star and another smaller speedboat are operated by Harrah's full-time mechanics that work for 'the garage.' Our motor pool is a fully-equipped vehicular maintenance shop with qualified full-time mechanics.

The boats are used for special guests and celebrities, with food catered by our kitchens. And of course, there are fully stocked bars on board. We furnish a bartender and a server for guest cruises on the Star.

Incidentally, the second largest boat on the lake is owned by George Worth, the chiropractor whose office is adjacent to Raley's parking lot—just a block from the nearest of the four major casinos. He's no fool. He knows that casino dealers, cocktail waitresses, and kitchen personnel are prime candidates for his services. He rakes in money as fast as any blackjack table in a casino; it just comes in slower, because it's all insurance claims.

The Star Suite - A two-story suite that starts on the 16th floor and reaches up to the 17th floor of Harrah's-Tahoe and is used exclusively for showroom headliners. Most of these highly valued entertainers get to choose if they want to stay in one of the Harrah's-owned homes in the Skyland area at Tahoe or at the hotel. If a headliner chooses the hotel, he/she gets to stay in the Star Suite, which is just plain stunning. It's for headliners ONLY—meaning it is never rented out to guests, nor is it comped to our biggest players, nor is it used for run-of-the-mill entertainers.

The Star Suite is staffed by a special crew of maids (who also cook) assigned to a tough old lady, Adeline Murphy, a personal favorite of Bill Harrah. After Mr. Harrah gives her

244

a car, she buys Nevada license plates: "THANKS." She accompanies him to help choose his two adopted children at the Mayo Clinic. I think her title is Special Assistant and she has enormous power when I first arrive on the scene. She runs the show at the homes and hotel rooms where headliners stay in both Reno and Tahoe. She and I have a bit of a rocky start, but we sit down on a bed at Villa Harrah one afternoon and work things out. After this, we become friends and I'm permitted to call her Murph.

The Trades - Under the HR leadership of Joe Spect, Harrah's was always smart about avoiding unions and union activity. Instead of having our own painters, wallpaper hangers, carpeting installers, electricians, and carpenters, we contract with top-drawer firms who have excellent craftsmen.

These guys are at Harrah's every day, five days a week, working on some part of the building, either doing repair work or major remodeling. Normally this activity would come to a screeching halt if any of these trades went on strike, but as they are employees of another company, Harrah's is not affected; we just go out and hire a new firm to do the work that the contracted company can't fulfill because its people are striking. The strikers have no beef with Harrah's, just with their direct employers, so no picket lines are ever set up on our sidewalks. Pretty smart.

Tuesday Sr. Management (from Reno) Visits - These visits are legendary. Today, as I write this, I don't remember

245

the full cast of players. I am only concerned with Rome (Andriotti), Joe (Fanelli), and Julius (Weiss). Others come and go, but I'm concerned with keeping Rome and Joe happy. Julius deals with Herbert or Horst in the kitchen. These guys don't always travel together, but until the expansion into New Jersey begins in earnest, they come up to the lake almost every week. It's like getting ready for an I.G. (inspector general) in the military service . . . only it's usually every seven days.

Uniforms at Harrah's - All are designed and manufactured under the watchful and tasteful eye of an egotistical old bag who used to actually work for the famed multi-Oscar winner of Hollywood costume design fame, Edith Head. Eventually I get out from under her mandated selections of staff uniforms, but only because she retires.

All dealers and cashiers wear black and white when I arrive. They buy their own uniforms until someone steals money from a lady who thinks the thief is a Harrah's employee. Then the company changes to colored vests which are supplied to the dealers.

Villa Harrah - Described tongue-in-cheek by R.J. as "a two-bedroom home that can seat 100 for dinner." This is one of the three Harrah-owned residences in a Tahoe development known as Skyland, which of course sits on Lake Tahoe. It has a boat dock that can accommodate either of the two Harrah's boats.

White copy machine paper for Reno/Pink for Tahoe enables us to quickly determine the source or intended direction of a document—pretty important, given that all the corporate execs operate out of Reno.

Work History Sheet/Work History Entries - A permanent record of each employee's life at Harrah's with name, date of hire, job title, rate of pay, promotions, pay rate changes, and most importantly, hand-written positive and negative entries by supervisors, which must be signed (acknowledged) by the employee.

Russ

Russ McLennan is everybody's favorite bad boy at Harrah's–Tahoe, full of mischief, full of fun. But he is also a very demanding keeper of the flame, who wants it right, always right, for Bill Harrah (even though he's dead about eighteen months before I arrive on the scene), for Rome, and for the company. It's guys like Russ, Ed Posey, Tom Yturbide, Joe Francis, Terry Pruneau, Lowell and Holmes Hendricksen, Joe Fanelli, Wayne Currie, and of course Rome Andriotti, who I meet and work with in my early years there. They are the leaders keeping the Harrah's-Tahoe ship slicing through the waters on the quality course. Quality about everything imaginable. This place doesn't get and maintain a Mobil Guide Five Star rating and a Five Diamond designation from AAA for 12 consecutive years just because

Bill Harrah put in a swimming pool (a recommendation in an annual review by AAA in the mid-seventies, after the property didn't get a fifth star).

Out of all these guys, I believe only three completed college—Joe Fanelli (Cornell) and the Hendricksens (U. of Utah). Back when they all started in the business, what mattered was a man's character and his performance; character and performance in the gaming business at the time had nothing to do with an MBA or a law degree. Still don't.

Russ is about 11 years older than me, and totally full of the devil. A truly great guy *if* he likes you—same as Joel Kunkel. *If they like you.*

Don't ask me why, but he takes a liking to me very early on. And since I am *the third guy to have that job in a nine-month period,* I am very grateful for his protection and affection. Don't get me wrong: if I mess up, I'm on my own. But because of some of the characters who have preceded me and haven't been cooperative or honest or trustworthy, the gaming guys tend to treat the food department manager like a necessary evil. And those less-than-trustworthy food guys don't last in the job. There is a joke among the other managers at the Rendezvous Lounge one night: they talk about wanting to put my name on a chalkboard mounted to the food office door. A couple of days later, a maintenance guy comes by and attaches a Harrah's name sign with its own chalkboard onto the office door. It's complete with a piece of chalk and an eraser, each hanging by its own string. This is a fun group. I'm going to like these people.

In the beginning of my time at Harrah's, when control of the department is decentralized, overseen by Joe Fanelli out of Reno, there is always an undercurrent of resentment caused by the fact that the Tahoe Senior Management pretty much has to go through Joe to talk to me about anything involving policy or procedure. Russ mitigates those resentful feelings with an occasional, *"Aw, Vinnie's alright."* I know he does this because after a while he tells me.

Moments with Russ

I'm at Harrah's just six months when we are at a corporate meeting at Ormsby House Hotel-Casino in Carson City. It is early June 1980. The last night we are staying there things get real loosened up, i.e., everybody is drinking.

A few of us go down to Harvey's gun club in Russ's truck to shoot skeet. The next morning at breakfast, one of the much older guys, Lew Powers (in his 70s) is MIA. Turns out they find him passed out in the wee hours in a classic drunk pose sitting on a curb in front of the Ormsby House with his back supported by a lamp post on the main drag running through Carson City. Russ finds out when we're on the buffet line getting our breakfast eggs, and says to me, "Goddammit if I'd only have known. I would have called up the funeral guy here and had them put Powers in a coffin.

Can you imagine what he woulda thought when he finally woke up?"

This is classic Russ McLennan. And cost is not an object if there is a good laugh in the deal.

****

He is notorious for getting on crowded elevators after leaving the Forest Restaurant on the 18th floor, and silently leaving one of his infamous, nasty beer farts for the unsuspecting guests. He knows that virtually everyone in the car is headed for the casino on the first floor (a long way down). So he'll keep a very serious face, perfectly time the silent fart, then get off at maybe the 14th floor, leaving all inside to suffocate the rest of the way down, none of them realizing it is Russ who leaves the 'gift.'

****

Once he and Ken Kettler are going "over the hill" (U.S. 50—Echo Summit) to the San Francisco Bay area. Russ gets Ken to drive and then keeps pushing him to drive faster and faster. Eventually they get pulled over by a California state trooper.

You have to know Russ to understand the talent this guy has for never, ever smiling when he's messing with somebody. The trooper comes over to the car, and *immediately* Russ tells him, "Thank God you stopped this crazy son of a bitch, officer. He had me scared out of my mind." And of course, Ken gets tagged for speeding: points, fine, the works! Russ never tells the cop he's joking.

****

He carries around more jokes in his head than any three comedians who earn their living at it. You can't start a joke without him finishing it with the punch line, usually about five seconds into the bit. But his favorite thing is the practical joke, the sight gag.

If we are eating lunch in the Sierra Restaurant, at what the staff call the Bosses Table (reserved for Senior Management), he may ask someone to sit down and visit for a few minutes, say Bob Stirling, or an assistant restaurant manager who might be walking by. He's the picture of hospitality, ordering a Coke or iced tea for the invited guest. After a few minutes, Russ finds a way to distract him or her, then pops a few shakes of Tabasco into that person's drink. Just for a laugh.

****

Another time after my friend Art Daub leaves Harrah's (having worked several years running the personnel department there), he decides to come over to the Rendezvous Lounge for an after-work drink. Art is now working at Harvey's across the street, and he runs into Russ at the 'Vous.'

'The Hill' where the four larger Tahoe casinos are located is a tight little community and everybody knows everybody else's business. Russ knows that Art is having pretty significant marriage problems. In fact, Art's wife Bev has thrown him out.

These two guys haven't seen each other for quite a while so they start gabbing away. Russ very gradually leads Art into a conversation about how dissatisfied he's become with Harrah's. At this point Russ has been there about 35 years and because Art is a personnel guy, Russ knows he'll be a good listener. Art changes the subject, never asking Russ what he'd rather be doing, but over a span of about 15 minutes, Russ continually peppers the conversation with reasons why he wants a career change. *Finally* Art asks the question for which Russ has been patiently waiting, "What do you think you'd rather do?"

And never cracking a smile, Russ answers, "I'm gonna be a marriage counselor." And very typically after a prank like this, straight-faced Russ *immediately* gets on his way, leaving the victim pondering, *"What just happened to me?"*

****

John Babcock on Russ (tongue-in-cheek): "I knew the guy for two years before I realized his first name wasn't Fuckin'."

****

For a time, Russ eats once a week with a friend at a coffee shop down in South Lake Tahoe. The owner of the place keeps putting a pair of Swedish Ry-Krisp crackers on every plate served. Russ hates these crackers and tells her repeatedly over several months that he doesn't want to see them on his plate. He literally throws the crackers across the dining area at one point.

Finally he's had enough. And when he spots a stray dog outside the window wall where he's seated, he loads a pair of the crackers with Tabasco, slips outside and drops them where the dog can be seen approaching the 'treat' through the large window facing South Lake Tahoe Boulevard. Russ hurries back inside the restaurant, and perfectly times the scene outside. He calls the owner over to the window and says, "Look out there."

She looks, and not knowing that Russ has doused the crackers with Tabasco, sees the dog take a sniff, and trot away.

"I told you those fuckin' crackers are shit," he scolds, "even the fuckin' dog knows it!"

****

He knows professional athletes from all over but has special relationships with those who are from the Bay Area, his home turf. When Billy Martin has one of his infamous fights with Yankee owner George Steinbrenner, Russ hides Billy for a few days in a room at Harrah's-Tahoe. When we run a charity basketball game to raise money for a gal at work whose husband—also a Harrah's employee—was murdered while on a Harrah's recruiting trip down in San Jose, Russ gets a whole bunch of 49'er players to come up and be the 'opposition team' facing the Harrah's managers— every winter for years. He's got a big, big heart . . . if he likes you.

****

He gets away with all kinds of ethnic ribbing to people's faces. It's no different for Rome when he comes up from Reno once a week to inspect the property and have lunch. We're eating with a man who has god-like power and respect, not simply within Harrah's but throughout the gaming industry. Rome is Bill Harrah's right-hand man, the very quiet and dignified but powerful corporate operations guy. Russ looks at him, and says, "Hey Rome, wanna hear a good Dago joke?" Before Rome can answer, Russ is off and running with the bit, and as usual, gets away with this kind of thing.

During the '80s, before the advent of Amber Alerts, missing kids are often pictured and described on the side of milk cartons. It becomes a trendy thing. Russ often tells me that his fondest dream is to see his ex-wife's picture on the side of a milk carton. But get him around kids, anybody's kids, and he is all heart. He lays more stuff on my son David than I could possibly remember: Oakland A's box seats on third base (more than once or twice), tickets to the National League All-Star game (which Dave shyly turns down), large boxes of bubblegum baseball card packs, candy, etc. He loves the kid.

And when it comes to mischief, most of the time he makes me look like a choirboy.

On one of his birthdays near the end of my time at Tahoe, the casino throws a roast for Russ. It's in the South Shore Room, a big party for friends, high-end gaming customers, and Harrah's management pals. The dais is filled with celebs. Unfortunately, I only remember Bill Walsh, Red Buttons, and maybe Norm Crosby, but it is a great fun night.

New Year's Eve 1979-80 and Beyond, at Harrah's-Tahoe – Moments & Things at Harrah's I Can Never Forget

New Year's Eve is the biggest of the year's big nights. I spend 11 New Year's Eves in the place, the first (1979-80) being the most memorable. Memorable because it's all so new to me, and because I can float throughout the night, and at midnight I can be anywhere I choose to be. As my first NYE approaches, I've only been working at the lake for a couple of weeks, and I am warned by several people that I need to learn to navigate the basement corridors and back of the house hallways, as the casino is far too crowded to attempt traveling from restaurant to restaurant taking the 'public route,' aka 'the floor.'

During Tom Yturbide's reign as V.P./G.M., we have a small buffet set up for the department managers in a departmental office vacant for the night, such as housekeeping or engineering. This is so that the managers can 'grab and go' if need be, and they won't take up valuable space in any of the restaurants on the busiest night of the year. It's a nice touch, giving us a catered break room, instead of forcing all to eat in the employee cafeteria, the only alternative if restaurant dining is out of the question. This is Tom—tough on the outside, but a good heart on the inside.

Getting ready for New Year's Eve involves its own set of idiosyncrasies, most of it to minimize blood and lawsuits: at about 4 p.m., bar glasses are replaced with plastic ones, bottled beer is not sold across the casino bars, and bar stools are totally removed from the casino floor. And cocktail waitresses are pulled off the casino floor by 10 p.m. (too dangerous for them).

After my second year, we paint the large Pony Express statue with a thick coating of grease, because on New Year's Eve 1981, some guy dressed *only in a diaper* climbed the statue to take a seat behind the rider (in spite of a wind chill factor of maybe 15 degrees!). Years later we abandon the grease and surround the horse and rider statue with a steep plywood pyramid that is impossible to climb.

Other than Halloween, when some casinos allow employees to wear costumes (we don't), New Year's Eve is the only time that dealers and cocktail waitresses can dress up in their own outfits. Most of the guys usually don't do anything special, but the women go all-out on this night. They buy beautiful cocktail dresses, get their nails and hair done, and look spectacular, which of course adds to the festive atmosphere. The women are not required to wear their pit aprons on this night. Pit aprons are still required for the male dealers, to prevent chips, aka 'checks,' from being slipped into their pants pockets or waistbands. In fact, some clubs disallow any pockets in dealers' pants.

The casino has multiple venues for invitees, and these can vary in their demographics from year to year. Depending upon what day of the week New Year's Eve falls, usually the two or three nights preceding the 31st and a night or two after we have the hotel at 100% occupancy, and all rooms are comps only. In other words, a paying guest cannot book a room at any price during this period. Unless you qualify for an 'RFB' (room, food, and beverage 100% comped), you cannot stay in one of our rooms.

New Year's Eve Venues

There's the South Shore Room (showroom) where both shows will be packed: 820 seats for dinner and 1,048 seats for the cocktail show. The cocktail show is pretty much comps only, and always has a balloon drop at midnight; it's always a touch-and-go thing as to whether the drop will go as planned.

The Summit is our fine dining venue on the top floor of the building, and the late seating will be comps only. When midnight rolls around, only comped guests will be in the room looking out at Lake Tahoe.

Our banquet rooms usually have one very large, comped party for a buffet, while two other rooms are filled with smaller comped parties, also buffets, but not necessarily the same food. For example, there may be a group from the Dallas area eating very different food than the players we bring in from Mexico.

This model of comps in various venues on New Year's Eve is followed in virtually all decent-sized successful casinos everywhere.

In the beginning, I try visiting different venues within the casino to experience each one at the stroke of midnight. In my later years at Harrah's, after I'm satisfied that those spots in the casino are the same old hat, I spend two or three midnights outside, up on the fifth story parking garage roof. From there I can look down onto Highway 50, between Harrah's and Harveys. Every year the teenagers and twenty-somethings 'take the street,' and it's just bedlam for about 45 minutes or an hour—insanity, really: guys launching empty bottles of all shapes and sizes, hitting total strangers in their heads, others throwing firecrackers at innocent bystanders, and a fair number, having nothing other than their fists, throwing punches. It's chaos.

When the cops have had enough, they form a flying wedge made up of vehicles and guys with night sticks walking alongside. They start about three or four blocks east of Harrah's and slowly clear Highway 50 of the rabble, right up and through the state line into California.

These random acts of violence out on the street, along with various forms of misbehavior within the hotel and casino, are the reason that the cops back a school bus up to our loading dock every New Year's Eve. As the perps are arrested, they are taken to the bus and handcuffed to their seats. It's freezing cold in that bus, and the cops don't run the heater for the 'passengers.' They are made to sit there until enough bad boys have been rounded up to make the winding trip worthwhile, down through scads of hairpin turns on Kingsbury Grade (17 miles) to the Douglas County Jail in Minden. Sometimes they must sit in the cold for hours. Years later, they finally build a jail up at the lake, on the 'Nevada side.'

Shaking Hands

The first time I meet Terry Davis, it's also the first time I go to the Summit Restaurant for dinner. It's April 9, 1980, and Charlene and I are celebrating our anniversary. I'm on the job since December 17, 1979, but far too busy herding cats in the casual restaurants to sit down for dinner in the problem-free crown jewel dining room of both Harrah's properties. We are barely seated by Maitre d' Claude Oertle when waiter Terry approaches to introduce himself to the new guy (me). As he sticks out his hand to shake mine, his pinky catches my water glass, dumping ice water straight onto my crotch. The poor guy is mortified. I try to tell him it's no big deal, and I remain seated for the next 70 minutes, soaked right through my undies, never indicating how uncomfortable I am.

The rest of the crew waits till Terry gets back to the kitchen where no guest (including me) can hear them, and they bust his chops without mercy. Years later we laugh about it. Well, not Terry so much, but the rest of us. Truth is, I love this guy, and it is a pleasure watching him develop from busser to waiter to captain to assistant restaurant manager to restaurant manager, and years later, in 1996 to maitre d' when together we open White Orchid at the Peppermill in Reno.

August 1980 - "All I hear is Bomb, bomb, bomb"

(Loudly, to the crowd sitting on the grass in front of Raley's Food and Drug at South Lake Tahoe) "All I hear is 'Bomb, bomb, bomb.'" "Big fucking deal. I've bombed plenty of times, and nobody made a big thing out of it!"

-Comedian Rip Taylor, Harrah's-Tahoe Cabaret Headliner (at the time of the bombing)

This scene takes place a block west of Harrah's. Taylor is sitting out on the grass on a sunny Tahoe afternoon with a crowd of people who have been evacuated. He is accompanied by Sue Lowe of our entertainment office, who gives me the quote the next day.

In late August my boss R.J. Lukas travels to Atlantic City hoping to transfer to the new Harrah's (it will be the company's first operation outside of Nevada), scheduled to open in 1981. A day or two after he leaves for the interview in Jersey, I am called to V.P./G.M. Tom Yturbide's office. As it turns out there are several department managers who

262

had been summoned to the office. It is about 10 a.m. on August 26. Tom explains that Harvey's Hotel/Casino (right across the street) received a *serious* bomb threat during the graveyard shift.

I say "*serious*" bomb threat because during this era, casinos frequently get bomb threats. It's just part of life in the clubs. Players get angry because of gambling losses, employees get fired and try to get back at the club, etc. Sometimes attempted extortion is involved; on other occasions, it's just people making prank calls. But in any case, there are protocols to follow for clearing the building— meaning we must search, but in this instance, we don't find any suspect packages.

By now, Harvey's has been evacuated, but the threat is not fully understood or known by anyone outside of law enforcement or upper casino management. We are to be on alert until further notice. We go back to work under orders to tell no one, not staff, not guests, no one. I believe some made-up story is used to get everyone out of Harvey's. I just don't remember. This is pretty much the way things always are with bomb threats and other extortion situations. Those who need to know are told, and they quietly carry out the procedures for such an event, never telling other employees or, God forbid, the guests and players.

It really is a wild west atmosphere up at Tahoe during my early days there. In my first three years, shots are fired three times during robbery attempts on Harrah's casino

263

floor. And down the road at Harvey's Inn the bad guys even sprayed the place with automatic weapons about 2 a.m. one night, causing my friends Hadji, Perry, Hassan, and a few of the other South Shore Room captains to dive under the coffee shop tables. Bullet holes in damaged walls are patched up and painted within hours, and life goes on.

This thing at Harvey's is no prank. The FBI quickly discovers that two men dressed in white overalls delivered a 'replacement' copy machine to the executive offices. No Harvey's employee questioned this graveyard-timed delivery. The perps have left an extortion note with instructions. The note warns that if moved, the bomb will detonate.

The FBI brings in an x-ray machine along with experts from across the nation. It's amazing how fast—relative to our semi-remote location—all this happens. They soon discover that the bomb is real and that the quantity of explosives locked inside it is huge, and that it is far too complicated and dangerous to dismantle. Later, after lunch, I happen to be up on the 18th floor of Harrah's, looking down on the street, and I see two flatbed trucks coming down Highway 50 toward Harvey's from the Nevada side. The trucks are loaded down with sandbags, and it's obvious to me that they're going to pack-in the bomb, in an effort to minimize damage if and when it gets detonated or accidently explodes.

We stay around the building, waiting till around 11 p.m. while the FBI, Harvey's people, and local law enforcement are making plans and, of course, contingency plans. For a while I hang around with Entertainment Manager Bob McClure in his office across the hall from mine. He plays a Kip Addotta record for me, we laugh a lot, and finally we are permitted to go home and get some sleep.

About 8:20 on the next morning, we now begin evacuation of Harrah's. Hotel and restaurant guests and casino players are moved out in a very orderly and professional manner. This happens smack in the middle of breakfast on Wednesday, August 27. Of course, everything is comped: hotel rooms, food, everything. After all guests and players are led to safety outside, the process of counting and securing every single table game's bank of cash and chips must be completed. All slot machines are 'dumped,' (coins removed) and the employees are then evacuated. Never before have all gaming tables been emptied of their cash/chips inventory, nor have all the slots been completely emptied. Never.

About 30 minutes after our evacuation, I walk through my entire areas of responsibility, making sure that everybody is gone, employees and guests, and that all the gas lines in every kitchen and the bake shop are turned off. A few unforgettable scenes will be with me forever, most notably in the 24/7 Sierra Restaurant, which is the largest and busiest coffee shop we operate.

It is a surreal scene, normally the busy, bustling center of the property's activity during breakfast time. I'm totally alone in this moment; the room now empty of guests and staff is a bit eerie. There are several food servers' jack-stands sitting with full trays of plated breakfasts, the one nearest to me still with its stainless-steel covers on the plates, except for one. And that one without its cover is obviously about to be served: an order of scrambled eggs, hash browns, and bacon (now ice cold). I move downstairs to the employee cafeteria's kitchen prep area, where I find half a canned ham intact on a maple cutting board, the other half in a neat pile, diced. Laying a couple of inches away is a 10-inch French knife. My mind flashes on what I imagine in history to be the Last Day of Pompei, where every sign of life is in suspended animation, a freeze frame containing the moment of disaster.

Upstairs on the casino floor, the corporate guys, Rome Andriotti and Joe Francis, arrive from Reno. Rome is standing at an empty blackjack table in pit 4 out in front of the Cabaret. He's talking to Tom and me while with one hand he deftly 'laces' (shuffles) two side-by-side stacks of chips over and over again. I see a few others do that on slow games over the years but watching this older guy, who hasn't dealt in decades, is an eye-opener for me, a real mind bender. It is *always* done with *one hand*. Try it some time. Although he is a definite type-B personality, he is clearly concerned this morning. He is such a class act, such a respected gentleman. I feel badly for him, that he is thrown into this position: a serious threat to the building and to our staff and guests.

Building Engineering Manager Jay Osborne, his crew, and the QD Construction guys do an excellent job prepping the vulnerable spots. Windows facing Harvey's are quickly 'x'ed' with protective duct tape and covered with plywood. Armed state troopers are stationed at our doors and at our first-floor elevators and escalators. We need the troopers because the building's entrances are not equipped with locks. (Why would you build locks into the doors of a 24-hour business? It would be a waste of construction dollars.) About three dozen key management employees stay behind. For the most part, once the employees and "civilians" are out of the building, we hang around in the employee cafeteria, which is in our basement and classified as an official bomb shelter.

It is boring just hanging around, and so I take a walk every so often. At one point I am up on the 18th (top) floor just walking around with Jay Osborne and a food shift supervisor, when Jay receives a radioed scanner call from law enforcement over at Harvey's, *"Three minutes to detonation, three minutes to detonation."*

Ok, now we have to move it and get down to the basement. We take the public elevators, because they are nearest, but we have to get off at the ground floor and run down the escalator, which has been shut off. As we round the curve of slot machines lining the exterior wall of the Rendezvous Lounge, a state trooper spots us moving fast and draws-down his weapon on us and commands, "Halt!"

Now we have to explain that we're the good guys, and we need to get to safety in a few seconds, as an explosion is about to occur. He holsters his weapon and lets us go. A minute or so later, at 3:43 p.m., we are in the employee cafeteria, and *feel* the bomb go off across the street. It is a power-packed charge made up of a thousand pounds of Hercules Unigel dynamite sticks stolen from the construction site of the Helms Power Plant at the Wishon Reservoir near Fresno, California.

The cost to rebuild Harvey's? Eighteen million dollars and nine months of lost revenues.

We all leave the basement and start the process of reopening. I get with Tom and Joe (Francis) and talk about timing needs and priorities. I quickly lay out a plan for them, suggesting that we stagger restaurant openings based on the time of day, complexity of the restaurants involved, and availability of staff. The process of communicating all this to employees in an era when cell phones don't exist takes a bit of doing, but it all comes together in a beautiful way, mostly because 90% of the people working at Harrah's-Tahoe during this era have pride in their workplace and a sense of duty. You can't buy that.

And *I can't buy* that these guys who run the company see me (only in the casino biz for nine months at this point; just turned 36) reacting in an emergency situation, the likes of which nobody has ever seen in *any* casino—let alone theirs—and effectively dealing with it. I accidently make my bones in a 24-hour period. The truth is, I just happen to be at the right place at the right time . . . and so is my boss: if he had been with us at the lake, instead of in Atlantic City looking for a transfer, life would surely have turned out differently for me. R.J. never even calls during the emergency. Kind of unbelievable.

A few weeks later, they get rid of R.J. He doesn't get the job in Jersey. He's totally out of Harrah's and I now report direct to Joe Fanelli. This reporting relationship only lasts about two months, because Joe is sent to New Jersey to oversee the opening of our newest casino there. By November I'm reporting to Joe Francis, who has been promoted to Corporate Senior V.P., working out of Reno.

What feels equally good is that, as a consequence of Harvey's being closed up for the next nine months, our restaurants' covers and sales are up by 23% . . . every month! *Thank you, dumb-ass bombers,* who, BTW, get arrested, tried, and sent away pretty quickly.

By six p.m. on the night of the bombing, we have Room Service, the Sierra Restaurant, the Employee Cafeteria, and the Snack Bar open. The following day we're open everywhere else: the Forest Buffet, the Summit, the New York Deli, the Carousel Restaurant, the Seafood Cove,

Banquets, the South Shore Room (our showroom) and Winner's Circle.

We are plagued by copy-cats for the next several days. It's tiring, because each time one of these morons makes a bomb threat call—and it's almost always at night—we have to go back in to work and deal with it. The funniest one occurs when a guy makes an extortion call and tells us to drop the money to him at such and such a time, and he'll be waiting at the drop point—which happens to be the phone booth from which he's making the call. Idiot.

Life at The Lake in the 1980s

Living and working at Tahoe during our time there sometimes feels as if we're on an island. This is partly because of weather-related events and infrastructure failures and the fact that the area is a bit remote.

- Mail is not delivered at our house, so we get a post office box and learn to stop in at the P.O. every day.
- Power outages occur frequently so we have a supply of big fat candles and matches at the house. On the other hand, Harrah's has a big bank of generators which can supply necessary limited power to essential parts of the building.
- Heating the house is very expensive during our first year. Fortunately, our landlord is a good guy and buys a woodstove for us. But then, of course, as with many up at the lake, we are dependent on firewood. Every late summer and throughout the fall, we are on the hunt for wood. And we learn how to harvest, age, and split it.
- We learn how to deal with major drops of snow and huge icicles. It's fun for the most part, providing you have

appropriate clothing and equipment. Charlene, Tim, and Jeff build a toboggan run in our very steep backyard and we have great times sliding down on plastic bags and cardboard. The long decks and eaves must be continually cleared, but for me it's enjoyable exercise.

♦ Retired cop Ralph is our next-door neighbor. He lives with Sonny, his big German Shepard, and fades in and out of dementia. He likes my son, David, but always calls him Mike. One day Sonny starts barking at me and with his front paws on my shoulders, pins me to the exterior wall of the house. A close shave with death. Lucky for me, Ralph has his wits about him this day and saves me.

♦ Shopping for the nice clothes I need for my job or for the kids' Christmas presents requires trips over the Sierras to Sacramento. The choices we have in Reno (56 miles away) just don't cut it for the clothes, and there's not even a Toys R Us there during the years we live at Tahoe.

♦ What we *do have* is a beautiful view of the lake every single day we live at Tahoe, plus clean air accompanied by the sweet aroma of downed pine needles that bake in the sun. These features contribute to a number of visits from friends and family from all over the country, and it's great to see them.

♦ And because Harrah's is such a mecca for entertainers, we even re-connect with entertainment friends with whom we've worked in Colorado and Wyoming: Katy Moffatt; also, Ricky and the Redstreaks.

A Cross Section of Perps, Victims, and Everybody In-Between

Over the years—and I suppose this is true in all major casinos—we have an odd collection of quasi-celebrities on staff, all hiding in plain sight (well, one, a former IRA hit man really *is* hiding):

♦ A poor unfortunate soul who survives the Bataan Death March as a fourteen-year-old boy. He was an American kid over there because his dad was stationed in the Philippines working for one of the big oil companies. He is a coffee shop sous chef when I arrive, but sadly, a classic PTSD victim of the experience.

♦ A blackjack dealer who is a former Cy Young winner.

♦ A former IRA hit man (also a coffee shop sous chef).

♦ A former Olympic Track Team member (1968).

♦ A platinum album winning road manager from the singing group The Commodores.

♦ A couple of former NFL players, both Corporate and working out of Reno.

♦ A National Trap Shooting Champion.

♦ Another National Trap Shooting Champion, but this one in the Junior age group at the time he won.

♦ Two former FBI guys, working out of Reno; one, our Corporate Director of Security, was allegedly pretty close to J. Edgar Hoover.

Winter 1981 - The Jarrari

One of the top oddities in Harrah's Auto Collection is the "Jarrari," an orange Jeep Wagoneer, which Bill Harrah has his H.A.C. technicians fit out with a special drivetrain and a Ferrari engine. The frame actually has to be extended to make it workable.

For all the world to see, it's just an orange 1970-something Jeep Wagoneer housed in a Sparks warehouse along with 1,200 other collectible, well-cared-for autos. Only if one reads the museum's framed description of what's under the hood and the explanation of the conversion process does the true story of this freak of a vehicle unfold.

One winter evening, on the way home I stop to get gas at the Round Hill Shell station on Highway 50, a couple of miles east of the Tahoe casinos. It's at the base of a fairly steep hill, and as I'm standing next to my car filling the tank, I hear the scream of an engine and look up to see Joe Francis in the Jarrari, flooring it up that hill on his way back to Reno. It's an unforgettable sight and sound, with bad Joe Francis at the wheel. Who's gonna tell Joe he can't take the Jarrari out of H.A.C. now that he's just been promoted to Corporate

Senior V.P.? Who's gonna tell Joe even if he hasn't been promoted? Bill Harrah? Maybe. But the fact is, I never meet anyone who would dare try to question this guy about very much (you had to know him). *Maybe* Bill Harrah, and *maybe* Rome, and that's as long a list as I can create. But Bill Harrah is dead when Joe flies up that hill, and Rome is in Reno, 56 miles away.

February 1981 - Lesson for a Lifetime

One day Joe Fanelli calls and asks me to go eat at a well-respected dinner house in South Lake Tahoe. In the restaurant trade, this is called 'shopping' the competition. The next day he calls me to ask about the experience:

"So, what did you think?" asks Joe.

"Oh, Joe, we're way better than they are," I confidently tell him.

"That's not what I asked you," he says. "Never compare yourself to somebody else. Compare the experience to *your own* standard of excellence. You have a good education and a good background. I expect you to use them."

It is an uncomfortable moment for me, but *a lesson for a lifetime*—one that I recount often to others.

Joe is a complicated mentor during my early days with Harrah's. He can mete out some tough verbal lessons one day and be a loving uncle the next.

Dr. Paul Bunyan at Your Service

In late 1981 I begin asking a few of the guys at work about their vasectomy experiences. After talking to Charlene about it, we go visit the doc who does the procedure in South Lake Tahoe. Everybody goes to the same guy. (Tahoe pretty much has one guy for this, one guy for that. Small community.) Art Daub and Ed Posey both use the local vasectomy guy and recommend him. I trust them.

The deal is, you go sit in the doctor's office, he asks the husband and wife a bunch of questions, explains the procedure, has you sign some papers, has you make an appointment, then sends you home to think it over for two weeks. You come back, and he does the procedure right in his office. But this is Tahoe, and the guy dresses like a lumberjack, complete with the heavy plaid flannel shirt and full beard. *I'm gonna let a lumberjack put a knife to me? There?*

On the day of the procedure, I'm alone in his office waiting room. I pick up a copy of Sports Illustrated and I begin reading an article about a young guy who lives in Yosemite Valley and free climbs frozen waterfalls—no ropes! The article is fascinating, engrossing. After a while, a nurse comes to get me, and tells me, "The doctor is ready."

Oh, is he? 'Cause it looks to me like he's still doing a pretty good Paul Bunyan impression. And while we're at it, Doc, where are the latex gloves? What? You're allergic? Go find a new career.

The nurse tells me to take my pants off, pull a sheet over myself, and lie down on the examining table. She leaves. And I get back to reading about the ice climber while I wait for Dr. Paul Bunyan to ride in on Babe the Blue Ox.

The guy is middle-aged and kind of 'country.' He's really a pretty congenial character, especially for a doctor. He tells me what he's going to do, but I truly want to get back to my reading. To take my mind off his razor and shaving and the numbing injection, and to learn about the insane ice climber, I get back to the magazine. The doc goes away for a few minutes while I get numb where I need to be.

He comes back and goes about the business of performing the procedure, which at the moment is painless. I hear the famous 'snip-snip,' and feel a tugging sensation as he's sewing me up, but that's it. It's finished. And he looks down at me and says, "So, how was that article you were reading?"

"Um, I guess I stopped reading before I finished it," I answer.

"Yeah," he says with a big-ass grin, "I've had only one calm, cool customer over all these years, who just kept on reading through the whole thing. But I took one look at you, and I knew you weren't gonna be like him."

Another part-time comedian.

The next day, a Saturday, I'm alone at home, lying in bed recuperating. I'm not in pain but lying in bed is definitely preferable to being on my feet at the 'post-snipping' stage.

We don't have a phone in the bedroom. We have only one phone, which is a mile away in the kitchen area of the great room; and my buddy Art Daub knows this and is fully aware of how slow one has to move right after a vasectomy. At about eleven o'clock the phone starts ringing. I gingerly get up out of bed, and slowly, with some discomfort, make my way to the phone, now on perhaps its eighth ring. When I finally pick up the phone it is my friend Art Daub, who is having a good laugh at my expense. Another wise guy in this whole process. Several months later, you will see, I get even.

Winter 1982

During the winter of 1982 Russ hands me a ticket for an annual Ducks Unlimited dinner which will take place across the street at Del Webb's Sahara. We go over there with a few management guys from Harrah's-Tahoe and two or three of Russ' East Bay (San Francisco area) pals—who also are players—and by the end of the evening, Russ decides Harrah's needs to 'own' this event for next year.

Through Russ's connections in the hunting community, we get the event for the next *several* years. They are pretty amazing affairs, with a big dinner where the guys in attendance are regularly peppered with interruptions from an MC who is cajoling them into buying raffle tickets from wandering 'hostesses.' Later around dessert time the raffle winners are called. But these guys are so well off, and they like their charity so much, that many just donate back the prizes, including hunting dog puppies, which are brought to them at their tables. And there's also a big auction after dinner.

My first couple of times going with Russ to this dinner, I always enjoy the 'Duck Walk.' A craps table is fitted with a set of doors built into its sidewalls, and plywood painted layout placed on top of the regular felt (which is protected by Visqueen). The layout is nothing but a field of two-inch squares with numbers.

Ducks are kept in a cramped cage where they are fed all day. But they are unable to raise their heads, and therefore are unable to poop until released. Dinner attendees purchase a few numbers, hoping that the duck, when released, waddles through one of the craps table doors and well, poops on one of the squares they buy.

This organization has huge bucks and many of the prizes are very rich: expensive top-of-the-line shotguns, trained hunting pups, training schools for the pups, trips to hunting lodges, etc. I never win a thing at these events but they are always fun.

Another kind of fun are the prize fights of the 1980s. In my lifetime, I am able to go to two Mohammed Ali fights at Madison Square Garden (the first one, when he is still Cassius Clay and not yet champ). But the 1980s, after Ali retires, are the peak of boxing's popularity, mostly because of middleweights, but some memorable heavyweights are also in the mix. Once again it is Russ who sees to it that I get to come along with the big boys. There are six of us. We go next door to Caesars-Tahoe for two or three of the great middleweight bouts. A few are also televised (closed circuit) at Harrah's.

This period has an amazing group of middleweight fighters, and we see bouts occurring often, with Tommy Hearns, Marvin Hagler, Sugar Ray Leonard, and Roberto Duran, also heavyweights Michael Spinks, Evander Holyfield, Larry Holmes, and Mike Tyson.

My most memorable moment is right before the infamous "No mas" fight of Duran's. Our group is in a crowd being funneled through the doors to the seating area at Caesar's Showroom entrance, our gold tickets in hand. We're in a crush of guys trying to get through the narrow entrance. I'm right next to Tom (Yturbide), who, if I haven't mentioned it before, is a big man and not shy about using his size to remind you to stay on your side of the fence. Two local, flannel-shirted, work-booted twenty-somethings decide they'd like to get into the showroom in front of us. They're solidly built, probably Tahoe construction workers. They make a move on Tom and *attempt* to squeeze past. He looks down his nose at both of them and snickers, saying, "You don't think you're gonna get past me, do you?" There is silence from these two, and we move forward past them. Oh, to be that big!

May 1982 - West Point

On one of our early recruiting trips to CIA, knowing that Art Daub and I have some time to burn before our flight out of Newark, the ladies in the school's placement office ask if they can set up a tour of the West Point kitchens for us. *"YES! We'd love that,"* I tell them.

Over the years I get to tour behind the scenes of famous resorts, world-class restaurants, the big Orlando theme parks, four- and five-star hotels, major league slaughterhouses, huge trade shows, culinary schools, etc., but nothing is quite as cool as the United States Military Academy at West Point. And because so many times I am alone when going on tours, it's nice to share this one, especially this one, with Art, because we are both patriotic. We are there only a week before graduation. If we had taken the CIA trip a week later, we'd have missed seeing the place buzzing with cadet activity. We are *very* lucky.

CIA arranges that we meet a driver at the famous Hotel Thayer on West Point grounds. I know the place well and stayed there a few times on recruiting trips during my Harrah's years. It's full of tradition related to the military academy and just a great old hotel.

We drive over to Washington Hall where the cadet meals are served. With the driver (Bob), we are guided through the food production areas in the lower portion of the massive building. As you can imagine, in order to feed as many as 4,400+ people at the same moment in time, all the equipment is on a grand scale, even the dumbwaiters that transport the food upstairs to the mess hall. The place, although quite old, is spotless. The only kitchens I ever tour which are USMA's equal for its cleanliness are those I see when I'm interviewing at Eli Lilly headquarters (of course a big pharma company is going to be spotless) a few years later.

Writing about this visit some 37 years afterward, aside from the level of sanitation, what stands out most about the production areas is that they are breaking sides of beef in the meat cutting room. I never see anyone breaking sides in a feeding establishment, only at packing houses. It's pretty amazing to see this is still done at West Point in 1982; it's really unforgettable.

Also unforgettable is the next part of our visit. We all thank our USMA tour guide and Bob takes us outside, adjacent to the stone entrance steps facing the famed 'Plain.' We get to watch the entire corps of cadets form up in their companies, then march up and into the mess hall.

From Wikipedia: *"The Plain rises approximately 150 feet (45 m) above the Hudson River and has been the site of the longest continually occupied U.S. Army garrison in America since 1778. In its early years, the entire academy was located on the Plain and it was used for varying activities ranging from drill and mounted cavalry maneuvers to an encampment site for summer training to a sports venue. Currently, the Plain refers to just the parade field where cadets perform ceremonial parades."*

And then for the grand finale of the tour (Art and I are not expecting this), Bob sneaks us back into the mess, telling us we are not supposed to be there at this juncture and to quietly melt into the wall where we are standing. The enormous room gets completely quiet. Seconds later, a voice heard over wall-mounted speakers throughout the place commands, "Take your seats!" And 4,400 of the very finest young people America produces do just that. They are standing at attention behind their chairs, and when given the order to take their seats, the noise they create by moving 4,400 chairs is a sudden explosion. Six minutes later, all have been served, and are beginning to eat. What a system: every table seats ten, each waiter serves ten tables; all foods are served family-style; the waiters serve the entre, vegetable, starch, sides, bread, etc., with ten portions on each platter. Six minutes! The cadets actually get twenty-four minutes for the meal. It's amazing.

August 1982

It's time for another recruiting trip to CIA. Art and I fly into Newark, landing in early evening. We rent a car and head north on the New Jersey Turnpike.

In the early days of these trips to the East coast cooking schools, the personnel department is footing the bill. Because neither of us has yet been given a Harrah's credit card, Art is carrying the cash needed for our expenses. Prior to leaving the lake, Art simply goes over to the casino cage and signs out the money, all in hundreds. (In 1982, only Nevada has full-on gambling. New Jersey has limited casino gambling, so most people outside of Nevada—unless they are very wealthy or involved in criminal enterprise—don't commonly see hundreds.)

The Jersey Turnpike leg of our trip is very short, with a $.65 charge at its northern terminus. As we come into the toll area, the road is a massive sixteen lanes across, eight for each direction. It's getting clogged up as we approach a tollbooth on this hot summer evening at 6:30.

Art, who is driving, looks over at me and says, "All I have is hundreds."

I've got what he needs, but even though, and maybe *just because,* Art is such a good friend, I'm not letting the chance for some fun to get away. Besides, what about the time he calls me the morning after my vasectomy?

With as serious a face as I can muster, I tell him, "Sorry, I figured you were covering us, so I didn't bring anything."

He stares at me for a moment, as if to say, "You've got to be kidding me."

But I stick to my story, and tell him again, "Honest, I've got nothing."

So Art hands over the $.65 turnpike ticket, along with a 'c-note,' to what has to be the sweatiest little fat guy that I ever see. He must be roasting in the sauna-like prison of the tollbooth. The guy looks down at his hand holding both ticket and currency in disbelief, shaking his head and repeating, "Yeah, yeah, oh yeah." He then grabs a clipboard, leaves his booth, and heads for the rear of our rental car, where presumably, he writes down the license plate number. Unfortunate drivers who choose to follow us into the lane for that particular booth are now getting backed up into a long queue.

Returning to the tollbooth, sweat dripping from his chubby red face, he counts out ninety-nine singles, along with $.35, and hands it over to Art. He sticks it to Art, as if to say, "Think you're gonna have some fun with me, boy? This is New Jersey. We don't get mad; we just get even."

We take off northward, laughing. And for the next day or two, Art has to pay the price of our laughter by carrying a big wad of singles in the pocket, gradually trying to 'sell' them to restaurant cashiers along the way. I never tell him until the trip is half over that I had the money for the toll at the time. I just had to get even with him after that post-vasectomy phone call he made to me.

April 1983

A couple of months prior to the Symposium on American Cuisine down in New Orleans, I learn about it, and find out it's going to be a fantastic food experience, both for the dining opportunities as well as the educational agenda. It's also going to be fun, and as it turns out, an unexpected reunion with many old food industry friends.

It'll even be a whole lot more fun if my pal Moose can come along. I'm working for Harrah's-Tahoe at the time, and Moose is working in Denver for Doug Bessant at a free-standing restaurant. It works out that my plane will land in Denver, where Moose will board, and we'll get to fly in together.

One evening we're walking down in the French Quarter and two young local teenagers approach us. Because of where I was brought up, and who I am, I ignore street people. But Moose is the essence of an affable people-person, so we have to stop and listen to these two trying a hustle on us. Well, one of them, anyway:

"Hey mister, betcha two dollars I can tell you where you got them shoes," the kid claims. Moose is somewhat intrigued, but we keep walking.

The pair persist for a couple of long, annoying minutes. I'm not only annoyed with them; I'm also impatient with Moose. Finally Moose agrees to the bet and the kid says, "You got them shoes in the State of Louisiana, in the City of New Orleans, in the French Quarter, on Royal Street. Now pay up!"

Moose smiles, looks DOWN at this kid, and quickly tells him in no uncertain terms, what most people don't need to hear twice, coming from a 6'3, 270-pound guy, "Fuck you!" And we move on down the street, unimpeded.

November 1983

I get a call from my mother that my grandmother has been hospitalized with severe stomach pain and that they are operating on her. Soon afterward, another call: Gram doesn't make it through the surgery. An intestinal blockage results in a rupture, which poisons her abdominal cavity. She is gone.

I make quick plans to go back for the funeral. There's no way I can bring Charlene, and it's no place for the kids, so I will go alone. Luckily, Art and Bev Daub are going down to Sacramento the next afternoon, and I can stay at their friends' house overnight. We plan that Art will take me to the airport down there at 5 a.m., so I can get a direct flight, and also save some time and money, rather than fly out of Reno.

In the meantime, I have to stop in and get something off my chest with Tom Yturbide. Because the company is putting a managerial lineup together, pressure is mounting on me to accept a transfer to relocate to Atlantic City to open "Harrah's at Trump Plaza." And I know the 84-page N.J. 'Key Employee' Gaming License Application requires that

I answer questions concerning any appearances before a grand jury.

Minutes before I have to hop into Art's car to head for Sac, I go to Tom's office and explain that what I'm about to tell him is going to put me in a very vulnerable position, but that I can't keep this from him, as ultimately the company could be embarrassed—and I don't want that. I give him a three-minute version of the Matty Feldman/Emerson's Limited story. I'm pretty surprised at his reaction. He smiles and tells me it won't be a problem and to relax. Whether he's right or wrong I feel a great relief.

I go to New York, where I meet up with my parents and Mer at the St. Regis. We sleep in connecting rooms, just like old times, Mer and I in queen beds in the same room. It is surreal to re-experience this set-up at 39 and 41 years of age, respectively.

Late Winter 1984 - Atlantic City (A.C.)

Two days before I'm scheduled to fly out to the East coast on a recruiting trip to CIA, where I will work a Harrah's-Tahoe booth at the school's semi-annual job fair, I get a call at my office at 7:30 a.m. It's a Sr. V.P. who tells me to stop what I'm doing and drive to our corporate headquarters in Reno. I'm asked by company President Dick Goeglein to meet with Corporate V.P. of Food and Beverage, Joe Fanelli, who is temporarily working in Atlantic City (A.C.), about taking over the F&B job at the soon-to-be-opened (eight weeks hence) Harrah's at Trump Plaza.

During the previous summer, Rome and I take the Trumps (Donald, wife Ivanna, and his brother, Robert) on a tour of Harrah's-Tahoe, as the company is in serious partnership talks with The Donald. This is a top-to-bottom tour through our crown jewel property, and my role is to be available to answer any questions about the food operation. It is all pleasant chit-chat. I barely know who the guy is.

Why do they ask me to jump onboard with only a matter of weeks before the scheduled opening? Because they are suddenly forced to fire their Hungarian Food and Beverage man. The word on the street is that this guy takes a group of the pre-opening team out for dinner in A.C. one night, and as he's finishing up with payment at the podium, asks the young hostess, "Want to know how we pull up our socks at Harrah's?"

Before she can answer, he drops trow to the floor, pulls up each of his socks, picks up his pants, zips up, hitches his belt and catches up with his dinner mates.

Harrah's, unlike some of the professional sports teams and TV networks at this time, will actually fire somebody for bad behavior. There's a reputation to protect, not to mention gaming licenses and credibility with shareholders. Previously, when the question of transferring to Atlantic City comes up, I indicate that I have no interest in leaving Tahoe. But with only about eight weeks before the casino's grand opening, I am the only one they know and trust.

After the CIA job fair and interviews are over, I grab a prearranged ride to Atlantic City from old Tahoe friends who have also been working the event and are now assigned to Harrah's-Marina in A.C. In the hours it takes to drive from CIA to A.C., they give me an honest picture of casino life there. By the time I check in to Harrah's-Marina I know more than ever that this is not a gig I want.

The next morning, a Saturday, Joe Fanelli swings by and picks me up at the Marina, and we head over to the Fairmont Tavern. Located in a pretty run-down neighborhood, this place is a local favorite of Harrah's A.C. people. It's got great down-home Italian chow. I've been there before, on another business trip to A.C. Of course, the joint is not open at 10:15 a.m. when we arrive, so we don't approach the front entrance. Joe takes me around the side of the building and knocks on a door. Owner and local celeb Sonny Mancuso lets us slip in and locks the door. I get introduced, and we are led to a table in the back of the darkened restaurant.

Joe and I sit down, and after bringing coffee for 'Mista Fanelli,' and tea for me, Sonny disappears. We're alone in this darkened back room of an old Italian restaurant sitting on bentwood chairs at a table with a worn red and white checkered tablecloth—no music, no white noise—just us. And for more than a moment it feels like every cliché of every mob movie ever made. I'm waiting for Al Pacino to come out of the men's room blasting away.

We're just talking for maybe ten minutes, and Sonny comes back asking, "Hey, Mista Fanelli, you want some pasta fazool?" Joe looks at me, I nod, and Sonny lays down two cups of pasta fagioli and leaves again. I'm really not interested in soup at this moment, but I'm being polite, so I take a couple of sips. We talk some more and now Sonny returns.

"Anything else, Mista Fanelli?" he asks. And looking at me, my mostly untouched soup, then me again, "Hey somethin' wrong witchya pasta fazool?" And before I can answer, Sonny is grabbing my spoon, *my spoon*, and sampling the soup from my cup. It's an insane scene, maybe only possible in an old-time neighborhood in New Jersey. And as bizarre and hilarious as it is, I sorta love it, and sorta love Sonny too. Sonny leaves. Again.

Another ten minutes of talking and Joe looks at me, and says, "You really don't want this, do you?"

"No, Joe, I don't," I tell him.

Then a rhetorical question from Joe, "Those people at the lake are like family to you, aren't they?"

And as my mouth is saying, "Yeah, Joe, they are," my mind is thinking of the night before I leave Tahoe for this particular East coast trip I'm on. I'm walking through the casino, and as I pass by the Cabaret Bar on my way to the car, I hear Russ's voice calling to me, "Hey, Vinnie boy."

And yeah, he and many others are family, and I'm not at all ready to leave them or the place. And Joe says—in as fatherly a way as I ever hear him speak to me, "Don't worry. I'll take care of this." And that's it. Not another word is ever mentioned to me about transferring to Jersey. No "what'll it take to get you to leave Tahoe?" (which has happened in previous months and weeks). No nothing. Joe, Freddy Rufe's classmate at Cornell; Joe who allows me into Harrah's-Tahoe, the only five star/five diamond rated hotel casino in the entire United States for twelve consecutive years. Joe, the benevolent uncle . . . *if he* likes you. Why are these "*if* he likes you" guys in my life???

April 1986

At some point during the summer of 1985, Tom gets word from the folks at Mobil Guide that his lobbying has paid off: Harrah's-Tahoe has been selected for the Mobil Five Star Awards Weekend, to take place in April 1986. I have mixed feelings about this. The idea of putting ourselves on display for 150-200 guests representing the best of the best may be the ultimate corporate ego trip in some people's minds, but for me it's the ultimate test for an entire non-stop weekend in April, a time of year at Tahoe when outdoor activities are very limited and the weather always questionable. Only 34 qualifying hotels and restaurants will be sending their top people, along with associated industry giants, such as the *Mondavi family, Dan Duckhorn, Manfred Esser, Justin Meyer, Sam Sebastiani, Janet Trefethen, a few other top-end winery people, and several food and wine writers. I know that most of the weekend events will be on me, because at Tahoe during April, we will pretty much be indoors.

*Can't remember if all of these are there for this particular event, but they and many other big names in the

biz are often our guests/speakers at our Annual Wine Weekends.

We get moving right away, and I begin by arranging three menus to be served in the Summit private dining room to a small group of us over three nights during late August and early September (1985). We end up doing a bit of mix and match on the menu items, but by the end of September we have that part of the following April's weekend "in the can."

As winter begins to draw down, we rehearse what we can, and for everything else, rely on our experience with high-end events to pull us through. What I don't see coming is a bit of a curve ball . . .

On the Wednesday preceding the event, at about 4 in the afternoon, a delivery guy from Thunderbird Printing (in Reno) rolls a hand truck into my office with boxes of all the printed materials for the weekend. Thunderbird Printing is owned and operated by Pete Peterson, whose knowledge and skills are so valuable to Harrah's that even when the company opens in Atlantic City, Pete prints the menus and ships them from Reno to New Jersey. How does this relationship become so strong?

Pete tells me the story: Back in the late 60s or early 70s when Bill Harrah is looking for a printer to create custom Christmas cards for his big personal mailing, he gives newcomer Pete a try. Mr. Harrah is so impressed with Pete's work that he orders that all high-end work be done by

Thunderbird. And it stays that way even after Bill Harrah dies. It stays that way because Harrah's lieutenants, like Joe Fanelli, never stray from the quality required by Mr. Harrah. And then when newcomers arrive on the scene, as I do later on, we are taught how to keep the flame of quality lit. It's not like that anymore, and I feel very, very lucky to have worked for and with the old timers. Years later, when I'm with the Peppermill in Reno, I use Pete's menu printing skills until he retires and sells the company.

After the delivery guy leaves, I look at Susan Newbre, my all-time favorite Tahoe front-of-the-house ops person, my right hand, a loyal and really amazing leader, and for no apparent reason I say to her, "Wouldn't it be a bitch if there was something wrong on this stuff?"

I begin looking through all the boxes that hold the various pieces of printed materials needed for the weekend: welcome messaging, the weekend schedule of events, the separate piece listing the Five Star recipients, the menu for the awards dinner, and the Sunday brunch menu. The menus . . . *hmmm, let's have a look at them.*

And there it is, jumping off the paper, so clear, so obvious: a typo that makes all of us look like complete and thorough imbeciles: the Brit showroom maître d', the Swiss fine dining maître d', the assistant executive chef, the secretary who types it up, and yours truly. Weeks before, each of us proofed the Saturday night awards dinner menu, and it passed muster. We didn't see that the first item on the

299

menu, the one I intend to be 'Chilled Medallions of Maine Lobster in Chardonnay Aspic with Caviar,' is all good *except* that Maine is spelled Main, as in 'my main man.' *Oh, my God!*

My life, my career, passes slowly before my eyes. I'm dead! I call Pete the printer, a guy who—thank God and Joe Fanelli—loves me. I immediately tell him that a mistake's been made, and he and his crew are not to blame. It's my fault. I just want to know if he can correct it.

Pete's a classic type B personality: a calm and cool slow talker, easy-going dude, somewhere in his mid-fifties. He's thinking out loud, over the phone . . . very s-l-o-w-l-y, "Well, let's see. I have to get more stock flown in from Sacramento, I need more gold foil, I have to print and die cut the job . . . Geez, I still have to print a big job before the weekend for the Eldorado. That may be a problem . . . Yeah, **I think** I can do it by Saturday afternoon."

I'm quiet, and scared, and thinking, but not saying, *You THINK you CAN???*

I thank him and hang up. Now comes the dreaded walk down to Tom's office, and a conversation I don't enjoy thinking about. I tell him what's going on, and he tilts back in his chair, and gets a nice big grin on his face, enjoying my suffering, "Ah, you'll do fine. You'll get it done."

I live in some sort of suspended zombie world that night, and next day, and most of Friday. The guests are arriving late Friday afternoon. Suddenly, at about four o'clock the menus arrive. Yes! A day early! I can breathe again. And sure enough, when I go to Tom's to report that all is well, he grins again and says, "*I knew you could do it.*"

Yeah sure, I'm thinking to myself, and remembering the time Kunk watches me through his rearview mirror, being pulled over by a state trooper, me with a car FULL of stuff he steals from a restaurant, and later telling me, "Ahh, I said to myself, Oakes will chill him out."

Yeah sure.

Anyway, the entire weekend is spectacular, and really a tribute to the ultra-talented food team I'm blessed to work with at Harrah's-Tahoe. When the big awards dinner is over, it's late at night, and a number of us go upstairs for drinks at the Summit Restaurant. I'm invited to sit with Robert ("*call me Bob*") Mondavi and others, and it all feels pretty good: cigars, drinks, compliments, a beautiful view of Lake Tahoe's twinkling boat lights off in the distance. And I know one thing, for sure, one thing I won't forget: I owe Pete the printer, *big time.*

June 1986

In the winter of 1986, I am invited by Ferdinand Metz, President of the CIA, to be the June graduation speaker at the school. It is quite an honor, and I soon regret not spending the airfare for Charlene or one of the kids to come along. I still have major regrets about that. The graduation day is Friday the 13th, but as it turns out there is no cause for concern . . . well, maybe just one, but I'm getting ahead of the story.

The entire time I am there, I am continually bombarded with little wonderful things: they tape an interview with me for their archives of graduation speakers, they take me to dinner at American Bounty, and the menu has printed on it, "Welcome Vinnie Oakes," and well-wishing chefs and staff members come by the table and greet me.

On the morning of the graduation, I am thrilled to be greeted by Jack and Mary Bogrette and two of their eight children in Ferdinand's outer office. Jack was one of my teachers at CIA, and his son David, born when I was Jack's student, will be in the graduating class that day. David will be going to work under Rod Stoner in an apprenticeship at the Greenbrier. During the five-month winter break for apprentices, he will be coming out to work in our kitchens at Harrah's-Tahoe.

Ferdinand's secretary pins a flower in my lapel and quietly tells me that the entire event, including my speech, is being taped by NBC for the Today Show. I don't have time to be nervous; we are soon to go downstairs for the graduation luncheon. There are about 350 people seated for the meal and ceremony.

As the meal is winding down, the ceremony begins, and through the main aisle of the very large room, the graduating class in their whites begin marching toward the stage at the far end of the room. A recording of Pomp and Circumstance is played, and not out of nervousness but because I'm so sentimental, I get goose bumps. Real goose bumps. Even the hair on the back of my neck stands up! After the kids are in their places, and after the traditional graduation formalities take place, I am introduced. My speech goes off perfectly, and they make me feel like a million bucks.

After being pampered beyond anything a casino food guy could dream of, it's time to say all the thank-you's and goodbyes and drive down to Newark to catch a late plane heading west. First I have to stop at Ron Peterson's, where I've been his houseguest, pick up my bags and leave. I change clothes and load the car. But wait . . . nature is calling. Back into the house I go and unleash 24 hours' worth of both casual and fine dining at CIA. Ron is not home but has warned me of a touchy toilet system in his old country house.

OMG! It's overflowing! It's attacking me with a fury of output equal to the input that I so unwittingly, so rampantly, forced down into it. Quickly I look for the plunger. There *has* to be a plunger—after all, the guy *warned* me he has a touchy toilet. No, there is *not* a plunger. No time! I'm scrambling—with my pants around my ankles—for the tank cover. I get it off, and grab the shaft thing that controls the water, but too late: I'm standing in a half inch of water. Luckily, nothing else has escaped the bowl (*too heavy*, I guess). I shut off the water from the wall handle, pull up my pants, mop the water up with bath towels, throw them into the tub, wash my hands, and get out of there.

I must call Ron, but where? I can't find him at the school on a Friday afternoon, after a graduation. Impossible. Cell phones are not invented yet. I must get going. I've still got a plane to catch after I drive an hour and three quarters, turn in a rental car, check my bags, and wait for the plane. After leaving a note explaining the situation, and saying that I will, of course, cover any associated costs, I hit the road.

On the beautiful drive down to Newark—well, beautiful on the upstate New York part—I regain my composure and enjoy the drive. What the hell . . . they treat me like a rock star and the speech is perfect. I'll call Ron when I get to the airport and again offer to pay for any damage that occurs.

I get on the plane without a hitch, and when it stops in Chicago, a mother and daughter take the two seats next to me. After about 20 minutes of flight, the mom looks at me and asks, "Are you Vinnie Oakes?" This is a stranger! My mind is racing trying to figure out how I can be so well known only hours after I give the address to the CIA graduates; she can't have seen the Today Show taping. Before I leave the school, they tell me it won't air for two weeks!

"Yeah," I answer.

And here's what brings me back down to my proper place on earth:

"I'm Cindy Kaiser," she says. "I know you from DU."

OK, so she doesn't see me on national television, and I'm not famous after all, but at least she doesn't say, "Yeah, I heard you were the guy who left a shit mess in your friend's guest bathroom upstate. Heck, everybody's heard about you."

Summer 1989

For the past couple of summers, I receive a summons for jury duty from the Carson City County Court in Carson City. On each occurrence I write a letter to the court, explaining that summertime is our busiest season at Harrah's-Tahoe, and due to my position, being away puts a significant strain on the property. I have my boss sign it, and each time they excuse me. But in the summer of 1989, they are not having it, and my request is rejected.

The case I'm being considered for involves the former local sheriff of Carson City, who has been removed from office and accused of financial malfeasance.

When it's my turn to be asked a bunch of questions to determine my fitness for actually sitting on a jury, here's how it goes:

Judge Michael Fondi gives me some instructions and we move forward.

Prosecutor Noel Waters opens with, "Mr. Oakes, would you please tell the court if you know me."

I respond with, "Yes, I do."

Waters asks, "And would you please describe for the court the nature of our relationship."

I tell the room, "You were my neighbor for a few years, living across the street, and our kids used to play with each other. When my daughter became old enough, she babysat for you."

Waters asks, "And is that the extent of our relationship, Mr. Oakes?"

"Yes," I reply.

Waters then asks, "Mr. Oakes, would our relationship in any way affect your ability to be objective in your determination of the guilt or innocence of the accused?"

I answer, "No sir."

Waters then asks, "And Mr. Oakes, do you personally know anyone else in these proceedings: the accused (points to him), the defense attorney (points to him), the judge (points to him)?"

Again, I say, "No sir."

Waters requests, "And Mr. Oakes, would you please describe for the court what knowledge you may have of this case."

"Not much really," I answer. "I know that guy over there (motioning toward the accused) has been accused of some improprieties, but honestly, I haven't read about the details in the paper."

Waters closes, "Thank you, Mr. Oakes. No further questions, Your Honor."

And now it's the Defense's turn, and after a handful of simple questions, he seems satisfied, and the judge is about to move forward to the next citizen in the jury pool. But before he does, he asks, "Before we move on, is there anything you'd like to add to your testimony, Mr. Oakes?

Now reader, please understand, what happens next is not planned by me in any way, shape, or form – just like many things I do or say in this life.

I say, "Well, maybe just one thing, Your Honor."

Judge Fondi asks, "What's that, Mr. Oakes?"

"Well, you see that guy over there (pointing to the accused)?" I ask.

Judge Fondi, says, "Yeah."

And here I tell him very honestly, "Well, I think that about nine out of ten times, for him to be sitting over there at all means he's guilty."

Judge Fondi simultaneously speaks and motions with his right hand playfully wiggling side-to-side, "Hmmm, I don't know about nine out of ten, but…" (and his voice trails off). Then: laughter in the courtroom.

He continues, asking me, "OK, Mr. Oakes. Now I think you were probably alive when President Kennedy was killed, right?"

"Yes, I was," I answer.

"Then you're aware that Jack Ruby shot Lee Harvey Oswald, right?" asks the judge.

I answer, "Yes sir, Judge, saw it live on TV."

"OK. So tell us, Mr. Oakes, do you think that Jack Ruby should have been given a trial for the murder of Oswald?" he asks.

"No way. What would be the point? I watched him murder the guy on live TV," I say.

And right then and there I love this Fondi guy. LOVE him! The defense dude tries to act like he's not flustered, and they actually call the next potential juror.

But I know it's all over. And sure enough, right after they are done with their questions, the defense stands up and says, *"Uh, Your Honor, the defense would like to excuse Mr. Oakes."*

And the next morning, I'm back where I belong, back at Harrah's-Lake Tahoe.

Winter 1990 - Adrift Again

After reporting to ten different bosses over a ten-year span at Harrah's, the eleventh turns out to be a guy who can't take a joke I played on him in front of Tom Yturbide in 1986. Tom sure loved it. But this guy doesn't forget about it. His gargantuan ego can't take it. And after becoming the G.M. of the property, he waits until the time is right and then dumps me. It's hard to take because I love the place and most of its people. Bob Stirling helps me load my car and is in tears, but it is what it is.

Roughly two weeks prior to the day the new G.M. cans me, I sense what he is about to do. So I make a few calls, searching for something else. Almost immediately I receive a call from a headhunter down in the Branson, Missouri, area, a place I know nothing about. He's offered the job to my friend, Ron Peterson, and Ron tells him to call me.

The job is for Director of the Foods Division at Silver Dollar City Theme Park (SDC). Only after I have the job for several months do I realize another amazing coincidence in my life: when I was a senior at DU one of the restaurant trade magazines offered to put a free ad in its classified section for

Hotel and Restaurant students looking for a job after graduation. I took them up on it, and one of the responses I got was from—in its very early stage of existence—Silver Dollar City. I was not interested in going down there in 1969, but the whole thing is kind of amazing.

"Never Mind the Mule is Blind, Just Load the Wagon" ... and other Ozark Expressions

Many of these come from my Silver Dollar City friend Jim Hunt, a native of Harrison, Arkansas. Jim is a great blend of country boy and sophisticated, street-smart businessman, educated at the very unique College of the Ozarks, just outside of Branson. He is one of the most intelligent and pleasant individuals I get to work with in my entire life.

Many of these metaphors have a story attached to them. Being a city boy, I never hear people express themselves so colorfully and so effectively. I quickly fall in love with their use of language and begin to write down what I hear in the relatively short time I spend at SDC. Some of these expressions would pop up in serious business meetings with the senior management team, out walking the park, or in conversations in the Food Office:

"You won't get no trouble outta me, and if you do, it won't be my fault."

"We've got our thumb up our ass, and our mind in Georgia."

"Hangin' in there like a hair on a cheeseburger."

"Fine as frog hair split five ways."

"Hangin' in there like a wad of bubble gum on a cat."

"Don't bury the dog with his tail sticking up out of the dirt."

"Ineffective communication is like winkin' at a girl in the dark. You may know what you're there for, but nobody else does!"

"If you want to get milk, you don't take your stool to the middle of a field and hope the cow backs up to you."

"That dog won't hunt."

"What's the use of havin' a dog, and then barkin' at yourself?"

"I'm just walkin' around to save funeral expenses."

"Oh Vinnie, if God had liked a liar, he'd a loved you to death!"

"You don't have to leave, but you can't stay here."

"Are you Ed Smith? I'm what's left of him."

"Shinin' like a diamond in a goat's ass."

Sign: "Friends welcome . . . Relatives by appointment."

"Any jackass can kick a barn down, but it takes a good carpenter to build one."

"Like putting a new dress on an old whore."

"Happier than a cat at a fish fry."

"You make more racket than a jackass in a tin barn."

"Stronger than nine acres of onions."

"When you do Spring cleaning, you find everything 'cept dead men and money."

"Be careful of the sand in her sugar."

"Plain as the nose on your face."

"Like wet dogs at a wedding."

"Too poor to paint, too proud to whitewash."

"He's got more money than a dog has fleas."

"I don't have a dog in that fight."

"You throw him out the door, he comes back through the window."

"You can put your boots in the oven, but that don't make 'em biscuits."

"They're workin' me like a *borrowed mule."

*My friend Jim Hunt would pronounce "borrowed," as "borried;" as in "I need to borry some money from my bank."

"We wait for the mule to die until we buy the tractor."

"You're going around your elbow to get to your mouth."

"I'm sweatin' like a pig that knows he's dinner."

"Dropped down quicker than a fat kid on a seesaw."

"Tougher than the back wall of a shootin' gallery."

"Tougher than a dime steak."

Late Summer 1991

In late summer my boss at Silver Dollar City asks if I'm in for the long haul. I tell him, "No." I let him know that I love the people I work with, but the culture shock of moving from a Tahoe job to the Ozarks is just too weird. Soon afterward the company generously employs the same headhunter who brought me there to help me get re-settled into another job elsewhere. Until I leave, I work on some restaurant development projects for them.

Meanwhile, Moose and I travel to the big Florida theme parks on a trip that has been planned for some time. Even though I'm not staying with the company, they send us on a very expensive research and development experience.

Fall 1991 - Roadkill, Anyone?

Popular lore has it that roadkill is regularly consumed by folks living in rural America, maybe rural anywhere. In our time living in the Ozark mountains of Missouri, I am amazed at the abundance of wildlife, but even more so by the number of dead animals scattered up and down the highways. The accumulated scenes of dead animals just about every single day on the way to work kinda gets to me on some mornings. Fresh kills constantly come into view, and after a while the blood and guts on the asphalt can be depressing.

In the beginning (the spring of 1990), seeing a military-like column of six or seven turtles marching in single file in the slow lane, of course, I can't help but wonder if all of us—the turtles and my family—are headed to the same mall in Springfield. To see so many creatures out and about "in public" is a point of curiosity for me: armadillos, deer, foxes, rabbits, raccoons, skunks, snakes, turtles, etc. I like seeing the live ones better than the alternative; well, except for the snakes. There are blacksnakes and copperheads in abundance down in the Branson area.

Early on during my first summer 'on the park' (a term used by Silver Dollar City employees to describe being at work), I watch a busboy catch a long blacksnake, interrupting its travel through an area adjacent to an outdoor dining spot. He's got it between his legs, his right hand out in front of him gripping the creature right behind the head, and his left behind him, holding it much lower down the thing's body. I watch with eyes as big as saucers, I'm sure, as this kid awkwardly makes his way thirty yards away, through the tourist traffic and nearby attractions to the edge of a steep drop where he flings the snake into the wooded abyss adjacent to the park, then quickly heads back to his station in the dining area of one of the food outlets.

The funniest animal adventure comes on a foggy morning before work. I'm running laps at Branson High School at about six o'clock. And with visibility down to maybe thirty feet, my peripheral vision keeps picking up some sort of unfamiliar movement parallel to me on the grass alongside the track. I slow and turn a bit to see two albino armadillos running along as if we're all members of the school's varsity team. Albino armadillos are way creepier than just plain old armadillos. It actually happens a number of mornings at that track.

On another occasion, during my second summer (1991) at SDC, Tom Anderson, one of our shop leads, reaches up to grab a box from a darkened supply shed shelf about six feet off the ground, and is bitten on his hand by a blacksnake. I find out about this when Tom shows up at my office, his hand wrapped in a rag, announcing in his easygoing manner that he's been bitten by a snake, and will need somebody to watch his area while he has the bite looked at by the park nurses.

But maybe the scene most illustrative of life in the Ozarks and the people who live there happens on the highway that takes me to SDC every morning. One fall day in 1991, about a quarter of a mile ahead I see a woman crossing the road and heading up the bank towards her cabin, casually holding a dead raccoon by one of its hind legs, obviously planning her dinner menu as she strolls homeward bound. No need to shop for *her* protein!

Winter 1991 - Dolly Meets Chef Moose

At some point during the winter of 1991, the brothers Jack and Pete Herschend, owners of Silver Dollar City Theme Park, are getting ready to open their own Nashville-styled Grand Old Opry show venue in Branson. The plan is to run country acts on The Nashville (cable) Channel out of there, and through their long-time friend and Dollywood partner, Dolly Parton, they get Glen Campbell to sign on as the host.

There is a flurry of celebrity visits as things are moving along towards the opening of what will become a short-lived venture for the Herschends, 'The Grand Palace.' Any sort of entertaining of these country music stars or other notables is done either at Jack's or Pete's house.

A few months before this, Moose comes to work with me at SDC. On one occasion we send him and his wife Bonnie out to cater a dinner, working out of Jack's kitchen. About 20 minutes before meal service, Dolly comes in to see what's going on. The ever-gregarious Chef Moose introduces himself and proceeds to charm her, as he does with just about everyone he ever meets, male or female.

It is important at this point that you know Moose isn't called Moose by mistake. He is 6'3," and during this time of his life his weight runs anywhere between 270 and 325. He has normal-looking legs and rear end but carries a hefty belly out front. And he is very funny, a natural comedic wit with a keen sense of timing.

After some small talk, he takes a big risk and leads Dolly Parton into this conversation:

"You know, you and I have something in common," he claims.

Dolly, intrigued, asks, "What's that, Chef?"

And Moose delivers, "Neither one of us have seen our feet in the last 20 years."

Luckily for Moose, she cracks up.

December 1991

On Pearl Harbor Day 1991, Moose and I head down to Orlando. We're to spend eight days and nights studying Universal and Disney theme parks for ideas to take back to Silver Dollar City.

We're to check into Dixie Landing, a Disney property, for the first few nights, then move over to the Grand Floridian (Disney's flagship hotel at this time) for the latter part of the visit.

The first full day of touring Universal Studios Theme Park is good. I have a connection that gets us a behind-the-scenes tour of the food production areas, which of course is a great experience for us. We also have a very nice day on the park, enjoying all that it has to offer to two guys on an unlimited expense account. We never "take advantage"—we're not *that* way—but we do have a very good time checking out the food operations and of course, the rides and attractions.

Later this night, we've got reservations at a suburban Orlando restaurant called the Bubble Room, a place that is recommended for its unique interior and inventive menu. All this to tell you that a 'classic Moose' moment occurs, an example of his lightning-fast verbal skills and humor. At the end of the meal, he flags down the waiter and the following brief exchange takes place:

Moose, being the nice guy he is, asks, "Can I talk you out of a towel?"

Waiter, being a smartass and ballbreaker with Moose the tourist, says, "Yeah, go ahead." (and stands in front of Moose waiting).

Moose, not at all tickled by this kid's disrespect, says, "OK, how 'bout I break your face?"

The kid quickly leaves and brings back a towel. And that's how it always is with the Moose: a really nice guy, rapid dry sense of humor, produces the most laughs of anybody Kunk and I hang with (and that's saying something), but when he thinks he needs to remind somebody how big he is, has no hesitation.

Late Spring 1992 – Drifting Back to Nevada

A couple of job opportunities crop up during the winter and spring, but nothing is just right, so Charlene and I decide to move back to Carson City. We sell the Branson house and hire a mover to bring our stuff back and store it while we figure out where to live. We drive one car back to Nevada, ship the other, and stay with friends until we can find a little house to rent.

A casino industry friend tells me there's nothing going on in northern Nevada, and that I need to "get my ass down to Vegas." She arranges a few interviews for me and I line up another. I do get a job at Sam's Town out of that trip, and begin working almost immediately, but after I'm there only five weeks, I get a call from the one Vegas interview that I had lined up myself. And that call takes me through some twists and turns, resulting in my becoming vice president of food and beverage at the Desert Inn Hotel and Country Club.

I go to this new job after a handful of meetings with just one guy: the seventy-three-year-old legendary gaming industry figure, Burton Cohen. We always meet in a local Jewish deli. It's always in the morning, and it's always filled with a bunch of old-timers, all of whom know Burton, but nobody knows me. If we were to meet in a casino, things might be different—and that would be a problem. I take the job knowing full well that the place is for sale, because it's owned by financier Kirk Kerkorian, who is in the process of building the world's largest hotel (the MGM Grand) on the corner of Tropicana and Las Vegas Boulevard (The Strip). Kerkorian will take several key people from the 'D.I.' to open the MGM Grand, and that's why there's an upcoming vacancy in the F&B job.

Sure enough, after I'm at the D.I. about nine months, Sheraton comes in to take over the property. I stay a few more months into the winter of 1994, but I know that I can't possibly smile every day at the guy Sheraton places there. I make a couple of calls and end up moving the family back to northern Nevada, to take a food and beverage job at the Peppermill Hotel Casino in Reno.

Back to Northern Nevada: The Peppermill

The Peppermill is an interesting experience and I work with some great people there, but after a couple of years they fire my boss, and gradually put everybody he hired, including me, on the street. And that's how I end up at family-run John Ascuaga's Nugget Hotel Casino, a few miles away in Sparks. I start there in June of 1997.

May 1998: John Ascuaga's Nugget Casino

We're a few months away from opening Restaurante Orozko at John Ascuaga's Nugget, and John decides he and his old, former right-hand operations guy, Tony Lubbers, are going to the National Restaurant Association Show in Chicago with Stephen (John's youngest son) and me. For me, this will be like being on a dog leash.

As soon as I find out that we're *all* going, I book a flight for Stephen and me, but a different plane than the one his dad and Tony will be on. A few days before the trip will be made, the old man finds out about this and is not amused. He loves an entourage, and we're going it on our own. Stephen knows damn well what I am up to and is fine with it. It's an unspoken thing. We blame it on our personal schedules, which is pretty much the truth. Besides, what John and Tony want is that Stephen and I will bond during this trip, as they now have me reporting to him. He's just a young guy, and they'd like him to learn the food business. So it's for the best that we're alone anyway.

It's about a four-hour flight, so we end up talking to each other about our prior adventures. And because both of us went to college in Colorado, although a generation apart, we have some common ground for starters. Of course, it's impossible for me to talk about those days without bringing Joel Kunkel into the conversation. Pretty soon we're making each other laugh with some crazy Colorado stories. And it's fun to make this young kid (29 at the time) laugh. He has a great joyful laugh, and is a regular guy, so it's easy to become fond of him.

We get to town and to the hotel just fine. No sooner do we check in than Stephen gets a call from his dad. It's about dinner arrangements. I've made resy's for all of us at one of my favorite Chicago joints, Frontera Grill. It's great chow, and as we're finishing up, I spot chef/owner Rick Bayless (a CIA grad) walking through the dining room. I go chat with him a bit and get him back over to our table where he signs his cookbook for each of us. This is one of those rare, happy times with John where everything is perfect, and he is kind enough to buy the book for each of us. Stephen and I leave the two older gents and take a long walk across town to hear a couple of sets at a blues club, then go back to the hotel.

The next day we meet John and Tony at the show, but remarkably we are left on our own to actually walk it. I invite Stephen to come with me to a CIA alumni mixer at the Union Club, so we head over there in early evening. As with all CIA functions, it's a very nice affair, and we run into many old friends of mine. We're talking to each other when I feel myself being lifted off the ground from behind, in a sleeper hold. I am turned around by the lifter, and it's Joel, who gives me a big hug and kiss (on the cheek). I can't believe my eyes. What a great surprise!

"What are you doing here?" I ask.

Kunk says, "Aw, I won a trip here in a drawing from the Colorado-Wyoming Restaurant Association show a few months ago. This is my girlfriend, Ann."

I tell them, "This is my boss, Stephen Ascuaga."

We get together with Marcel Desaulniers and a few others, and all go out and eat dinner together. It's a great night with old CIA friends and Stephen, a new friend.

When we're finally alone, on our way back to the hotel, Stephen says to me, "You know I thought you were just bullshitting me with all those Kunkel stories on the plane, but then I got to look into the guy's eyes, and I knew they were all true."

July 1999

It's right after the Ascuaga family puts me in charge of their warehousing and purchasing (in addition to food and beverage operations). I get a phone call from Chief Building Engineer Tom Newell on a Friday afternoon. There's an infestation of tiny black bugs out at the motor pool and carpentry shop building. Tom asks me to come out and have a look.

The building in question is a couple miles from the hotel/casino complex. It's pretty standard in the industry for large hotel/casino operations to have off-site warehousing and workshops for the trades to do their fabricating, repair work, etc. What's unusual about this situation, however, is that the 'shops' building is about 40 yards away from the main off-site warehouse structure which also happens to house Nugget Meats, the family-owned processing facility that sells meats all over northern Nevada.

I get out to the warehouse area and see that there is such a large number of the little black bugs on work benches that it appears they form a coating of sorts. This occurs in the smaller building just east of the meat plant. I am very concerned that they'll migrate to Nugget Meats in short order. I'm standing with Tom outside the smaller motor pool building, and I notice a field of about three acres just across a barbed wire fence to the south. I don't own a cell phone, and don't even know how to use one at this point but ask Tom to use his so that I can talk to our on-call contracted exterminator. I ask Terry, the head exterminator guy, to come out and give us an immediate quote on treating all of the smaller building, inside and out, and also to hit the full perimeter of the main building (warehouse and meat plant). I ask Newell to stay there and show Terry around the property, while I go back and try to discuss this with John (always a good idea when you're about to spend his money).

I get back to the office and find John. Typical of his persona, he hits the roof and just goes into a rant—and this is without even getting the quote from Terry. I ask him if he wants the job done, but he won't give me an answer. Within 30 minutes, Terry calls me at my office and quotes his price. It's something like $800 and change. Without asking John, I tell Terry to go ahead. There really is nothing to talk about. It's a Friday afternoon, and we're talking big bucks tied up in the meat inventory, not to mention the possibility of bad publicity. I'm not happy that John wants to shoot the messenger, but this is not new behavior for him.

I find Tom Newell in his office on the following Tuesday (I'm off Sunday/Mondays), and I ask him how things are looking out at the meat plant. He smirks and tells me the whole back story.

A week before the bug infestation, John is out at the motor pool building. He looks over at the field to the south, beyond the barbed wire fence, and doesn't like what he sees. He calls Newell from his car and tells him to call the owner of the adjacent field and tell the guy that his property is an eyesore for visiting Nugget Meat customers. It's tall prairie grass, and John wants the guy to have the field mowed.

So sure enough—and amazingly—the guy has the field mowed. After all, this is *the* John Ascuaga doing the asking. John's the local celebrity casino owner in Sparks, Nevada.

Apparently, after the grasses are mowed, the little black bugs from the field migrate to John's side of the fence. Nobody knew the bugs were even there in the neighboring field. Of course, the old man figures it all out and is livid. On Monday, he finds out what the exterminator charges for last Friday's work, and he then tells Tom to call the neighbor up again. Only this time he wants Newell to tell the guy that the infestation is from *his* bugs (I swear this is all true), and he wants him to pay for half of the exterminator's bill.

Newell calls the guy and tells him exactly what John says to tell him. The guy tells poor, innocent Tom, in no uncertain terms, "You tell your boss to go FUCK himself!"

I hear this story, and for only the second time in my life, literally drop onto the floor—in my suit and tie—laughing.

September 1999

John has two elephants doing the opening act in the Nugget's Celebrity Showroom for decades, but in the late '90s there's mounting pressure from animal rights groups to donate them to a zoo or wildlife sanctuary. Sadly, Bertha, the older of the pair, becomes quite ill in 1999, and arrangements are made to truck her down to the veterinarians at U.C. Davis for medical help.

The day before she's going to be transported, John asks me to take a walk with him down to the elephant house. The house was specially built years before to keep the animals safe and isolated from the public. It's located in a casino parking lot west of the property, and I've never been in it before.

It's a touching scene as I watch normally tough little John trying to comfort his very large pet. He's simultaneously talking to Bertha and reaching up, rubbing her rib area. It's a tender side of John that I only see this once, and I can't help but feel badly for him. The next day after they load her onto a trailer, she just gives out and dies before they can get her to Davis. Angel, Bertha's younger partner in showbiz, is later transported to a sanctuary. Don, their trainer, gets a job at the Seattle zoo. An era ends. It's a sad time, and a signal of the inevitable for the entire business.

October Vay-cay 1999

Who doesn't love to take some vacation time in the beautiful month of October?
But before I leave, I grab my right-hand superstar, Jim Moritz, and tell him to ask Hugh Stone to replicate the beautiful fall pumpkin display that he created when we all worked together at the Peppermill Hotel Casino during the mid-nineties. After I leave, Hugh designs a beautiful combination of pumpkin colors and varieties, along with a collection of seasonal props for placement at the entrance to our buffet. When I return from my week off, I'm very happy with the work the guys did and don't give it another thought.

Later in the morning when Jim gets to work, naturally we go over the highlights of the previous week. It is then that I find out that my absolute favorite casino food and beverage pal, Jim, gets blindsided by John Ascuaga while I'm away and not available to take the heat myself. Apparently, John has a very different view of the pumpkin display, and after questioning Jim about where the pumpkins come from (we buy them from a vendor), the old man comes unglued, telling Jim, "I could have grown them on my ranch, if you guys would have asked," adding, "If we did need to buy some, why wouldn't you call my friends at the Ferrari Farm?"

Why? Because we'd no more ask John to grow pumpkins for us than we would ask him to grow tomatoes or potatoes for the restaurants; and oh yeah, we've never heard of the Ferrari Farm. True to form, Jimmy never tells John the whole thing is my idea, and once again we have a good laugh (well mostly, *I* have a good laugh) over another of John's blasts; Jimmy taking a beating about spending a few dollars.

September 2001 - Live From New York, It's Tuesday Morning (and it's REAL)

In 1975 a new TV comedy show called Saturday Night Live is created. In the early days of the show, it typically begins with a very realistic, but somewhat surprising skit, usually sounding like a news show opening. Just when you'd begin wondering what the heck is going on, the camera zooms in on one of the actors, who looks straight into the lens, and says, "Live from New York, it's Saturday Night." And you realize that you'd once again been suckered into thinking that you were watching some real event. After a couple of weeks, the SNL opening is no longer a surprise, but it still occurs every Saturday night to this day.

On Tuesday, September 11, 2001, I find myself awake at 5:20 a.m., so I head for the "computer room," where I sit down to read my e-mail and watch the early morning news on TV. At about 5:50, I'm listening to a couple of a.m. anchors doing their usual small market shtick on Reno's ABC affiliate, channel 8, when one of them announces that we're switching to NYC where there's been a report of a plane crashing into the World Trade Center.

Sure enough, they are showing the twin towers with smoke coming out of one of them. I'm thinking as I've been trained to think, from decades ago when I was a child watching King Kong movies: *O.K., some small propeller-driven general aviation plane has crashed into the towers.* ABC is too slow in providing information. They seem confused so I switch to CNN. Immediately they begin interviewing one of their executives who describes watching the crash live from his office window in the CNN building. As he's repeating his story for the second time, the camera is on the towers off in the background, showing the growing smoke billowing out. Suddenly the guy sees that another plane is bearing down on the other, undamaged tower. He instantly, almost franticly, describes what we're all seeing LIVE on our screens. I watch stunned as a full-sized commercial passenger jet flies into the tower, a giant fireball following its entry.

Instantly, I realize our Middle East enemies are attacking NYC (there is no thought that it could be anyone else), and that I must cancel our planned 9/15 vacation flight to Seattle, because nobody's going to be flying *anywhere* real soon, and that our country is going to war. I'm thinking it's gotta be my generation's Pearl Harbor. I continue watching for the next half hour, and finally wake Charlene.

The event is indescribably shocking to have witnessed, so horrific and so sad in its result, yet from a military standpoint (and I hate to say it), brilliant in its planning and execution.

For several days, the skies over the entire U.S. are empty of non-military aircraft. And so reminiscent of the days immediately following the assassination of JFK, the nation is glued to its TVs.

On Friday afternoon at work, John arranges for priest friend Father Frank to hold a prayer service outside the building, at the base of our flagpole. Afterwards, The Lettermen (I think), our Celebrity Room headliners for the weekend, lead us in singing "America." It is 'a moment,' that's for sure. A few hours later Charlene and I are at a surprise birthday dinner party for John's daughter Michonne. The family likes me (well, at the moment); I am one of only three management people invited from the casino. But three years and three weeks from now, after seven years at the Nugget, and after my departments contribute more profit than they ever have in any previous year, the family will end the party for me because, while I usually get along well with the kids, John and I are just not very compatible. We have very different values.

Some People's Kids - Casino Incident Reports

You'd be justified in thinking that I'm making this stuff up, but the details of the incidents that appear on any casino's 24-hour security reports are many times just plain unbelievable. And depending on the demographics of a particular club, they go from unbelievable to bizarre to, *Yeah, ok, I get that it happened **there**.* So without naming names, or getting into the kind of information that would identify a particular casino, here are a few summaries (please understand that while many, many of these are suit worthy claims, after investigation a bunch prove to lack substance):

♦ All manner of bodily injury reports concerning foreign matter in food, insect bites, food spills, food-borne illness, allergic reactions to various foods, burns, broken teeth, slips/falls, cuts/lacerations, etc.; also, allergic reaction to dealers' perfume, tipped-over wheelchairs, etc.

♦ All manner of car break-ins, property loss, and/or property damage in casino parking lots and garages.

♦ All manner and locations of homeless sleepers, *and yes, campers* in otherwise unoccupied space: in banquet rooms, under pianos, in unlocked cars on casino property, in closed restaurants (under tables in booths), in keno chairs.

♦ All manner of mischief such as fire alarms being pulled, vandalism causing property damage, poop found in hotel swimming pools (they then have to be closed-down, completely emptied, cleaned, and re-filled), poop found outside hotel room doors, graffiti, fires started in public restrooms, people jamming public toilets with wads of TP to intentionally clog them, hard-boiled eggs thrown out of hotel room windows, bomb threats, urinaters.

♦ All manner of property loss from hotel rooms, mix-ups with valet parking (missing cars).

♦ All manner of sexual activity—none in the privacy of hotel rooms, but all taped of course, because video surveillance is everywhere.

♦ All manner of employee theft and embezzlement.

♦ Personal property damage due to food and drink spills/property loss due to claimed theft.

♦ Theft from slot players' buckets/racks (back when coins were still used), pocketbooks, etc.

♦ Rapes/brawls/fights/domestic battery.

♦ Property damage in convention/meeting room areas (mostly cause by people/machinery moving equipment in or out).

♦ All manner of gaming cheats, con artists, pickpockets, scammers talking people out of their money (in a slot area for instance, when coin racks were still in use: "M'am, let me take those two heavy racks to the cashier for you. You just keep playing, and I'll bring back a couple of one hundred-dollar bills for you)."

♦ Counterfeit bills being passed, slugs in slot machines (when coins were still used).

♦ Swimmers not registered as hotel guests using the pool(s).

♦ Medical situations such as heart attacks, chest pains, strokes, dizziness, diabetic issues of all sorts, people passing out, injuries resulting from brawls, injuries resulting from domestic abuse.

♦ Exclusion of individuals threatening staff members, harming staff members, inappropriately touching staff members, smelling bad, "not contributing to the welfare of the casino," consuming discarded beverages in the casino, inspecting slot machines for unearned credits (formerly sea gulling or silver mining when slot players used coins or tokens), trespassing, verbal disturbances.

♦ Mechanical problems with elevators, escalators, HVAC, kitchen equipment. Fire suppression systems being accidently activated, etc.

♦ Solicitation (usually sexual favors).

- Dine & Dashers, Non-payers walking through a buffet line and snagging food, even putting it in filthy slot coin cups.
- Lost and Found items, including cash.
- Minor and major fires.
- Deaths: they happen, and whether they are medically brought on, or suicides, or homicides, most casinos refrain from placing them in the regular reports.

OK, I lied. Here are a couple of security reports that I can't resist providing just a bit more detail:

- "John Doe (town of residence) was excluded from (casino) for choking his wife in (restaurant name)."
- "On (date) I was informed by (maître d') of a (subject) urinating on the floor of a kitchen storage room. This was the third day this has happened. Subject enters the room, goes to his immediate right, lays a towel on the floor (in the corner), and urinates on the towel.
  - On (next day) the chairs in this room were arranged so someone could observe this area without being seen.
  - At (time) on (date) I positioned behind a stack of chairs in the (restaurant) storage area. At approximately (time) a male subject entered the

room, closed the door ¾ of the way, turned off the lights, and proceeded to urinate into the corner behind the door.

- o Upon leaving the room, I followed the subject to the adjacent room (kitchen) where he washed his hands. Subject wore a name badge, (name).

♦ (Name of officer)

♦ (Name of subject) was brought to the security office, where conversation was taped. (Name) admitted to urinating on the floor. He was suspended and told to come in and see the Executive Chef and Vinnie Oakes."

♦ (Name of Security Supervisor & Signature)

♦ "Jane Doe (town of residence) claims that $80 in credits she unknowingly left behind in the (Name of Area) of the (machine name) machine at Bank # XXX were taken by the white male subject who had coerced her into playing the machine by 'guaranteeing' her a win."

♦ (This one because of an incorrect spelling by the reporting security officer): "Jane Doe of (town) claims that "a cryogenic tank filled with seamen (sic) had been tipped over while under valet's custody." *(I sure hope the "seamen" regained their footing. VO)*

♦ "John Doe (town of residence) claims his golf bag was missing from the bed of his (vehicle brand) truck. Value of missing items was $250.00." *(Wait, you park in a casino garage and leave your golf bag in the bed of your truck? VO)*

♦ "John Doe (town of residence) claimed that shoeshine stand employee (name) had threatened to put his foot in his derriere."

A few things quickly learned while working in casinos:

1. Cameras are everywhere. Sometimes, even people who know this fact forget and do things they later regret.
2. NEVER leave anything of value in *any* hotel room or a parked car.
3. *An awful lot of people* who are walking free around these United States ought to be locked up in jail or prison. *You have NO IDEA.*

Winter 2006 - A Surprising Change

The Nugget job is over and I am now sixty years old, beginning to experience firsthand the difficulty of a "senior" job search. After several months of doing nothing, I begin volunteering at the Food Bank of Northern Nevada. Ironically, I learn about the Food Bank from Stephen Ascuaga who volunteers there during the 2003 holiday season.

After volunteering for just short of a year there is an opportunity for full-time work. Although it takes them an astounding three and a half months to get their act together, I begin working at FBNN on March 13, 2006.

There is a lot to learn. I'm involved with a world in which I have no prior experience other than putting cans of food in boxes. It's way more complicated than that, and for a social justice organization bent on helping those in need, an effective 'onboarding' of new employees is not part of the culture at the time of my initiation. Nonetheless, I somehow manage to survive the first few years, and settle in after creating a sensible day-to-day role for myself as the director of food procurement. After the two-legged problems go away, I begin to really enjoy what I do, and for the most part most days are rewarding, fun, and when COVID-19 comes along, filled with an exciting, pressure-packed roller coaster ride of challenges.

February 2010 - Heart Attack(s)

On the morning of February 18, I have a good workout at the gym and get home for a shower. After I am dressed, I start gathering up my camera gear and waiting for my oatmeal to finish cooking. I have taken the day off to photograph the eagles that annually migrate from Oregon down to the Carson Valley, near Minden, Nevada. It's about 7 a.m., and as I'm drifting between the family room and the kitchen, loading my camera backpack and stirring my oatmeal on the stove, I'm getting an unusual feeling: a gassy fullness in my chest causes me to try "burping it out." I am burping away and packing the bag for a few minutes. But then, before I can begin eating, the burping becomes a bit acidic and then I start getting a sweaty feeling from the neck up. It takes a lot for me to sweat, and I'm pretty sure I know what this is. For a nanosecond I look at Charlene's closed bedroom door and instantly dismiss the idea of asking for her help. She's asleep. I quickly get in the car and drive to St. Mary's Hospital. Along the way I remember what all the little brochures say about heart attack and begin coughing to try to stave off the effects by "lining my lungs."

I park in the ER lot at the hospital, walk in and tell the lady at the admitting desk that I think I might be having a heart attack. Of course, I have to produce my ID and insurance cards, but soon enough they take me into an examination room and begin assessing my condition. A chest x-ray is ordered (portable machine), and blood pressure and pulse are rechecked, because both are perfect out in the ER. A nurse with a clipboard begins asking, "Do you smoke? Do you work out? How often?"

Always seeing the humor in a situation, I'm thinking, *what is this, a singles bar?*

The doc orders a Plavix IV, but there's none of the blood thinner in the Saint Mary's ER. *"Do you want me to run down to the pharmacy?"* the orderly asks. Doc says, *"Yeah."* but he's not happy about the necessity of a 'run.'

I'm thinking facetiously, why would you have heart attack meds in the ER?

They decide to take me to the Cath Lab, and everything moves into high gear. As I'm lying there, pressure increases in my chest, but no pain. And then, as they're beginning to shave my upper right groin, prepping me for catheter insertion, my leg begins uncontrollable shaking, then my whole body starts to flip around like a fish out of water. They insert an IV into my hand and knock my ass out; then they take pictures and implant a stent.

They keep me at St. Mary's for about four days, and a week later I go back to work. But while I'm at home, I am unsure of how to let friends know what has happened. It's a bit of an awkward thing for me to approach. I'm not looking for people to feel sorry for me. Then I hit upon an idea to head the email with: 'Lucky Day.' And I describe not only that I survived the heart attack, but that just before the symptoms I happened to put on a brand new pair of underpants after my post-gym shower, and isn't it *lucky*, because in humorous stories every little boy's mother tells him to "wear clean underwear, just in case…"

A number of people think that the email is some of my typical kidding around, but Kunk knows better, and immediately sends this:

****

From: Kunkel Joel
Subject: Re: Lucky Day
Date: February 26, 2010 9:46:14 AM PST
To: Oakes Vinnie

doc; i take it that this is not a joke. i hope all is well. my thoughts and prayers are with you. Love, joel

****

****

From: Oakes Vinnie
Subject: Re: Lucky Day
Date: Fri, 26 Feb 2010 10:12:15 -0800
To: Kunkel Joel
Not a joke. But they put a stent in there, so I'll ride it out.
No weakness, because they got to it so quickly, so virtually
no damage, but they told me to take the week off from work.
"Oh, do I really have to?" Shucks!
XXX,
Yo' Roomie

****

From: Kunkel Joel
Subject: Re: Lucky Day
Date: February 26, 2010 10:23:27 AM PST
To: Oakes Vinnie
that's great, well not great but you know what i
mean. take care of yourself doc, i need you in this world.
you know it's all about me, don't you dare go first....
the kunk

****

. . . and in retrospect, if that wasn't strange enough—ok,
spooky—here's what he sends two days before he leaves us

(remember those Irish folksingers we love in the New Haven days? The Clancy Brothers, his favorites, are the most famous of all of them. Google them if you don't know.).

****

From: Kunkel Joel
Subject:
Date: March 14, 2010 11:33:25 PM PDT
To: Oakes Vinnie
hey doc; hope your doing well, here's one we missed, cut his last album at 73.
http://www.youtube.com/watch?v=VUgEYl4V_AE&feature=related
the kunk

****

This is the last I hear from The Kunk. Days later, after he doesn't show up for work, the Bluffton, S.C., cops call Joel's older brother, Jay, asking for permission to break into his apartment. They find his body on the floor slumped up against his bed. Heart attack. And of course, Jay calls to tell us the news.

I am truly happy for him, that he is able to "cash in his chips" the way he does. It is a shocker to hear of his passing and I am still consumed with flashbacks and grief, but he has peace forever, and that's a great thing.

So Rest in Peace, My Brother. You'll always be missed, but never forgotten.

In Memoriam

This is the memorial that I write for his family and our mutual friends.

Joel Alan Kunkel

April 19, 1943—March 16, 2010

(Written to be read at his memorial service)

My mind is flooded with unstoppable memories of him: attacks of overwhelming sadness, and of smiles, too, all triggered by the finality that we will never speak again, never laugh again, never share the many common bonds of brotherly love and mutual respect that held us close in some wonderful magnetic force for 47 years.

We met in 1963. And over the next several years before we moved away from each other, we shared so much. And in many ways that sharing continued, no matter how far apart we lived. We shared a love of working with food, and both went to The Culinary Institute of America (in New Haven, at the time), he ahead of me. He held the record for the fastest cake decoration job for the Yale Birthday Cake Association, and he graduated seventh in his class. We had the same teachers and took the same classes. His skills as a Pastry Chef, in the early years, and an Executive Chef later on, were exceptional. During the time we spent in or near CIA, we both learned to enjoy Irish folk music, and loved to go listen to the live shows in the little basement bars of New Haven. Later in Colorado we became big fans of bluegrass. He bought a banjo, took lessons, and became more than competent in the difficult style of frailing.

We roomed together at The University of Denver (aka DU). We studied together and we discovered a love for the American West together. We took long car trips, often spending nights in one of our cars. We hunted and we fished together, and we chased girls and partied together. Oh, did we chase girls and party. And truth be told, we also got involved in one heck of a lot of mischief and mayhem together. It was all insane, all of it. Decades afterward we'd be talking on the phone and he would often say something like, "I was sitting in my car, at a red light the other day, and I just started laughing out loud at some of the f----n s--t we used to do."

"Yeah, I know what you mean, man, same here," I answer.

We worked at many of the same places, mostly for the same bosses, in our younger days when we were learning the biz. Sometimes we worked side by side, and other times we experienced those same places separately, but we shared it all in our backgrounds: The Harborside Inn on Martha's Vineyard, and Restaurant Associates; and Le Profil, and the Royal Platte River Yacht Club, both in Denver. We designed and set up Soup's On together, again, in Denver. When I opened Stouffer's Denver Inn, he came over and helped me put together a grand opening buffet table. His work on that occasion was remarkable for its creativity, speed, and flawless execution. He helped me get jobs, and I helped him get jobs. I worked Steamboat, and then he worked Steamboat. Then there was the R.A. stint in Ann Arbor with Moose and Burke, working with him; and where he met my sister, while she was at U. of Michigan. The guy could do anything, and I mean anything in a restaurant. And he did it better than any of us.

He was an artist, a person who was never formally educated in any aspects of art, but who naturally came by an appreciation for works well executed, and who had a God-given ability to create his own stuff, whether on a cake or a sketchpad, or whatever. And when I would e-mail a set of my recent photographs, or other craftwork to him, if I got an attaboy from him, it was worth something special to me, because that praise came from a guy whose skills I couldn't match.

He was as badass a dude as I've ever hung out with. He enjoyed fighting, for almost no reason, and you knew no matter what the odds were in a given situation, he'd have your back. One night at The Yacht Club five guys decided they were going to rough up Billy Gross, a college kid that was working as Joel's Assistant Manager. Joel, working in his office, hears a ruckus out in the saloon. He walks out to these guys with a baseball bat in his right hand and a large can of mace in the other. Their backs are facing Joel. He screams a very loud, "HEY!" They all turn around, and he asks, "Who's first? No? Then get the f—k outta here." And they did. FIVE GUYS! And I think Kunk was just a little bit disappointed that he didn't get to try out that combination of the Louisville Slugger and mace.

He didn't like everybody he'd ever met, but if he liked you, he was the most sharing and generous friend you could have. He really did teach me, by his own example, how to share. That, in and of itself, was a gift he gave me soon after we met. And there were many more gifts, some tangible, some intangible. When we lived together at DU he had to work hard to pay the bills. It wasn't easy for him. But with all his financial struggles, as an example of his thoughtfulness, he always found the time and money to put together occasional care packages for his Bridgeport buddy (I think it was Bill Devon, or John, but I can't be sure) who was over in Vietnam. I learned an awful lot from Joel, and much of the time he never even knew that he was teaching me.

We also shared our wedding ceremonies. He was my best man in my second wedding; I was his in his first.

He never wore a wristwatch in all the years that I knew him. He used to drive me nuts with being late. He was 20 minutes late for my wedding—and he was the best man! And could he sleep! In spite of having an alarm clock loud enough to wake a firehouse crew four city blocks away, he needed (and requested) my screaming or several kicks on his bed frame to actually awaken.

He was one of the brightest and most gifted people I've ever known. The guy could do just about anything. But he never was going to be a corporate suit dealing with the intangibles of management. Don't get me wrong—he was certainly a leader, but he just liked the nitty gritty of working in the trenches. He had those gifted hands and was compelled to use them.

He became a talented chef, but along the way he learned it all, and excelled in anything he touched.

You know Joel quit high school when he was 16, and he kind of drifted around before he figured out what to do. Even after he discovered a passion for working with food, and graduated from CIA, it wasn't until he ran a jackhammer on a job in California, that he realized he needed to go back and get an education. I often wonder if Jay knew what he was doing when he 'helped' his younger brother find a job getting his brain rattled, and his whole body shaken running a jackhammer all day long. According to Joel, it didn't take very long before he realized he ought to get back into school. And it didn't hurt that he got a little push eastward from some law enforcement types in California, who took issue with his love of guns.

So this high school dropout goes back to Bridgeport and signs up to do his junior and senior years (academic courses) of high school simultaneously. He gets ALL A's and B's;

and by the way, he's working full time at night as the Pastry Chef at Restaurant Associates' Mermaid Tavern, with occasional evening work on the floor as the maitre d'. As I said, the guy could do anything. They wrote up his story in the Bridgeport paper. He was awarded a Centennial Scholarship to The University of Denver, and was accepted to Cornell's School of Hotel Administration (the finest school in the world for hotel and restaurant management), but was insulted because Cornell gave him a 'conditional' acceptance, and so he went to DU.

For the most part he was highly successful academically at DU but became disenchanted and impatient with the student life and its constant financial pressures. So he left, to continue working with food and restaurants, always doing impressive work, always with a passion and a love for good food, good times, and good friends. The demands of being grown-ups eventually pulled us geographically apart, and life rolled on. But we never were really apart, and so it is now. He'll always be with me.

I had a heart attack on February 18th, and after about 10 days I let a few friends know what had happened. I did it in a humorous way, and some just thought I was having a bit of internet fun, but he knew better, and as you've read, he left me with a light-hearted demand that will be with me forever (FYI, he used to call me "Doc"): "Take care of yourself Doc, I need you in this world. You know it's all about me, don't you dare go first...."

January 2012 - Clapple at Apple

This is a story about how to do things right in business. It has nothing really to do with my life story, except that it is something more people ought to know about . . . and YOU are those people. And it should come as no surprise that the star of the story is Apple Computer.

Soon after Apple puts a store into Reno's Summit Sierra Mall, (c.2005) I begin taking lessons there. They are one-on-one—just an instructor and me for one hour at a time. And it's very, very worthwhile for a non-techie like me.

Over the years I go there, I meet a handful of instructors who can handle teaching the photographic software that I use. Some move on to other careers, one or two get promoted within the store, but my favorite is Hillary, a sweet kid somewhere in her late twenties. She is patient, encouraging, and kind. After several months of working together, she gets promoted and I can no longer take lessons from her.

About a year later, my old Denver/Steamboat friend Jay, who works at Apple, tells me Hillary is getting promoted again: to assistant manager at a new store down in Vegas.

Hopefully, I'm thinking, I will get to say, "Goodbye, good luck, and thanks again," before she actually leaves.

One day, weeks after I learn she is leaving, I happen to be taking a one-on-one lesson. The store is very crowded, and there's a bit of a commotion at the back of the store. Apple staff members near the back are beginning to clap . . . a very slow clap. I look up, but can't see what's going on, so I ask my instructor what's happening. He tells me it's Hillary's last day; she's leaving the store for good at this very moment. As she makes her way through the store, she's taking a path that will go right past me at my worktable. The clapping gets louder, more intense, and faster. As more of the staff now realize what's going on, they stop what they're doing—selling, teaching, whatever—forming up in lines on each side of the store's depth. She stops where I stand. We wordlessly hug and kiss, tears beginning to form in her eyes, and she continues toward the front, the noise now deafening; customers who have no idea what's going on are joining in on the applause. It is a moving experience (no pun intended), and I'll never forget it—not just because it is so nice to see how much they all love this girl, but because it's part of the company culture, something they create, and like many things Apple does, no other company can pull it off with the equivalent panache.

A little more than a year later, I'm talking with Jessie, another of my former teachers—my first—who is now in management, a very talented, bright, fun, photographic instructor, and I tell her about my impressions of that last day of Hillary's.

Her response, "Yup, we clap 'em all in, and we clap 'em all out."

I'm surprised, and ask, "All of 'em?"

She nods, "Yup, all of 'em."

The entire staff's clapping is the first day's greeting for newbies, and the last thing anyone leaving from their job in that store will remember. Maybe their send-off won't be as loud or as long as Hill's, but still . . . how can you beat that kind of goodbye?

Speaking of doing things right in business...

It's ironic to me that people who are so caring about feeding the hungry can be so inconsiderate about sharing space with co-workers. At some point a few years after we move into the beautiful new food bank building, I've had enough of people leaving their messes in our staff lunchroom, and I tape this note to one of the cupboard doors:

> **To whomever leaves crumbs, coffee grounds, and stains on the countertops:**
>
> If you don't know how to properly wipe-down a countertop, please come see me. I'll be glad to show you.
>
> If you're too important to clean up your mess, please come and see me. It would be an honor to meet you.
>
> ***Vinnie Oakes***
>
> *I will always love this message!*
> *Sue*

My friend, Sue Eckes, wanting to keep the peace, took it down after a couple of weeks, but unbeknown to me, saved it. Then, when she retired, she left it for me with an attached Post-It note.

At some point pretty soon, it'll be time to say "Goodbye" to the Food Bank of Northern Nevada, get two rocking chairs for the little front porch and enjoy all of life's good memories. In the meantime, I just want to leave you with a handful of vignettes and some remarkable big and little coincidences that occurred along the way . . .

Unforgettable Moments – The Desert Inn – Las Vegas

- One Sunday night at the D.I. we have a bunch in from Taiwan, probably fewer than two dozen players. They go through 21 bottles of Louis XIII cognac. I have to borrow a case and a half from my counterpart at Caesar's. Current retail cost at Total Wine per bottle is $3,600. They probably take half of the bottles home in their baggage.

- In early winter of 1993, I buy a case of 1982 Chateau Petrus from a San Francisco wine broker for $27,000, and it is all for comps: to be given away one bottle at a time. Again, most of it probably goes right into suitcases. That would be just a bit under $49,000 in 2020 dollars.

- There is a guy who used to fly up on his private plane from Mexico. Somehow he gets my name and begins calling me during his flights. In one of our early conversations, he says, "I'll be there in an hour and a half. I want you to put some chocolate in my room that I've never tasted before." This is a guy who could lose or win $2 to 2 and a half million on Saturday night. So, "Yes, sir."

♦ The last time I deal with him, he calls me for an early room service breakfast for his son and him the following morning: scrambled eggs, toast, orange juice, coffee, and a pound of Osetra caviar. Who orders a pound of caviar for two people at breakfast? *That* guy does. So, again, "Yes, sir."

Did You Ever Live in Seagate? - Life's Coincidences & Connections

We have a family joke about my father when I am growing up: whenever we go on a vacation trip, my father is continually striking up conversations with strangers, and frequently finding that he has some small connection to them. Often he is off doing something which takes him temporarily away from us, such as checking us into a motel, paying at a gas station, golfing, etc. The most frequent "coincidence" being that the person with whom he'd spoken had lived in or knew someone who lived in the little resort village of Seagate on the ocean side of Brooklyn, near Coney Island. This was the place where my parents met in the 1930s, so it has special meaning for my father. But after he meets two or three people from Seagate, over the course of our travels, we always give him a hard time when he begins a story about meeting someone. My mother would say, "Oh, another person from Seagate, Al?" And then, of course I jump in for a shot or two. Merilee is too nice for this sort of kidding aimed at our father, and rarely participates. But we're just kidding him.

For example, my parents are on vacation in Scandinavia. While in Oslo, Norway, they run into Seymour Zabalski, a Teaneck guy and local Chrysler dealer who is a friend, and from whom my father buys several cars—for himself and others (with their money, of course). Later, on the same trip, in Bergen they are in a restaurant for dinner and find that the only way they can be seated is if they share a table with strangers. The strangers agree to the arrangement, as do my parents. The guy turns out to be my father's kindergarten classmate!

So all that background is to tell you that maybe I inherit this business of having coincidences in my life. There are several. I wish I could remember all of them. But some of the ones that I can remember will make some readers think, 'That couldn't have really happened. Only in the movies.'

In all honesty, I don't know that my life is so unique; it just seems that people's paths cross in strange ways, or as the saying goes, 'Truth is stranger than fiction.' Maybe this kind of stuff just happens to *everybody*. I don't know, but these things begin occurring to me when I'm a young adult in the 1960s.

Coincidences - You Can't Make This Stuff Up

New Year's Eve in Times Square – c.1956

This is a story about somebody else's coincidence, but it's a pretty good one, and I was connected to him in the 70s, so I put it in this decade.

When I work for Marty Sussmane at Steer Palace (Madison Square Garden), he is 36 years old, and as I've mentioned, about 300 lbs. I don't know what he looked like in his early twenties, but I'm confident that he was big and a force to be reckoned with. Marty tells this story:

It's New Year's Eve, circa 1956, at Times Square. He's on college vacation, taking his fiancé Kay out to the movies before a late dinner. They are waiting in line in the chilly night air. Like a lot of young people in this era, Kay is smoking. Some wiseass in need of a smoke comes along with his buddies and grabs the cigarette from her lips. Marty takes issue with this act of rudeness, aka disrespect, and beats up pretty good on the kid. Marty and Kay then get their tickets and enjoy the rest of the evening.

It's about two weeks later, and Kay's younger brother returns to his dorm hundreds of miles away, at Ohio State.

He and a few friends are talking about what they do over the Christmas vacation. This guy does that, another guy saw this, etc. One of them says, "Well, I got attacked by a gorilla in Times Square when I tried to steal a cigarette from some girl."

Kay's brother looks at the guy, and says, "That wasn't a gorilla, that was my future brother-in-law, and the girl was my sister!"

Harry Feuerherm at The Yacht Club Denver, c.1973-74

After Kunk and I do our stints at the Royal Platte River Yacht Club, two crazies, Johnny Borg and Wayne Dunstan, take over in the kitchen. Both are pretty unique characters and have their own stories (maybe another time for those). Every once in a while, I drop in for a visit, and on one occasion, Wayne tells me there's a guy from Teaneck who knows me, who is also cooking there. He tells me when I can find the guy at the job.

I go back a few days later, and it's Harry Feuerherm (from my THS Class of 1962), whose dad owns the Teaneck Diner while we are in high school. Harry tells me he's got a degree in chemical engineering, but he's decided to just see the country for a while. He travels with a dog and lives in the back of a pick-up truck/camper combo ("Travels with Charley?"). I see him every once in a while on my Yacht

Club visits, and then he moves on. But it's pretty strange to see him there that first time. He could choose to work at just about any other restaurant in Denver, and I wouldn't run into him!

A Late Summer Business Trip, 1975

At some point during the short time I spend at Shakey's Inc., I fly out of Denver to L.A. on business. I'm there to meet with the presidents of two companies: one is the giant food distributor Rykoff (since gobbled-up by US Foods), the other is Elster's, which builds walk-in refrigerators.

The afternoon I fly in, recently married Mer picks me up at LAX and we drive to a restaurant where her husband Zan and his kids meet us for pizza and spaghetti.

The next day I meet first with Rykoff President Roger Coleman, then get driven over to meet with the Elster guys. These meetings, when you've traveled to get there—always, and I mean *always*—start off with the same polite small talk: "When did you get in? How was your flight? Where are you staying?"

This particular conversation with one of the Elster brothers, who is a very warm and friendly guy, seems to have legs, and so, not ready to get down to business, he continues with more questions, "Oh, so you're staying with your sister and her husband. Where do they live? And what do they do?"

Now this guy is developing a freaky look on his face, and asks, "Your brother-in-law is the Psych Department Chair at Cedars? What's his name?"

"Zan Sperber," I answer.

At this point the guy almost needs to be physically restrained. He yells—I mean YELLS—for his brother who is in a nearby office. He can't believe this is happening and has to share it. And while we wait a few seconds for the brother to arrive, he tells me, "Dr. Sperber is my therapist!"

The guy was right to look freaky! What are the odds?

Katie Slingerland

Back in N.J. when I'm 14 I get juiced into a job caddying at the golf club in Englewood. It's summertime and toward the end of July there's an annual youth tournament at the course. It's sponsored by the Star Ledger, Newark's newspaper. It's a pretty well-known event and creates a certain amount of excitement among teen golfers (boys only, back in the 1950s) every year. Bobby Cannon is an amazing athlete, so it's no surprise that he signs up for the tournament. I caddy for him, but he doesn't win. The son of a local North Jersey club pro named George Slingerland wins. Bobby would later proudly coach his own son to victory in the N.J. High School Golf Championships when Matt is only a junior.

About 24 years later, I'm at a youth soccer game up at Lake Tahoe, watching my David play on the same team with a little girl who has a familiar name, and it turns out that her dad is George Slingerland Jr, same guy who won that tournament back in 1958. He is a casino host right across the street from me, over at Harvey's—about 24 years and 1,800 miles from that golf course in Englewood, N.J.

Crazy!

The 60 Minutes Connection – Part One

In the late spring of 1980, Herbert (Exec. Chef at Harrah's Tahoe) asks me to interview a guy he thinks he'd like to hire as a sous chef in the Sierra Restaurant. It's an unusual interview because the guy is an Irishman, and here in America we don't exactly revere food prepared by people who learn to cook in the British Isles. He's a barrel-chested bull of a guy, maybe 5'8" or 10; pleasant to speak with, not overly friendly, but a nice enough person. For the job that needs filling, a coffee shop sous chef, he should be fine. So we hire the man, and as I would do with any new hire in that capacity, I check in with him every few days to make sure all is going well. And it is, but after about three weeks he's gone. In a building which at the time has 4,400 employees, there's just so much time you can spend wondering/worrying about what happened to so-and-so. You move on, fill the slot, and keep things going in the right direction.

369

About eight months later, it's a Sunday night and I'm home watching 60 Minutes, and Mike Wallace is interviewing our guy (only shown from behind), the Irish chef who scooted on us. I can't believe my eyes or my ears, but this dude is a renegade IRA lieutenant, on the run and hiding from them. He's been a hit man, a pro, and you just don't retire from that field. As soon as I'm sure it is definitely our guy, I grab the phone and call Herb at home.

All I say is, "Hey Herbert, are you watching 60 Minutes?"

All he says is, "Yeah, that's the guy."

Only in the movies . . . unbelievable!

Layne Holmes – Another Popper Upper

I work for Layne Holmes at Village Inn Pancake House Corporate Offices in Denver. Strange guy, a sort of hipster, a year or two younger than me—a smooth talker (BS'er) with whom I always get along very well. But somehow you have to figure this guy is carrying around a few stories that you just are never going to hear.

It's the winter of 1974, and Layne's nowhere to be found. He simply disappears from Village Inn. Without him around, I have to deal with a cranky old curmudgeon named Jim Mola, the founder of the company.

Fast forward about thirteen years, and I'm at Harrah's-Tahoe. One late afternoon maybe in 1987, I get a call from a bartender at the Cabaret Lounge, who tells me there's a guy wanting to say hi to me. I go down there, and it's Layne Holmes. He lives across the lake over in Incline Village and is with a client of his. He is doing consulting on the guy's new restaurant. I never ask him about his disappearance back in 1974. People have their reasons (just as when a very good friend once asks me for the best criminal defense lawyer in Reno; I never ask for details). We have a nice visit, and he pops in every few months over the next couple of years.

Fast forward even more—another 14 or 15 years—and now I hear from a Sausage Factory (Carson City) salesman that Layne sends his regards. He's selling meat for the company up at the Lake. We talk on the phone a couple of times, and then when I've moved on to the Food Bank, I hear he's died from some terminal illness. But I have a feeling that he'll turn up again. That's just the way it is with Layne Holmes. Nice guy. And like Jay Margulies, he just keeps popping up in my life. This isn't so much a coincidence as an example of the constant weaving into and out of my life that can and does happen with people connected to the food business. It's an illustration what a small world the food business is.

"John the Greek"

"John the Greek" is Marty Sussmane's Assistant Restaurant Manager for most of the time I am at Steer Palace at Madison Square Garden. After I move to Denver, excepting a quick phone call or two to Sous Chef Ralphie in 1971, a couple of 15-minute visits in the late 70s, when I'm dashing in and out of the city, and the brief time I am involved with the Emerson's Ltd. grand jury, I have no contact with anyone from my Madison Square Garden experience.

One day in 1985, when I'm working at Harrah's-Tahoe, I get a call from one of the bartenders that somebody wants to see me down on the casino floor. I am pleasantly shocked to see it's "John the Greek." After leaving New York, the guy moves to the Walnut Creek area and makes a lot of money selling houses. He likes to gamble at Harrah's, and at one point, because he is an old restaurant guy, asks about the person running the restaurants. Neither of us can believe that we find each other in this chance encounter with fate. He comes to visit from the Bay Area every so often, and once we have a great time getting our old Steer Palace friends Marty, Virginia, and Ralphie, on the phone, all of whom are still working together in a Manhattan restaurant.

I sometimes wonder how many people I know from my past, yet don't get to see, who visit Harrah's-Tahoe during my ten years in the building.

It's OK to Look at Someone's Face During an Elevator Ride

One Saturday afternoon in maybe 1988, I get on the elevator heading up to the 18th floor restaurants at Harrah's-Tahoe. There is already a couple in the car, and when I look at the woman, there is a vague recognition in both our eyes. I have to ask, *"Do I know you?"*

She replies," I think I know you too."

It's the former Voris Mitchell, who is my friend Albie White's girlfriend when we all are at DU. I take Voris and her husband to dinner that night and we have a nice visit. We stay in touch via the internet and get together again years later when she visits Reno while I'm working at the Food Bank.

The Larimer Square Crazies - Nora Jones (No, not THE Norah Jones)

At some point within my first couple of years at Harrah's, I am having a casual conversation with Beverage Department Secretary Nora, whose office is one door down the hallway from mine. The subject goes to where we both live before coming to the lake, and when I tell her Denver, she asks me an improbable question. (At the time there are maybe 1.4 million people living in the Denver metro area;

it's the 21st largest city in the U.S.). She says, "Oh, I have an uncle there. Do you know Dennis Cassidy?"

I can't believe this. Dennis, a great guy, is one of several characters I know mostly through Kunk, down at Larimer Square. I like him. He's a big, friendly, beer-drinking Irishman, who (before I met him), Joel described as having "hands like hams." This is an important point to Kunk, because when fights break out with strangers in the Yacht Club bar, it is good to know which locals one can call on for a little help.

And so it goes: It's a very small world . . . at least *my part of it* is.

60 Minutes Redux:

Charlene and I are on a rare vacation without our kids. It's about 1985, and we're down in the Carmel area. We have our bikes with us and leave the seaside, heading north for a couple days of touring the Napa Valley. We stop to see the Mission at San Juan Bautista. But as I'm making sure that the bikes are secured to the car, I accidentally reset one of the combination locks to an unknown number. I'm fit to be tied, and I cannot relax and go see the mission until it's dealt with. So we drive around the town and soon find the little police station. We make the acquaintance of the police chief, who kindly offers to help us. He's an unusual character, a middle-aged sort of cowboy-dressed guy, with the boots, the weathered straw cowboy hat, and a big six-shooter strapped to his hip. He has us follow him down to a local garage, where he walks in, borrows a bolt cutter, and takes care of business. I give him a twenty for his trouble, and we head back to park at the mission. Now all I have to do is find a good hardware store to replace the lock on the way to San Francisco, where I want to see a Richard Avedon photo exhibit at the Museum of Modern Art before we move on to the wine country.

About two years later we're watching 60 Minutes one Sunday night, and there's the gun-toting police chief from San Juan Bautista. He's being featured in a Morley Safer piece—all because of the "cannon" he openly carries around in his cowhand holster in a quiet little town in California.

What's with this connection to 60 Minutes? Are they following me?

Eric & Oliver Saucy

After graduation from DU, I end up at the Newark Airport with Restaurant Associates. I'm very disappointed, because I've been promised a back-of-the-house management role in Manhattan. But between that promise, which occurs during Christmastime of my senior year, and my August graduation, new guys take over at RA. Joe Baum and the Cornell crowd, who consider me one of theirs, are gone.

They put me in the infamous (and sometimes famous) management training program at Newark Airport. Jim Cohee, when he's interviewing me for my first food and beverage job years later in Denver, would refer to it as "the boot camp of the restaurant industry." The old Newark Airport, in the words of Layne Holmes at Village Inn Pancake House, is "a toilet." But the airport's food operations are handled by R.A., and they do TEACH well.

I'm assigned as manager of the Coffee House, which is the main coffee shop at the old airport. The assistant manager, a Swiss guy, is introduced to me as Saucy. I don't realize it at the time, but Saucy is his last name. I think it is a nickname. I'm calling him Saucy for about two days, when he finally announces to me, "My name is not Saucy. It is Eric, or Mister Saucy!"

The guy obviously has a problem with me being brought in as his supervisor. He lets me know it when he comes in and quits about ten days later. He's got his little five-year-old kid with him, and while we're waiting for his check to be cut, he mellows a bit and tells me about the job he's moving into. I don't take it personally and shake his hand when he and the little boy leave.

About 13 years later, Eric Saucy turns up as a chef instructor at CIA when I'm recruiting there for Harrah's-Tahoe. Maybe because I have so many influential friends at CIA during this time, he ends up being a pretty nice guy toward me, and I make it a point to visit with him when I'm at the school several times every year during the 1980s. It turns out that the little boy he'd brought along his last time in the Coffee House at Newark is now a student at CIA, and Eric puts him with me at Tahoe for his externship—a strange twist to what begins as a very uncomfortable relationship. A few years after his graduation from CIA, the kid, Oliver, goes on to fame (and I assume) fortune in his own restaurant in Miami.

Sam Sebastiani

When I'm working as the F&B director at the Hitching Post, aka 'The Hitch,' in Cheyenne, Wyoming, aka (according to four-year-old Allie) 'ShyWhy,' one of my areas of responsibility is the hotel's retail liquor store.

At some point I decide I want to promote Sebastiani Wines. Since we're in the middle of nowhere, I write a letter to the company requesting a retail end-cap display, like I see in a large grocery in Colorado. Much to my surprise, not only do I get an answering letter promising to ship the display, but it is written and signed by winery president Sam Sebastiani.

About seven years later, we decide to have a series of annual Harrah's-Tahoe 'Wine Adventure' Weekends. These are pretty elaborate affairs, with wine education activities and some fine dining events with celebrity speakers, etc. Summit Maitre d' Claude Oertle invites the speakers, and I never bother to check on who they are. Sam Sebastiani is a featured speaker at maybe the second year we run one of these weekends, and he has a wine served at the big Saturday night dinner. We end up sitting at the same table. I tell him about the nice letter he sent to me in ShyWhy, and the favor he did for me with the display. We have great chemistry, and since his daughter is working as a weekend dealer at Harrah's while she's earning a master's down in Sacramento, we see each other frequently over my remaining years at Tahoe.

At some point in the late 80s, Sam gets pushed out of the presidency by others in the family. He notifies me that he's got his own vineyards and winery and invites me to stop in next time I'm in the valley. I do, but soon I find myself in Branson, Missouri, and lose touch with him.

Fast forward another ten-plus years, and I'm at the Nugget, where I begin buying the Sebastiani label again. One day I get a call that people from the winery have stayed overnight in the hotel and would like to meet me. It turns out to be Sam's sister Mary Ann and her husband Dick. We also develop great chemistry, and Charlene and I visit their home and guest cottages in and around Sonoma often while I am at the Nugget. They even sell my photo note cards in the winery gift shop. They are great friends in this period of my life, and I am quite fond of them. All because of a letter Sam answers to a stranger in ShyWhy.

Pat Rocco

There are connections (the CIA connection, the R.A. connection, the DU connection, the Harrah's connection, etc.) that harbor ghosts (good ghosts) who seem to return, ghosts who cycle through my work life in one way or another. Take Pat Rocco, for instance:

In the fall of 1964 (my senior year at CIA) it's a big honor for me to be chosen by Chef Emile Delorme to work on a four-man team to put a piece in the Société Culinaire Philanthropique Salon, a competition held each November during The National Hotel & Motel Exposition, aka the New York Hotel Show. It's even a bigger honor that we win first prize for students' work, but the truth is, without Chef Delorme "advising" us, it wouldn't happen.

The event is at the N.Y. Coliseum, and two of us must man our table before and after the judges come by to score the work. Friends and family stop by over the course of the two- or three-day show. My mother brings a camera, which I borrow, and begin to shoot slides of some of the amazing work in the room. There's some absolutely incredible pastillage work adjacent to our table, and I am drawn to this remarkable piece, a perfect scale replica of St. Peter's Basilica in Rome.

Flash forward: One day in the early days of 1994 when I am V.P. of food and beverage at the Desert Inn (known as 'The D.I.' in the gaming industry), Executive Chef Michael Ty asks if I would mind putting on a retired baker friend of his for the winter. This guy would come out from the Albany (NY) area, and winter at his daughter's house in Las Vegas. We need another guy in the bakeshop, so I readily agree.

The guy's name is Pasquale "Pat" Rocco. He is 12-14 years older than me. He is a warm, friendly guy, and usually stops in at the chef's office in the early mornings for a cup of coffee. He knows all the old-timers (instructors) back at CIA, so that gives us a connection. After he's been with us a few weeks, we get to talking about pastillage work, which I'd been told was his specialty. Pastillage is a highly specialized art form that can only look good if done by a highly skilled pastry artist. Done correctly, it looks something like a sculpture made from white mat board, the kind used to mat a photograph within a picture frame.

I tell Pat that when I was in my senior year at CIA, I was lucky enough to be on a team that had a piece being exhibited at the New York Show in of November 1964. And I go on to say, "At the time, I saw the most amazing exhibit of pastillage work I can ever remember seeing, and that I still (30 years later) have a photographic slide of the piece. It was an exact replica of St. Peter's Basilica in Rome." I tell him in a gushing manner, "Whoever this guy was, he was one of the most talented pastillage guys I'd ever seen."

Pat's sitting at the chef's desk sipping his coffee, and looks up at me, and calmly says, "That was me."

The next day Pat brings in his scrapbook and there it is: St. Peter's Basilica. And I'm with the guy who put it together—30 years later and almost 3,000 miles from where I photographed it. It sat a few steps from the CIA exhibit where I stood watch, looking at it for two solid days during my time at the 1964 Hotel Show. Unbelievable!

Two for the price of one

The deal at the Desert Inn is that V.P. of Food & Beverage Leon Schelbert is to stay on with me for a month, teaching me the ropes while construction on the MGM Grand proceeds to the point where he can move into an office there. These two hotel/casinos are both owned by Kirk Kerkorian, so it's a friendly deal in all respects. They are sister properties—although only an idiot would believe that Kerkorian would hold on to the D.I. after the MGM Grand is scheduled to open in early winter 1995.

Leon finds no need to spend much more than about a week with me, so he begins to show up just here and there during that first month. One day he calls and arranges for me to meet his new executive chef, who just arrives from a big job in the Orlando area. Of course, the guy turns out to be Swiss, *because Leon's Swiss*, and that how it works with Europeans in many important food operations. As my friend Frankie Hubbell once explained, "When you go to a party with strangers, you bring a friend."

"I know this man"

We meet for lunch at the D.I. one Saturday, and we're both staring at each other across the table, trying to figure out why we look familiar. I ask the guy, Bruno Wehren, a couple of questions, and we realize that we spent a whole day together in Hyde Park, NY, at a c.1985 CIA job fair, tables side by side, while we were recruiting kids at the school. Bruno says to me, "While I'm looking at you, I'm saying to myself, I know this man." We became instantly comfortable with each other. A pleasant coincidence.

A couple of weeks later, Leon is running around my new offices at the D.I. having our secretary (his former/my current) arrange for an important meeting with the consultant who is helping him (Leon) with restaurant concepts at the MGM. After Leon leaves, I hear the secretary making arrangements, and she mentions the name of the consultant. Can it be? The same guy I've known since junior high school in Teaneck, the same guy who I introduced to people at CIA, when he decided to go to school there? Yes! Sal Casola. The next time Sal comes to town, we also have a nice reunion lunch at the D.I.

Carlton Geer

Soon after I begin working at the regionally well-known Hitching Post (1978), a guy arrives in town who begins as F&B manager at our one and only competitor in Cheyenne:

"Little America." He's a cocky, brash younger guy who has just graduated from Cornell's famed School of Hotel Administration, and he's over the top obnoxious. We begin calling each other on the phone, borrowing both food and equipment. He starts by asking for spare chafing dishes; I reciprocate weeks later by asking for 109s (prime ribs). And so it goes. It's unusual but necessitated by a pragmatic approach to our mutual realization that we need each other because we are in ShyWhy, the middle of nowhere when it comes to food purveyors and restaurant supplies.

A couple of years later, without discussing it—we never have a warm friendship—we both end up working in the northern Nevada gaming industry. I stay with Harrah's for ten years, and he bounces around a bit but settles with the Peppermill. We never have reason to speak to each other, and time just marches on. Eventually he advances to the position of G.M. at Peppermill and hires me out of the Desert Inn (Las Vegas) in 1993 to be his F&B guy. We get along like brothers, and I never have a problem with my one-time cocky, arrogant ShyWhy competitor. The people in this restaurant universe inhabit a very tightly knit place!

Buddy Adler—A Surprising Lunch at The Red Lion Inn...But First:

One night in February 1996, while I'm working at the Peppermill Hotel Casino, I get home and start a meal of meatballs and spaghetti. I am alone in the house and while the food is cooking, I begin to read the mail. I open a letter from CIA and am astounded to read that I have been nominated for an award for "Outstanding Direction in Food and Beverage of a Hotel, Casino, Cruise Line or Airplane," in celebration of the school's first 50 years. It is a new award, called an "Augie," named after the iconic chef August Escoffier. As I read the letter, I am humbled beyond description. THE FIRST 50 YEARS??? My mind is racing. How could this happen? I am really shook. Ironically, the meal, which I am looking forward to, is a mess, because I completely lose track of time and overcook the pasta (I told you: I am *shook*).

The big 50th anniversary weekend takes place in May. I'm determined not to make the big mistake of my prior honor at CIA—giving a graduation speech in June 1986, when I was too cheap to bring along Charlene or Allie (Dave is too young). All the nominees for the various categories (Outstanding Accomplishments/Direction, etc., in field of F&B Communication; Practice of Culinary Arts & Science; Catered or Special Events; Baking & Pastry Confections; Restaurant Most Worthy of a Detour, yada, yada, yada) are participants in various panel discussions that take place on Saturday, with the awards dinner that night. There are maybe six nominees in my category. I do not prepare an acceptance speech, because there's no way I can win this thing. At least two of the guys I'm up against are seriously heavy hitters.

Dell Hargis, a dear friend who runs the Alumni Office, takes me aside and tells me that all the nominees are being told to make a quick speech on stage if they win. Why does she tell *me*???

But I do win, and because I am in true shock, I babble some useless, forgettable words, they take my picture (I can't even SMILE, I'm in such shock!), and I go back and sit down with Charlene and old friends Bruce and Joanne Harms. I can't figure out why or how I receive such a high honor until months later: it isn't about some abundance of talent as much as it was about how many people I hire (especially for the ten years at Harrah's-Tahoe where the need for help is so great) and help along their own career paths, while just doing my job. So maybe they were thanking me for helping them get a start in their careers.

Anyway, the next day we have breakfast at a fun little restaurant in Rhinebeck with old CIA friends Nobel and Robin Masi. We find that we have just enough time to drive up north to the Norman Rockwell Museum at Stockbridge, Mass., before heading back down to Newark where we'll stay overnight, after a visit with Bill Cannon at our hotel near the airport.

The museum is great, as is the surrounding Berkshire Mountains countryside, and we decide to eat at the famous Red Lion Inn in Stockbridge. We are seated in the restaurant, and while Charlene reads the menu, I immediately excuse myself to hit the men's room.

When I return to the table, Charlene asks me to look at what she's found on the menu. It isn't a dish she'd like, but a printed welcoming message from the innkeeper and his wife, old Oakes family friends Buddy and Hilke Adler—impossible connections not only to Teaneck, not only to my father's youth in Brooklyn, not only to my days at Restaurant Associates, not only to cousins in Allentown, P.A., but even to Harrah's-Tahoe. So here: let me bore you with the convoluted ridiculous back story explaining the connection I had to these two people, Buddy and Hilke Adler.

Way back when my father was in his late teens, he dated Ruth Weinberg, who later married Monroe Adler, and by coincidence they settled in West Englewood, an affluent part of Teaneck. My parents and Ruth and Monroe became good friends over the Teaneck years. We grew up with their somewhat younger kids. Every once in a while, Monroe's older brother, a butcher and meat market owner in Allentown, P.A.—where we have Meshirer cousins in the soda bottling business—sent his kids (Mollie and Ira) to Teaneck to visit with the Adlers. The kids are both older than Mer and me by maybe four to seven years. But we got to meet them a few times while we're junior high age. Then Ira graduated from the School for Hotel and Restaurant Management at Penn State and went to work with a company called Restaurant Associates where he was placed into a management training program at Newark Airport. Ira lived at the Adler's house in Teaneck for several months. He had no time to find his own place. Some guy named Al Cimetta was working him like a rented mule but liked him enough to give him a nickname: "Buddy." Ira became "Buddy" Adler for the remainder of his life.

Eventually Buddy, a rising star, was transferred into New York City and placed into Tavern on the Green, for further training where they continued to work him hard, but also teach him. In the meantime, I'm beginning to take an interest in hotel and restaurant management.

As I'm developing an interest in the business, my mother begins encouraging me to read interesting articles she finds. I begin reading a lot about R.A., and specifically about Joe Baum, its amazing detail-oriented, creative president. At one point, when I'm about 19 or 20, Joe Baum is profiled in a long article in the "New Yorker." Then, when I represent CIA at 'The Chicago Show' (National Restaurant Association Convention) in May 1965, Joe Baum gives the keynote address. I'm there in the front row with Mrs. Roth (founder of the CIA) at the feet of this genius and become quite inspired.

Buddy becomes like a restaurant big brother to me when I start at R.A. in the summer after my freshman year at DU. We are both in the city, both working long hours, but find the time to have two or three visits in his restaurant that summer. He teaches me restaurant rookie survival tricks; even tells me how to trim my hair with a razor blade held onto a comb, because there's no way I can get enough time to slip away to a barber shop (I'm working 14+ hours a day/7 days a week). No complaints—I'm loving this life and have great passion for the biz.

One night I go down to Paul Revere's Tavern in the Hotel Lexington, where Buddy is the restaurant director. That's where I meet his bride-to-be, a Scandinavian airline stew named Hilke. We all have dinner together and they offer to give me a lift home. The three of us pile into Buddy's little two-seater MG convertible and drive up First Avenue with the wind blowing all around us. It is a fun escape from my routine.

Over the years, I hear about Buddy once in a while or read his name in an advertisement for the Publick House (he's still with R.A. and this is one of their out-of-town properties) in Sturbridge, Mass., where he is Innkeeper. One time about 1983 I even have an opportunity to stop in for lunch when I'm on a Harrah's recruiting trip in New England. Coincidently, I even hire one of Buddy's former employees when I'm interviewing kids at Johnson and Wales in Providence, R.I. It's fun to reconnect with him, and a few years later, he calls me to ask for help placing his daughter, a Cornell hotelie, in a holiday season job at Harrah's-Tahoe. I do and get her a place to stay with an assistant maître d' of the Summit Restaurant.

Back to the story:

The years go by, and Charlene and I are about to have lunch at the Red Lion.
Charlene has only met Buddy's Cornell daughter, but recognizes his name in that "Greeting from the Innkeepers" on the menu, and remembers when we helped get the kid a place to stay, etc. Truthfully, I would have missed it, as I rarely read those kinds of menu 'messages.'

I immediately ask the waitress if Buddy is around. No, he's out of town, but his wife is here. So Hilke comes to the table and we have a happy reunion, talking about Teaneck and R.A. and our Allentown families. It's absolutely amazing to me. How can these crazy coincidences keep popping up in my life, this one almost 3,000 miles from home? I'm only sorry to miss Buddy.

We head back to Newark and have a nice quick visit with Bill Cannon that evening at the hotel, before getting our return flight the next morning.

Craig Welch

One evening about 2002 my pager buzzes. I'm working swing shift at John Ascuaga's Nugget in Sparks, Nevada. I get to a wall phone and the hotel operator hooks me up with a long-distance call that turns out to be Craig Welch, one of the sales supervisors at Silver State Liquors and Wine.

"Hey Vinnie," he says, "I'm down in the Keys in Florida at a sales meeting, having dinner with a bunch of guys, and I want you to talk to somebody. I'm thinking . . . *who could he want me to talk to? Maybe his supervisor, Larry Sapperstein?*

"Hey Vin," a familiar female voice says, *"how ya doin?"* I recognize her instantly. It's Patty Cannon, who is waiting tables in Key Largo, where she and Davie have been living forever.

Same routine as all resort-area waitresses (after the order's been taken, and the first round has been served):

Waitress, Patty asks, "So where are you guys from?"

"Reno," somebody answers.

"Reno?" asks Patty, "I have a friend there: Vinnie Oakes."

"Vinnie Oakes? We sell him his wine!" Craig answers.

(This was about 3,000 miles from Reno!)

I don't make these up, just record them.

Mario & Crystal Colombini

In 2009 when I'm working for the Food Bank, I pick up a new volunteer to help me with occasional graphic arts projects that pop up every so often. Mario works for Grafics Unlimited in Sparks, and I do a good deal of business with them; it's the big paid projects, like design and installation of large vinyl pieces such as banners, truck wraps, foam core work, etc. But I always need a volunteer—if he/she has the talent—to do small stuff that I sketch out in concept, and then they would finish, and spec to printers.

Mario helps me for free on the side while his wife Crystal is working on her Ph.D. at UNR. I try to let him know we appreciate what he does, so we go out to eat great hot dogs at a place called Sinbad's (in Sparks) every several weeks on the Food Bank's tab. Once or twice a year I'll fix them up with a real dinner, or maybe even a summer concert in the park.

One day we're eating at Sinbad's and he says, "Hey, I met your sister-in-law last weekend. I even took some pictures of her place on my cell phone."

I have no idea who he's talking about. I don't have a sister-in-law.

Turns out he and Crystal are up in Washington state on their way to a family wedding when they get stopped cold by a bad accident involving a big rig. Traffic is at a standstill for *hours*. They pull off the road (I-5), drive for a bit, and find a little roadside coffee house. The friendly gal serving them makes some conversation, and eventually asks where they are from.

"Reno," on answers.

"Reno?" the server answers. "I've got family there. Do you know Vinnie Oakes?"

"Do I know Vinnie Oakes?" says a shocked Mario, "I work for him!"

The friendly gal is the shop's owner, Vicki Miles, my brother-in-law Tim's wife. Mario's coffee is on the house.

Amazing!

Kim's "Annapolis" Son at the Reno Wedding

At the Food Bank my main job is to buy the food. And the main supplier at this time is another food bank—the Food Bank of Middle Tennessee (Nashville). I deal with a handful of people there but my main and favorite contact is Kim Molnar.

In the summer of 2010, Charlene is paying me to help her—when I have the energy—do some heavy lifting and digging at her main landscaping clients' homes. One of them requires a lot of work to ready the place for a June wedding reception. We have plenty of notice, and the work goes on for about three weeks prior to the big event.

On the Friday of the wedding weekend, I'm on the phone checking on an order with Kim. In closing she mentions that if I see a bunch of rowdy young guys with very short hair running around Reno, it'll probably be her son and his Naval Academy buddies—in town for a wedding, and they haven't seen each other since graduation day of 2009 (one year ago).

I don't think anything of it at the time, but during the weekend, Charlene mentions to me that her client's daughter is marrying a guy from Annapolis, and it all hits me: Kim's son, who's doing submarine training in South Carolina, is going to a wedding reception *at the one home in Reno, Nevada,* we've been prepping for the same event! I check it out with Kim after the weekend, and it's true. Her son was right there at that client's house. And it's just weird.

If You Work in a Restaurant, Remember These Things:

From my F&B orientation for new employees at The Nugget Hotel Casino...

- ♦ If you want the rainbow, you've got to put up with the <u>rain</u>.
- ♦ The <u>Guest</u> is the boss.
- ♦ Your reputation is only as good as the last meal you serve.
- ♦ Everything a dishwasher does ends up in front of the guest.
- ♦ You never get a second chance to make a good first impression.
- ♦ Not all companies have a reputation . . . only the best, and the worst.
- ♦ You can never be that good at guest service, at cooking, at making a drink, at cleaning, that you can stop trying to be better at it. (Think about Michael Jordan).

- Never argue with a Guest. You may win the argument, but you'll lose the Guest.
- Never give an excuse to a Guest, or to your supervisor.
- Yes, you *are* being paid to SMILE! Please do.
- Never eat at a place called "Mom's" unless it is.

Looking Back

Looking back on my career in the hospitality industry, I will always be grateful for my teachers and coaches. Yes, coaches. Because there is an undeniable transference from the discipline of my high school wrestling to success in a career. And where would I be without the good people I encountered at my jobs: those who gave me their best effort and who were reliable. If I looked good at times, mostly it was because of the people who surrounded me.

In recent years, I suppose because of so many memories popping into my head while I was deciding which stories to include in this book, I have thought a lot about the cast of characters in my food life and have mused about what a listing of "All Stars" would look like: who was the best executive chef, who would have been the most creative problem solver, who was the best wine company sales rep, who was the best help in the big complicated budgets we had to do at Harrah's-Tahoe, etc. I wouldn't dare put such a list in writing, for fear of hurting someone's feelings. So let me just say that I worked with some very talented, loyal, and remarkable people, and that I learned from each and every one of them, whether they were above me, alongside me, or below me on a given org chart, and that they know who they are, and I shall be forever grateful for their presence in my life.

The Last Words . . .

The wonder of the world,
the beauty and the power,
the shape of things,
their colors, lights and shades;
these I saw.
Look ye also while life lasts.

- From a gravestone in Cumberland, England

THE END

Special Thanks

Three people helped this technically challenged person with my story:

My nephew, Mikko Sperber, who patiently helped me with my first crack at formatting.

My former Food Bank of Northern Nevada colleague, Sue Eckes, who edited my writing.

City of Reno Poet Laureate, Dustin Howard, who also works at the Food Bank. Without Dustin's encouragement, and conversion of my typed-up sheets into the book you hold in your hands, I would still be wondering how to make it all happen.

Each of these people have my gratitude for their patience, knowledge, guidance, and kindness.

For Questions or Inquiries

For general questions or inquiries regarding readings, interviews, reprint permissions, or the use of any material contained in this book, please contact the author directly at: vinnieoakes@gmail.com.

About the Author

Early in his career, Vinnie Oakes had the unglamorous late-night responsibility of rowing restaurant garbage across the famous lake at the Bethesda Fountain in New York's Central Park. His collection of experiences culminated in the career high of being selected by his fellow alumni of the Culinary Institute of America to be presented with the first ever "Augie Award" (named for world-renowned chef, Auguste Escoffier) for "Outstanding Direction of a Hotel, Casino, Cruise Line, or Airline," in celebration of the school's first 50 years. He currently lives in Reno, Nevada.

www.ingramcontent.com/pod-product-compliance
Lightning Source LLC
Chambersburg PA
CBHW030906120626
46554CB00001B/18